Critical English Education

Critical English Education

Enduring Voices, New Perspectives

Edited by

ERNEST MORRELL
University of Notre Dame

NICOLE MIRRA
University of California, Los Angeles

ANTERO GARCIA
Stanford University

CATI DE LOS RÍOS
University of California, Berkeley

JAMILA LYISCOTT
University of Massachusetts, Amherst

NCTE

National Council of Teachers of English
1 E. Main St., Suite #260, Champaign, Illinois 61820
www.ncte.org

Staff Editor: Emily Smith Gilbert
Manuscript Editor: Michael Ryan
Interior Design: Jenny Jensen Greenleaf
Cover Design: Adrian Morgan

ISBN (print) 978-0-8141-0283-1
ISBN (EPUB) 978-0-8141-0284-8
ISBN (PDF) 978-0-8141-0286-2

It is the policy of NCTE in its journals and other publications to provide a forum for the open discussion of ideas concerning the content and the teaching of English and the language arts. Publicity accorded to any particular point of view does not imply endorsement by the Executive Committee, the Board of Directors, or the membership at large, except in announcements of policy, where such endorsement is clearly specified.

NCTE provides equal employment opportunity (EEO) to all staff members and applicants for employment without regard to race, color, religion, sex, national origin, age, physical, mental or perceived handicap/disability, sexual orientation including gender identity or expression, ancestry, genetic information, marital status, military status, unfavorable discharge from military service, pregnancy, citizenship status, personal appearance, matriculation or political affiliation, or any other protected status under applicable federal, state, and local laws.

Every effort has been made to provide current URLs and email addresses, but because of the rapidly changing nature of the web, some sites and addresses may no longer be accessible.

Library of Congress Control Number: 2025947029

Contents

Chapter One

Critical English Education: An Introduction

Nicole Mirra
Ernest Morrell
Antero Garcia

The definition of *literacy* is constantly in flux as public understandings of what it means to be a "good" reader and writer map onto broader social beliefs and anxieties about what it means to be an agentic human being in this world—and who gets to be one. Considering the continuous and overlapping changes facing individuals and communities today, the state of literacy simultaneously beckons us into the past and propels us into possible futures.

As we write these words, the subject of English language arts—the disciplinary home for literacy instruction within K–12 schools—is wrestling with the nature and purpose of the literate subject on several fronts. Questions about how to best teach children to read are being framed in falsely dichotomous terms between cognitive and sociocultural strategies, and the current ascendance of the cognitive approach—strategically dubbed by proponents as "scientific"—represents a swing toward a narrowly functional definition of literacy. From this perspective, good readers and writers are framed as those who can comprehend and produce words *correctly*.

This most recent swing is happening as frantic considerations about the impact of artificial intelligence and machine learning are also consuming our field. When literacy is defined as the proficient production of words strung together into (somewhat) passably coherent texts, and when large language models can be programmed to accomplish such tasks, where does that leave the humans generating and consuming such texts? While this question has led to hand-wringing about the meaning of both creativity and humanity itself, school systems are largely acquiescing to the inevitability of AI's stranglehold on ELA instruction, doubling down on the functional literacy paradigm.

And yet these concerns with the technical aspects of literacy cannot be divorced from the political. The pedagogies framing *how* reading and writing are taught through rote, mechanical processes go hand in hand with policies seeking to control *what* texts students can encounter in class—which in turn restricts *whose* voices, identities, and experiences are validated and welcomed in society. The proliferation of book bans seeking to exclude conversations about racial justice and LGBTQIA+ identities are a reminder that literacy is always a social and cultural practice in addition to a cognitive one. Readers and writers are those who exert *power* to name and impact the world.

These recent developments stand in stark contrast to a strain of literacy scholarship that has coalesced over the past sixty years into what we call here "critical English education"—a body of inquiry that conceptualizes readers and writers as historically situated representatives of cultures and communities and families and that insists upon literacy as a practice of self and societal transformation in pursuit of dignity, agency, and equity (Morrell, 2005).

Some might look at the state of literacy today and suggest that critical English education is a marginal endeavor. We reject such a cynical interpretation; rather, we posit that the reactive policies and practices of today demonstrate the tremendous successes of critical approaches to literacy over the past sixty years. Indeed, the current retrenchment only serves to amplify the tectonic shifts in how we look at text, who authors text, and how we author text that have been elicited by transformative scholars, including the contributors to this volume.

This volume brings together trailblazers in critical English education with innovative new voices to document the intellectual genealogy of the field and light the path toward further ground-breaking literacy scholarship. In moments that can seem defeating, this text serves as a reminder of how critical literacy has succeeded thus far and as an exhortation to continue to push forward into new horizons.

We synthesize here some of the cross-cutting themes that illuminate these successes before introducing the chapters to come, which offer a detailed examination of the various threads that make up the tapestry of critical English education.

Critical Consumption: Reading (and Reading against) Text

When reflecting upon the history of literacy instruction, we are reminded of the seismic shift in what it means to read—a shift from being well read to *reading well*. This represents a huge, inclusive, empowering, and critical shift in the consumption of text. In the nineteenth century, being well read would have been a status reserved for the very few who could receive formal education at that time and would have implied familiarity with everything from Homer's *Odyssey* to Dickens and the Victorian literature of the day (e.g., the "gentleman's library"). Literacy—a term that was not used then—meant ingesting a library of great books and great texts that would somehow make one a learned person and offer access to high culture, a kind of diction of vocabulary, and something to do in their leisure because they really didn't have to work much to get by (Scholes, 1998).

The idea of being well read shaped formal education, particularly when it was limited to a very small group of privileged people; however, the twentieth century in the United States saw a great many people who had not previously been permitted to be educated (e.g., women, African Americans) achieving access to public schooling. Great interlocutors emerged within these groups who, over various phases and through the early and middle part of the twentieth century, began to focus on the act of reading itself. For instance, Theresa Perry, Claude Steele, and Asa Hilliard (2003) declared that "Literacy is an act of freedom," and reading well meant a number of things successively that have been really powerful for us as a field. One of the biggest contributions was the shift from merely *appreciating* a text to acquiring a set of skills to critically *question* a text, to have ideas about text.

Nineteenth-century poet and cultural critic Matthew Arnold (2009) opined about how one should read a great piece of literature: Basically, go sit by a tree and wonder about how great it was. More contemporary theories of reading require that we critique the literatures we read; we pick texts apart, so to speak, to exert some agency over these texts and develop the ability to talk back to them. These activities and skill sets now cohere as critical theories of reading. These can include applying a particular stance, such as a feminist, postcolonial, or Marxist perspective (Appleman, 2000). Likewise, a reader-response approach meant that, all of a sudden, the reader had all of the power to bring a particular perspective to the text they were reading. Reader-response theory offered a crucial challenge to the hegemony of being well read in classics, precipitating a move toward serious discussions of what kinds of text could be part of classroom life (Beach, 1993). Many of the literacy scholars who came before us were moving toward multicultural texts—texts that came from diverse communities that could be part of what was happening in the classroom. They insisted that greatness did not just cohere in a small set of texts that had been deemed the progenitors of Western civilization. Contemporary authors could write texts that we could read, which we forget was somewhat radical considering that students in the late nineteenth century had to fight to get someone like Shakespeare into the curriculum.

To move from Greek to text written in English took a revolution. And to be able to read contemporary authors—people who look like us and who spoke like us and *to* us—is yet another transformative revolution. It is something we take for granted now. Today, we are expanding the literary canon—exploding it, even. This ongoing revolution wasn't just about what we read; it was about putting what we read in dialogue with how we read so that when we encountered texts that were written in the past, we did not look at them as if they were extensions of sacred text. We could speak back to them with our own power as readers (Freire & Macedo, 1987).

The shift toward an empowered reader was crucial. Sometimes we are tempted to mistakenly characterize reading/consumption as being passive and writing/production as being active and critical. However, the critical reading modality was an important one. We have been guilty in the past of talking about "moving from consumption to production" as if production was somehow more powerful (Mirra et al., 2018). Analyzing our past is also a moment of power, a moment of criticality, a moment in which the reader becomes centered in the dialogue with text rather than just the text itself.

Louise Rosenblatt (1978) conceptualized the poem as a kind of dialogue between the reader and the text. In the 1990s, many of us in the field defined critical literacy as the ability to bring theoretical understandings as leverage against the texts—printed or technological—we were bombarded with (Morrell, 2008). Yet many of these texts, particularly digital texts today, are mediated by corporate powers and in many ways are inculcated with hegemonies that are counter to the interest of the reader themselves (New London Group, 1996). One superpower was to be able to read those texts and read against those texts. Yet a concomitant and fundamental shift in the field was indeed the move toward embracing the student as a producer of text.

The Rise of Production: Students as Authors of the Present

In the year 2013, the professional organization that was once dubbed the International Reading Association renamed itself the International Literacy Association. Think about that. The idea that literacy does not just denote reading but is expansive enough to include writing or production is a huge move that was supported by scholarship in critical English education (Street, 1984). The idea that classrooms can be places where everyone can write and not just fill in short answers in worksheets, where a student shares their own thoughts and ideas in genres and through language that matters to them—this idea of writing text and being authors of text—is something that had to be fought for (Lee, 2007). A focus on writing, on student textual production, in print and in digital environments, has been a huge shift.

We are reminded of the intersections of this work with our personal histories. One year in the early 2000s when Antero was a Los Angeles public high school teacher and Ernest was a UCLA professor, Antero brought all of his students to UCLA during spring break to participate in a film festival. Soon afterward, one of those high schoolers ended up enrolling at UCLA and becoming a student in Ernest's class. When asked about the memory of that film festival she said, "The difference is he just asked us what we liked. We got to produce that." It's a significant shift in the technology of literacy pedagogy when you think of the student as the author of the present.

We are still writing with pen and paper at this moment, even as these tools have been joined by digital communication platforms that can greatly expand the scope and reach of student authorship. This idea of production and authorship underscores a certain kind of agency and a certain kind of power that introduces a wider conception of audience and impact into youth literacy practices (Shor, 1992). Writing for the teacher alone is not the same as writing something that is shared beyond the classroom with local communities; the focus on writing—and writing with authentic purpose for cared-for others—shows students that they have the power to name their world and potentially change how others think (Lankshear & McLaren, 1993). Innovations in the classroom such as youth participatory action research and syncretic testimonial have helped redefine classrooms as polyvocal and bimodal learning environments that transform normative ideas of who gets to speak and who has to listen (Cammarota & Fine, 2008; Mirra et al., 2015).

We do want to distinguish a bit between the framing of production and innovation. In some ways, we can view production as limited to composition in modes we did not create—in a sense, attempting to use the master's tools for liberatory purposes. However, in addition to this consideration, critical English education also asks: *What might it mean to invent literacies as opposed to manipulating the literacies that others have given us?* This innovation has always been possible. It has always been present (Freire, 1970). As we look at classrooms today, we prompt the field to ask: *What are the responsibilities that must be considered? What are the skills and ethical implications involved in organizing, curating, and archiving knowledge as part of digital citizenship?* Just as one innovative literacy practice is collecting and curating, we must consider the power implicit in such compilation. Inherent in being well-read, critical producers, we are digital curators as well as digital disseminators.

If these processes sound serious, it is because they are. However, we also need to remember the element of play at work across these modalities. "Praxis" can be a heavy word for a thirteen-year-old who might ask, "What do you mean? I thought we were gonna have some fun in class." It's not that the world isn't in a serious place, but doing serious things doesn't have to be solely a serious activity. Where does joy live in our pedagogies? What does it mean to play? What does it mean to make? What does it mean to invent? What does it mean to innovate? One of the challenges that we face at this moment is convincing reasonable skeptics that play and invention are the most intellectually rigorous activities that we can have our young people involved in. How do we make the case that this isn't something that is ancillary to intellectual work in the classroom and is the most intellectual work? We're all on the hook for this, so how do we show this? It certainly is at the core of a critical English education.

What do integral spaces for literacy-making look like in the future? If we as a literacy community deconstruct the barriers of risk, we can increase the scope of reward for youth and communities moving forward. We can set out tools in the space of innovation and play and productivity, where its high production and low stakes work. We suggest that this is going to be the most intellectually rigorous activity we can have as a field as we navigate the challenges of retrenchment across today's political and educational landscape.

We have to think really big in terms of uses of literacy and the uses of literacy in ways that are proactive more than reactive. We have begun to find these answers by returning to the lessons that have been passed down for generations in our families and communities and translating those into pedagogies of solidarity and kinship.

Historicity and Pedagogy: Speaking with and through Our Families

As we have touched upon already, there is a tempting pull to think about literacy studies through the frame of a forward-facing march of progress, whether it be progress through time or progress through modes of consumption and production. While there is indeed a sense of forward momentum, there is also beauty, enjoyment, and engagement beckoning us back into our collective pasts.

Critical English education scholars have woven historicity and an uplift of often muted and marginalized histories into literacy teaching and learning to add polyvocality to pedagogical praxis. Students are indeed authors of the present, but they are also representatives of cultures and communities and families, and they represent that knowledge. Honoring these connections has formed the foundation of sociocultural and critical approaches to pedagogy, as well as cultural historical activity theory (CHAT). Scholars like Kris Gutiérrez (2008) led us toward connecting that past to that present, conceptualizing spaces for students to use the skills they had to connect the past to the present.

In doing so, critical English education seeks to enlarge what we think of as the human corpus of voice so that we can speak with our mothers, grandmothers, fathers, and grandfathers. We speak with and alongside our elders and our ancestors. Consider the *testimonio*. A crucial, analog technology, we had to develop these tools of critical response. We have to intentionally look at such moments of innovation not just in terms of the technology created but also as the underlying pedagogical shifts that must happen as we interact with that technology or even the role of the students and teachers within those shifts.

We are able to literally live with our ancestors on the page. We as a field must pull these past moments into the future. Part of the problem with the present is that it has forgotten its past. When you are already in the future, you need to be continuously in dialogue with that past and present. Generative artificial technology recycles past texts as tools for regurgitation in ways that can look deceptively new and innovative. And so, when things like AI come along, poised to purportedly topple foundations of literacy, there is still a need—in fact, even more so—to look at Toni Morrison or to read a book. We haven't burned out or moved past the innovative tools of human thought and the printed word. We are still into books. The value of those texts is that it puts us in a conversation with the human condition. Importantly, this is not a one-way conversation. As long as we are able to speak back to those texts, we can learn from them, grow from them, and grow *with* them. A critical English education means evading historical amnesia while also not being bombarded with perspectives from the past that are neither empowering nor inclusive.

Critically consuming and producing text is not only a way to remember the beauty and the dignity in text. Rather, it is about developing the ability to read *against*. These are powerful skills, and what can get overlooked is the importance of pedagogy in supporting these skills. Our sociocultural theories of learning often emphasize all of the learning that happens without us being present as teachers. As a result, our theories of learning and literacy often do not focus enough on what can be learned from a place like school. Some people will reduce the literacies that we teach to a basic set of skills, but we as a field can push back against such a narrow interpretation. That's an imperative for critical English education.

Others might say people already enter schools with robust literacy skills, that schools are a site for convening people and preparing them to leverage the skills they learn at home and in the community so that they get high SAT scores and get into college. These are limited or antiquated ideas. We will tip our hand and propose that there is something to be taught in community with students, in dialogue with one another, and with a professional interlocutor who is someone like an educator. We need to discuss how literacy helps us to understand our own condition in relation to others, how literacy fosters polyvocality and dialogue, how literacy helps us to collectively unpack a constantly changing human condition, how to take really strong instincts and to refine those as part of a dialogic interaction with a community. Perhaps many of the reductive purposes of education, which you could get from Google or YouTube, just need to be removed from the classroom entirely. The classroom has to be a different kind of space. We have to convey to the next generation of educators and researchers what literacy pedagogy is going to yield that is important, what it means to us, why it is meaningful, and why it remains necessary.

New Tools: Expanding Notions of Textuality

There is another shift: expanding our notion of textuality. Take, for example, those critical literary theories that we had just begun to acquire in the post-war 1950s and 1960s. In the 1970s and 1980s, our field was applying those theories to look critically at film and television and newspapers. The decades that followed would look at hip-hop, digital media, and online communities. New literacy studies began to think about what it meant to navigate this technologically mediated world of text with the kind of reading power that we were used to considering more formally in classrooms. This look across formal and informal sources for textual consumption and production is still tremendously important today.

Critical English education in the years to come is not necessarily going to be defined by technology; that's an overwrought assumption. Rather, it will continue to be defined by our *relationship* to technology, our relationship to the classroom, and our relationship to space and movement of people. People want to make AI the new thing that's going to change everything. It is certainly significant, but we maintain that this next era of literacy studies is likely not going to be defined by some superior technological advancement that's going to change everything for us. We propose that it will be defined by thinking in more elemental ways about who we are and how we relate and how we learn. This is a humanizing process that will move us away from a crisis of modality that allows us to think about the connection between literacy and our humanity.

Inevitably, there will be new tools. Bill Gates (1995) said, "You will know it's a computer age when no one no longer uses the word computer." When the thing that comes after AI comes after AI, we don't need a new kind of pedagogy. Pedagogies that are unwittingly reactive to the moment can be more dangerous than any tool.

Right now, technology is not a word that has a lot of transport. It doesn't offer much. Literacy still does. Pedagogy still does. People still do. That is where we seek for this dialogue to move forward—by not responding but by projecting. What would literacy pedagogy look like if we weren't responding to something? Even as a speculative space. What does your literacy look like as a canvas? What does your pedagogy look like as a canvas?

At some point, we do have to be pragmatists, but we don't want to start there. Whenever we have started there, it has not taken us to the places where we want to be, which is engaged in revolutionary love and practice with beautiful and brilliant minds that are in front of us to do something that is eternal.

Looking Back to Go Forward

Our marching orders are mirror orders. It is to be extremely proud. The work that it has taken to create this kind of panic we see today in the American elite is not so easy to come upon. The idea that we have to go and change our intellectual outfits to imagine a future is not something that we think is true. This is a time for more perspiration and inspiration. The inspiration is here. The counter discourses that are part of our community are powerful, and the work of the people who have come immediately before us remind us to stay steadfast. We need to think about what kinds of particular transformations mean for us in terms of modes of communication and pedagogical practice.

We do not need an entirely new system of thought and action to continue to do good. So, the marching order for this generation is to remain persistent, to be able to transmit to the next generation what has been transmitted to us. As we lose our forebears, it becomes more and more clear the kind of genius that they brought, not only in what they did but in who they were. Now that is our responsibility. Every time we say goodbye to an ancestor, we get closer to becoming one, and that means a lot of responsibility. That means a lot of persistence. The things they dealt with were not any easier than the things we deal with now. We just have to remind ourselves of that. We have that kind of beautiful brilliance because we have been indebted to the folks that have given it to us.

Literacy is in a place now that is defensible by those standards of the last two generational movements, so we need to keep going. We need to keep going with all of the alacrity that we can muster. This is not a time to pause. So much is possible. So much has happened, but so much is possible. What do we want to do? What is the mark that we want to individually and collectively leave upon these people who call us mentors?

The Pages Ahead

The dozen chapters that follow all tell different stories of the myriad lives lived and enacted through critical English education. They are testimony. They are reflective, archival, playful, empirical, and joyful.

The first three chapters of this volume intertwine discussions of language, literature, race, and identity. In the opening chapter, Ofelia García and Kahdeidra Monét Martin articulate a "critical race-informed translanguaging English education" that "shifts the locus of enunciation from that of the school and the white listening subjects to that of all speakers/signers and learners in schools themselves." This centering of race then moves toward an intentional focus on how critical interpretations and engagement around race have supported transnational youth across settings. Gloria Ladson-Billings then builds on the legacy of Toni Morrison's language to explore how teachers enact and attend to themes of race and racial representation in classrooms around literature. Finally, Sabine Little and Jennifer Rowsell offer new possibilities for where and how multilingual approaches to ELA might foment in research practices and language pedagogy alike.

The following chapters take up various methodological approaches to pedagogical work in critical English classrooms. Maisha T. Winn brings the tools of historicity, offering methodological and pedagogical guidance for students to serve as both "worthy witnesses" and "practitioners of the craft" of critical scholarship from within our classrooms. Likewise, Limarys Caraballo builds on the longstanding traditions of participatory research to articulate a hopeful vision of intergenerational inquiry in English classrooms. Cati de los Ríos describes a tradition of "Corrido Poetics" in order to affirm literacy practices that sit at the natural confluences of politics, art, and youth expression.

The next set of chapters in this volume bring the critical lenses prominent in expanding literacy approaches to different aspects of critical English education. Mollie V. Blackburn shares the roots of queer literacy scholarship in order to articulate a critical English education that is deliberately layered with and entangled in "sexual and gender diversity, as well as other minoritized, surveilled, and marginalized identities." Next, building from the work of the New London Group (1996), Rubén González and Antero Garcia articulate abolitionist multiliteracies that build on literacy scholarship toward youth-centered freedom movements. Likewise, Stephanie Toliver picks up the threads of Ernest Morrell's initial (2005) framing of critical English education to articulate the ever-present force of speculative imagination.

The final collection of chapters in this book push us forward by reinforcing our roots as a scholarly field. Tracing connections across history, memory, and power, Jamila Lyiscott illustrates how Black English is a tantamount source of "both social inquiry and direct social transformation in teaching and learning." Next, Laurence Tan offers a narrative, built on two and a half decades teaching in elementary classrooms, to recenter the humanizing voices and ingenuity of young people who enter our schools each day. Finally, through carefully detailing multiple movements across her scholarship, Kris D. Gutiérrez links the field of critical English education to future-oriented work of social design-based experiments and research that intentionally builds on everyday knowledge.

The scholars who are in conversation with the paradigms of critical English education here represent some of the most dynamic kinds of thinking sharpening our methodological and pedagogical skills over the past three decades. Like the tensions described in this introduction's overview of the past, present, and future of critical English education, these are oftentimes unwieldy and vivacious directions to pull our myriad Englishes. And yet unifying all of them: commitments to young people and their teachers. Commitments to the dignities of young people and practitioners in our field. Commitments to the brilliance of young people and our field.

References

Appleman, D. (2000). *Critical encounters in high school English: Teaching literary theory to adolescents.* Teachers College Press.

Arnold, M. (2009). *Culture and anarchy.* Oxford University Press.

Beach, R. (1993). *A teacher's introduction to reader-response theories.* National Council of Teachers of English.

Cammarota, J., & Fine, M. (Eds.). (2008). *Revolutionizing education: Youth participatory action research in motion.* Routledge.

Freire, P. (1970). *Pedagogy of the oppressed.* Seabury Press.

Freire, P., & Macedo, D. (1987). *Literacy: Reading the word and the world.* Bergin & Garvey.

Lankshear, C., & McLaren, P. (1993). *Critical literacy: Politics, praxis, and the postmodern.* State University of New York Press.

Lee, C. D. (2007). *Culture, literacy, and learning: Taking bloom in the midst of the whirlwind.* Teachers College Press.

Mirra, N., Garcia, A., & Morrell, E. (2015). *Doing youth participatory action research: Transforming inquiry with researchers, educators, and students.* Routledge.

Mirra, N., Morrell, E., & Filipiak, D. (2018). From digital consumption to digital invention: Toward a new critical theory and practice of multiliteracies. *Theory Into Practice, 57*(1), 12–19.

Morrell, E. (2005). Critical English education. *English Education, 37*(4), 312–321.

Morrell, E. (2008). *Critical literacy and urban youth: Pedagogies of access, dissent, and liberation.* Routledge.

New London Group. (1996). A pedagogy of multiliteracies: Designing social futures. *Harvard Educational Review, 66*(1), 60–92.

Perry, T., Steele, C., & Hilliard, A. G. (2003). *Young, gifted, and Black: Promoting high achievement among African-American students.* Beacon Press.

Rosenblatt, L. (1978). *The reader, the text, the poem: The transactional theory of the literary work.* Southern Illinois University Press.

Scholes, R. (1998). *The rise and fall of English: Reconstructing English as a discipline*. Yale University Press.

Shor, I. (1992). *Empowering education*. University of Chicago Press.

Street, B. (1984). *Literacy in theory and practice*. Cambridge University Press.

Chapter Two

Critical Race-Informed Translanguaging for English Education

Ofelia García
Kahdeidra Monét Martin

For us, a critical race English education starts by questioning the concept of English itself. We question why English has been constructed as an entity with linguistic borders that privilege the language of some and not of others. And we explore the reasons why the institution of school views English in this way, as well as the tools that have been used for this ideological construction of a language named English. We write from experiences in English education across two generations with racial, linguistic, cultural, and geographical differences. Ofelia came to New York City from Cuba at the age of eleven. She has had a forty-plus-year career working as a teacher of bilingual education and TESOL in NYC, preparing teachers for those fields, and doing research on the languaging of minoritized people around the world and especially of Latinx students in the US. Kahdeidra came to New York City from Savannah, Georgia, at the age of two. In her twenty-year career, she has worked as a youth worker and administrator in after-school programs and community centers, as an administrator in independent schools, as a middle school special education teacher, and as a teacher educator on language, race, and religion, with a focus on Black/African-Descendant students in the US.

Cha-Cha-Chá Steps in English Education

One thing that age gives us is the ability to look back, reflect, and experience change; youth gives us the promise of a different future.

We share our thoughts on the development of English education from our different generational perspectives.

We might think of change as having a forward direction, but for Ofelia, English education has been more like a cha-cha-chá—steps forward and backward, creating movement yet standing in place. When Ofelia started teaching, there was no set English language arts curriculum. There were guidelines, yes, but the curriculum and the pedagogical practices associated with teaching English were not closely monitored and relied mostly on traditions of English teaching. From Ofelia's professional beginnings in the 1970s, the teaching of English language arts responded to the only tradition that was legitimized then in a mostly segregated country with little large-scale immigration: that of white middle-class Americans. Yes, her classrooms were full of Puerto Rican children, citizens of a US colony, who, like Mexican Americans and African Americans, were considered second-class citizens with little educational promise. And yet, the fact that standardized tests did not yet drive the curriculum and that technology could not yet conduct the surveillance which it does today made it possible for some educators of color to teach with their own voice from within (for more on this history, see García et al., 2025).

During the 1960s through the 1970s, many educators in racialized communities incorporated their own language and cultural practices, providing minoritized students with an awareness of the US history of domination, enslavement, racism, and imperialism. For Latinx communities, a bilingual education based on community rights to an equitable education made it possible to expand the English language arts curriculum with stories, poems, myths, and histories of the communities themselves, many times told in Spanish. The African American community had always had its own network of schools, and during the years that followed the Civil Rights era, schools with Afrocentric curricula grew. In these schools, the English practices of the local African American community were used as the norm in English language arts. But bilingual education schools, as well as Afrocentric schools, were soon hijacked by government programs that were said to support both communities. Yet the different categorizations by which the two groups were cast—racial for

African Americans and linguistic for Latinx people—ensured that their educational trajectories would never meet, making it easier to eventually disband grassroots efforts to leverage the communities' language and cultural practices, as well as their histories as enslaved, colonized, and racialized people.

As bilingual education and multicultural education became supported with public funds and "professionalized," English language arts reclaimed its role as the teaching of the language of the white middle class. Bilingual education became only a transitional program to teach English, in ways that rendered English as something that Latinx immigrants lacked rather than as another medium of communication in the Latinx community. And multicultural education programs that centered African American histories and practices were phased out, as Black students' language and cultural practices were silenced and ignored in mainstream English language arts classes.

In the twenty-first century, bilingual education was rebranded as "dual language," teaching language arts in two languages according to monolingual middle-class standardized norms. English as well as Spanish were taught as if they were languages "from elsewhere" (Mena & García, 2020) and not reflecting the bilingual dynamic practices of the Latinx community. The rebranding of bilingual education was seen as a way toward integration of Latinx students with others, but interestingly enough, the others were never meant to be the African Americans with whom they often lived, for those African American students were seen as not having English but a substandard variety of English and could not serve as "linguistic models" (García et al., 2024).

Today, more than ever, as Kahdeidra has experienced as a middle school teacher, English language arts is rigidly constructed away from the language practices of communities of color. In the monolingual programs where most Latinx and African American students are educated together (Seltzer & García, 2020), the "English" of English language arts simply reflects English language standards adopted by states that were constructed with white, monolingual, middle-class norms of practice. During the era of accountability that followed No Child Left Behind (2001), assessments were developed to reflect external standards of language that penalized the ways in which racialized communities used English. Academic English was constructed and defined by scholars as simply mirroring the characteristics of English use as written and spoken by those with institutional power (Flores, 2020; García & Solorza, 2020). By incorporating some famous African American and Latinx authors—for example, Toni Morrison and Sandra Cisneros—English language arts increasingly washed its hands from including local practices of doing English with features and practices of African American or Latinx communities.

As the diverse English-speaking Global South becomes an increasingly visible presence in the United States, the boundaries surrounding the English language in American schools have closed tighter and tighter. It is the features of English associated with white, US-born, middle-class speakers who are taught in English language arts classes, with other practices eliminated. The inequitable distribution of achievement in English reading and writing is felt now more than ever across lines of race, class, gender, and geography.

Yanvalou to Step Forward into a Future

If English education has as its goal the equitable education of *all* Americans, then it must be released from the structural constraints that has constructed it as the language of white, monolingual Americans with institutional power. Throughout our history, the art of teaching and learning often has been described as a dance, a dialogic exchange of ideas and bodies. For Ofelia, the future movement of the field must *not* be like a cha-cha-chá, only moving within the circle that has kept English reified as a structural entity with power. It is time for English language educators to move forward, voicing the sociopolitical role that English has had as the language of white male colonizers and educated slave owners in the past and the language of the Global North economy in the present.

From a critical race and abolitionist perspective on English education, we must be ever vigilant to notice what we are doing with, and to, our bodies during interactions and exchanges.

Learning to relinquish control and release the stress of dominant ideologies and assessments is critical to applying what linguist Anne Charity Hudley and colleagues call "liberatory linguistics" to the field of English education, a framework that centers the agency of African American and Black diasporic language users in their education (2022). By centering African American, Caribbean, Black diasporic, and Latinx language users, the field of English education can move forward in decolonizing racist ideologies.

Even further, a critical race English education must contend with the role of religion and religious literacies in reproducing white supremacist Judeo-Christian hegemony. For Kahdeidra, an African American practitioner of the Hoodoo ethno-religion and a priestess in Haitian Vodou, raciolinguistic ideologies and religious racism function in tandem; educators must work to understand and to uplift the African and Indigenous spiritual practices that are prevalent in Black and Latinx communities, even as they uplift their languaging. In 1996, Dr. Gerdès Fleurant, an ethnomusicologist and priest in Haitian Vodou, published the first text on Vodou music from an insider's perspective, *Dancing Spirits: Rhythms and Rituals of Haitian Vodun, the Rada*. In contrast to racist distortions from Hollywood and Eurocentric imaginations, Dr. Fleurant upholds Vodou as a "humanocentric" religious system that "reaches to the very essence of what it means to be human and spiritually connected to the family tree" (Fleurant, 1996, p. 9).

To adopt a humanocentric approach, a critical race English language arts can then move in the ways of the Yanvalou dance in the Haitian Vodou tradition in which the dancers emulate the ripples of a wave and the undulations of sacred boa constrictors that reside in the ocean, the embodiment of the deity Papa Dambala Wedo. Aristil (2022) notes:

> Yanvalou is easily distinguished from other traditional Haitian dances. Its unique *movements mimic ocean waves*. Then, to achieve them, the dancer must free himself from any muscular tension. He must *let himself go* by undulating his body from the base of the skull to the sacral plexus, passing through the pelvic girdle. When a dancer succeeds in achieving *total fluidity and letting go*, it is *because they have shed the negative energetic*

> *baggage that lived within them.* There is nothing more beautiful than seeing a dancer perform these movements. These ripples, like the movement of the snake, hypnotize and recall nature. Dancing Yanvalou *requires being present and mindful.* To be honest, it feels *good for the body and the mind.* (our italics)

To dance Yanvalou, one is required to abandon all bodily tension and "negative energetic baggage." What might critical race English education look like as a dance of Yanvalou? What ideological and curricular tensions would we still need to purge in order to be present in mind, body, and spirit? Addressing racism, and anti-Blackness in particular, is not enough. What's in our back pockets? What colonial baggage do we still carry in our fragmented concepts of humanity that we need to shed? Drawing from womanist theology and the work of elder Cynthia Dillard, Nana Mansa II of Mpeasem, we must cultivate classrooms that are "spiritual homeplaces" for Black/African-Descendant students, creating teaching and learning environments that are endarkening and healing (2021).

In order to truly fulfill the call of the Yanvalou to be free from "negative energetic baggage," we must be able to shed what Boaventura de Sousa Santos calls "abyssal thinking" (2007), the result of the abyss that was created during colonization to categorize people on one side of the line as human and all-knowing and the others as less-than-human and ignorant and folkloric (Wynter, 2003). It is this colonial logic (Mignolo, 2000) that has resulted in dismissing the epistemologies and knowledge systems of students of African descent. For example, African diasporic religious practices and literacies are even today not given the same respect as Judeo-Christian ones and are denigrated as irrational and black magic. Some limited value has been placed in Indigenous epistemologies and land-based spiritual practices by scholars, the result of work of Indigenous scholars such as Linda Tuhiwai Smith (2005). But the African diasporic religious literacies of Black American Hoodoo, Cuban Lucumí, Puerto Rican Espiritismo, and Haitian Vodou are seldom even acknowledged in the academy or classrooms. These are denigrated as simple primitive magic.

The future of English education for all Americans needs to promote not just linguistic justice (Baker-Bell, 2020) or social justice but especially cognitive justice. To end what Santos (2018) calls "the cognitive empire" of the West and Global North that has branded the epistemologies and practices of African descendants as impure and folkloric, their linguistic, religious, cultural practices and historical experiences must be included in an ELA curriculum for their academic value.

The role of English in the construction of "whiteness" must be acknowledged, as it has linked the notion of being a "native" speaker of English to being white and powerful. Thus, African Americans whose language practices when they were enslaved were smothered and who are today speakers of English only are robbed of being considered legitimate native speakers of English. We come up with descriptions of the varieties of English spoken by African Americans and Latinxs—African American English, Black English, Chicano English, etc.—and we come up with a list of languages that Americans of African descent name as theirs—Spanish, Fula, Haitian Creole. Yet we continue to separate the linguistic practices of minoritized and racialized people as different at best, often signaling inferiority and substandard practices.

English language arts programs today continue to focus on eradicating linguistic practices that do not conform to those of white monolinguals with power. Because of the ways that bidialectalism and bilingualism have been constructed, as the addition of two different codes (a standard/dominant one, and a non-dominant subjugated one), when bilingual or bidialectal pedagogies are proposed, they are most often interpreted as "code-switching." That is, features of what is said to be the variety of English or the other language of the racialized group are compared to the practices of white monolingual English speakers. Although this comparison might result in a greater sense of pride among students who value their bilingualism and bidialectalism, this is not enough to dismantle racism in language education (Saeedi & Richardson, 2020). As Frieson (2022) has suggested, this code-switching pedagogy often emphasizes "a color-evasiveness approach to languaging that operates from a position of anti-Blackness" (p. 51). African American English or Latinx Spanish are important concepts for racialized students' sense of pride and identity. What are named as dialects or varieties, or even languages, are real and have important material and identity effects. But their namings are social constructions, the result of historical processes designed to categorize people, with those associated with people of color always deemed as inferior.

Despite the good intentions of educators who think that Spanish for Latinx or an awareness of the features of African American English can help African American and Latinx students achieve success in American society, it is racism that lies at the heart of it all. The language of African Americans and Latinx students is represented through American society's raciolinguistic ideologies (Flores & Rosa, 2015) as emitted by visibly racialized inferior people who are considered "others." It is the ways that English, as well as Spanish, has been constructed in American institutions, especially in schools, that causes the inequities. What can we then do about it?

Translanguaging as a Forward Yanvalou

To Yanvalou forward, English education must disrupt the bounded circle of linguistic structures in which the English language has been constrained to benefit the few. It must liberate bodies, tongues, hands, minds, emotions, and the spirit, enabling all speakers to do English in their own ways with flexibility and creativity so as to become strong English users. What has been called *translanguaging* (García, 2009; García & Li, 2014) offers English language educators a way to Yanvalou forward, "deploying speakers' full linguistic/semiotic repertoire without regard for watchful adherence to the socially and politically defined boundaries" of what is considered the English language in school (Otheguy et al., 2015, p. 281).

Translanguaging has been often misunderstood as a practice of going across named languages—that is, as a practice in which only bilingual speakers like Latinx students can engage, thus leaving out African Americans. And sometimes translanguaging has been extended to include the practice of going across named varieties or dialects, which then includes African Americans. But as Privette and Saechao (2024) affirm, Black languaging is also translanguaging. Translanguaging is much more than simply going across what are understood as different codes. It emphasizes *the human factor in communication*, with speakers doing language with their own unitary repertoire as they orchestrate a network of linguistic, multimodal, social, cultural, biological, psychological, physical, and spiritual phenomena with which they make meaning for their own lives, with their own knowledge systems and onto-epistemologies.

Although all speakers engage in translanguaging, racialized and minoritized speakers (whether Latinx bilinguals or African Americans and other Black diasporic people or others) are rarely given the freedom in school to use many of the features considered "nonstandard" (that is, outside of the white monolingual production) in their meaning-making repertoire. Although translanguaging is the language practice most readily observable in communities considered bi/multilingual or bi/multi-dialectical, it is rarely permitted in institutions, especially in school. When Black/African-Descendant students, including African Americans as well as Latinxs, are given the freedom to language leveraging their full repertoire of semiotic resources, that is, their translanguaging, they are then said to be deficient. The difference then between white English middle-class monolinguals and racialized/minoritized users of English is one of freedom to act and to have agency. Although most white monolinguals are free to use their entire repertoire in state institutions and especially schools, racialized others are always asked to linguistically perform with less than their full repertoire. Most of the linguistic/semiotic repertoire of racialized speakers is seen as socially inappropriate in schools. Thus, these speakers are rarely granted the freedom to engage in translanguaging in the same ways that monolinguals do. Without recourse to their own semiotic and epistemic meaning resources, racialized speakers are thus rendered deficient.

The Yanvalou of English language arts must move the locus of enunciation (Mignolo, 2000) to African American, Caribbean, Latinx, Native American, African and Asian speakers of English, and other racialized/minoritized people, including the Deaf. We must all learn to listen, to understand people "doing" their own languaging without regard to the English languaging of white monolingual hearing speakers. That is, racialized speakers must be freed to perform their languaging, letting go and acting without the baggage of the "double consciousness" (Du Bois, 1903/1996) of always having to see themselves in the image of white folks.

Furthermore, the complex translanguaging behavior of racialized speakers must be understood as more than simply going across named languages or named varieties, as much more than code-switching. Their behavior must be understood as taking up the freedom, like other powerful speakers, of being able to draw from their entire unitary repertoire of meaning-making resources and in so doing, disrupting the power hierarchy that the English of white monolingual speakers has enjoyed in schools.

Critical Race-Informed Translanguaging in English Education

A critical race-informed translanguaging English education shifts the locus of enunciation from that of the school and the white listening subjects to that of all speakers/signers and learners in schools themselves. It is attentive to how race has been linked to language and dismantles the English language education project as simply teaching structural elements of what characterizes the language of white monolingual English speakers with power. A critical race-informed translanguaging English education would require the transformation of English language standards, curricula, texts, and assessments, which are unjust and irrelevant for racialized speakers of English. To do so, pedagogical practices that uphold colonial/white supremacist logic by maintaining the surveillance, marginalization, and policing of racialized students' translanguaging need to be challenged. Educators must be willing to refrain from practices that restrict racialized students' flexible use of their entire repertoire of meaning-making resources. English language classroom tools and norms, such as standardized assessments that reinforce whiteness and the exclusion of racialized speakers' language practices, would be continuously interrogated.

A critical race-informed translanguaging in English education would directly confront the racism—linguistic, epistemological, cultural, and religious—experienced by all Afro-descendant students. The distinction between calling a linguistic expression a "language" or a "variety" or "dialect" of a language is often determined by political elites, not language users themselves.

Scholars of color have fought back against the hijacking of the English language by white monolinguals with institutional power, away from racialized communities. Many are reclaiming historically marginalized expressions as languages. Creolists like Michel DeGraff (2005) have denounced the othering, "exceptionalist" lens placed on Haitian Creole (and culture) and have argued that all Creoles are languages. We'd like to argue further that all naming of languages and varieties, including Creoles, are social constructions; thus, all languages could be considered Creoles. When we center all speakers as equals in the act of languaging, we understand that what all of us are doing is orchestrating or assembling our own network of linguistic, multimodal, social, cultural, biological, psychological, physical, and spiritual phenomena to communicate and interact with others. The assemblage of resources to make meaning (Pennycook, 2024), and the ways in which we do English, differs significantly according to our own individualities, our socialization in different communities of practice, our interlocutors in different spaces, our race and socioeconomic status, and the power that we hold.

As a child growing up, Kahdeidra could be said to have been multivarietal because she used what are named as different Englishes—Mainstream American English, African American Language, Gullah Geechee, and Jamaican Patwa. We call Kahdeidra's use *multivarietal* to highlight the shared features that characterize ways of using language by racially or geographical distinct speakers. We usually would not call Kahdeidra's use of language multilingual because these are not socially regarded as different named languages. The difference between saying that someone is multilingual or bilingual like Ofelia or that someone is multivarietal like Kahdeidra is not linguistic; it is *social*. As Max Weinreich said a long time ago, the difference between a language and a dialect is that a language is a dialect with an army and a navy. It is not the language as a linguistic structure that determines its power; the power of a language or a dialect is determined by the social and racial position of its speakers. For example, Spanish in the US, spoken by immigrants and people who have been colonized and conquered over centuries, does not have the same power as Spanish in Europe, seen as the language of white Europeans, or even in Perú, where it remains the language of the white colonizers that dominated speakers of Quechua and other Indigenous languages. That is why US Spanish is often denigrated as simply "Spanglish," a dialect or variety with little prestige. The opposite process of turning what has been historically considered a dialect into a language also occurs, demonstrating the social nature of the construction of a named language. For example, Luxembourgish had been historically considered a German dialect. But after its occupation by Germany during World War II, Luxembourg started the process of standardizing the language spoken by its people away from that of High German. In 1984, Luxembourgish was declared the national language of Luxembourg.

The languaging—the action of orchestrating meaning-making using linguistic/semiotic/multimodal/psychological/emotional/spiritual/sociological resources—is the same across speakers, whether drawing on what are named as languages or what is said to be a dialect or variety. Again, the difference in the ways we see these practices relies on the institutional power and racial designations of the bodies doing the languaging. To be valued, racialized students in schools are forced to use only the features and practices from their repertoire that they share with white monolingual students. For example, Kahdeidra leverages different features and practices from her unitary repertoire when she is interacting with other African Americans, Haitians, and other Black diasporic people, depending on their characteristics and experiences. But when she teaches English language arts at the university, she is expected to suppress features and practices that are not considered part of the repertoire of white speakers, the only language that is considered "academic." In the same way, Ofelia is not free to use resources that are said to be Spanish when giving a lecture, even though at home with her husband, children, and grandchildren, she is free to use all her repertoire of resources. A critical-race-informed translanguaging English education would give all speakers the freedom to draw from their unitary repertoire instead of constantly having to arrange and rearrange features to fit the white monolingual discursive practices that have been socially invented as the only means to educate.

A critical race-informed translanguaging pedagogy would teach, strengthen, and celebrate the specific linguistic performances that all speakers bring to language-learning contexts, inquiries that are largely absent from scholarship on translanguaging, which has focused traditionally on what are seen as bi/multilingual speakers. Disrupting the bi/multilingual paradigm and encompassing all language speakers, including those who are seen as bi/multivarietal, would enhance what Kahdeidra calls *transvariant priming*—the ability to more readily notice linguistic variation so as to maximize communication and relationships (Hankerson et al., 2024). An example of this can be drawn from Kahdeidra's personal experience. When she was learning Spanish in high school, her teacher was a woman from Venezuela who praised her for having the "accent" perfectly. By this comment, the teacher was referring to her use of Caribbean Spanish linguistic features that were commonplace in her Brooklyn neighborhood but were often stigmatized in schools (Clemons & Toribio, 2021; Martin et al., 2019). These linguistic features are also common in the repertoire of many African Americans and people from the Anglophone Caribbean, which was already a part of Kahdeidra's own repertoire. Kahdeidra was able to then adapt these features, without prompting, as she was being taught with what was said to be the Castilian variety of Spanish.

We need to repair raciolinguistic language policies that erase and eradicate the linguistic abilities of Black American and Caribbean multivarietal language users, as well as those considered bi- or multilingual. To do that, there would need to be professional development for English language arts teachers to work with multilingual and multivarietal texts in their courses and equitable financial resources for the publication and award-granting of translingual and multivarietal student texts.

García, Cioè-Peña, and Frieson (2024) have delineated a number of principles for critical race-informed translanguaging practices that could be adapted for English language arts to ensure the inclusion of all racialized students. Centering the languaging and experiences of racialized language users, they recommend closely observing the speakers' actions and that of their communities without regard to the white monolingual gaze. They also advise focusing on the strength of these practices with purposes that are intellectually purposeful, and academic as well as social. A critical race-informed translanguaging would support the students' use of all their resources, linguistic or otherwise, to make meaning and interact purposefully. In this way, the students' own subjectivities, as well as those of their teachers, would be transformed so that their languaging actions can be considered creative and critical, regardless of their use of specific "standard" features and practices. The English language arts questions raised by educators would change. No longer would they ask whether the language is "academic" or uses "standard" features. No longer would they evaluate for deficiencies. Instead, they would ask whether the students' use of language enables them to think, to create, to be critical, to make connections, to relate to others, to engage with all types of texts, ideas, and people.

Taking up a critical race-informed translanguaging stance in English language arts would free our imaginations from our preconceived notions of "English." This may be the most difficult struggle we have ever faced as English language scholars. But as Robin Kelley (2002) reminds us, we "must do the complicated intellectual work of dreaming and imagining" (p. 62). And so, this essay is Ofelia and Kahdeidra's attempt to move us forward in Yanvalou to be free to imagine a very different English language arts profession.

For Those Who Want to Learn More about Yanvalou

https://haitiantimes.com/2020/09/21/exploring-yanvalou-the-sacred-dance-of-haiti/

https://centretoussaint.com/en/blog/haitian-traditional-dances-yanvalou/

Watch a Yanvalou performance from the JAE 2018 Haitian Dance Institute by Jean Appolon Expressions: https://youtu.be/nSMycgN8EuI

References

Aristil, S. (2022). *Traditional dances of Haiti: Yanvalou.* Centre Toussaint. Retrieved on July 20, 2023, from https://centretoussaint.com/en/blog/haitian-traditional-dances-yanvalou/

Baker-Bell, A. (2020). *Linguistic justice: Black language, literacy, identity, and pedagogy*. Routledge.

Charity Hudley, A. H., Mallinson, C., & Bucholtz, M. (2022). *Talking college: Making space for Black language practices in higher education*. Teachers College Press.

Clemons, A. M., & Toribio, A. J. (2021). Racializing Latinx bilinguals in K–12 language learning classrooms in the United States. *Journal of Spanish Language Teaching*, *8*(2), 129–142.

DeGraff, M. (2005). Linguists' most dangerous myth: The fallacy of Creole exceptionalism. *Language in Society*, *34*(4), 533–591. https://www.jstor.org/stable/4169447

Dillard, C. (2021). *The spirit of our work: Black women teachers (re)member.* Beacon Press.

Du Bois, W. E. B. (1996). *The souls of black folk*. Penguin.

Fleurant, G. (1996). *Dancing spirits: Rhythms and rituals of Haitian Vodun, the Rada rite*. Greenwood Press.

Flores, N. (2020). From academic language to language architecture: Challenging raciolinguistic ideologies in research and practice. *Theory Into Practice*, *59*(1), 22–31. https://doi.org/10.1080/00405841.2019.1665411

Flores, N., & Rosa, J. (2015). Undoing appropriateness: Raciolinguistic ideologies and language diversity in education. *Harvard Educational Review, 85*(2), 149–171.

Frieson, B. (2022). "It's like they don't see us at all:" A critical race theory critique of dual language bilingual education for Black children. *Annual Review of Applied Linguistics, 42*, 47–54. https://doi.org/10.1017/S0267190522000022

García, O. (2009). *Bilingual education in the 21st century: A global perspective*. Wiley-Blackwell.

García, O., Cioè-Peña, M., & Frieson, B. (2024). Bilingual education: Leaving (and not leaving) race and disability behind. In L. Padilla & R. Vana (Eds.), *Representation, inclusion, and social justice in world language teaching: Research and pedagogy for inclusive classrooms* (pp. 102–121). Routledge.

García, O., Flores, N., Seltzer, K, Li, W., Otheguy, R., & Rosa, J. (2021). Rejecting abyssal thinking in the language and education of racialized bilinguals: A manifesto. *Critical Inquiry in Language*

Studies, 18(3), 203–228. https://doi.org/10.1080/15427587.2021.1935957

García, O., Kleifgen, J., & Cervantes-Soon, C. (2025). *Educating emergent bilinguals: Policies, programs, and practices for English learners* (3rd ed.). Teachers College Press.

García, O., & Li, W. (2014). *Translanguaging: Language, bilingualism, and education*. Palgrave Macmillan.

García, O., & Solorza, C. (2020). Academic language and the minoritization of U.S. bilingual Latinx students. *Language and Education, 35*(6), 505–521. https://doi.org/10.1080/09500782.2020.1825476

Hankerson, S., Martin, K. M., Charity Hudley, A. H., & Mallinson, C. (2024). Critical metalinguistic engagement of Black language users in writing instruction. In R. L. Jones & C. P. Proctor (Eds.), *Pursuing language and metalinguistics in K–12 classrooms* (pp. 67–81). Routledge.

Martin, K. M., Aponte, G. Y., & García, O. (2019). Countering raciolinguistic ideologies: The role of translanguaging in educating bilingual children. *Cahiers internationaux de sociolinguistique, 16*(2), 19–41.

Mena, M., & García, O. (2020). "Converse racialization" and "un/marking" language: The making of a bilingual university in a neoliberal world. *Language in Society, 50*(3), 343–364. https://doi.org/10.1017=S0047404520000330

Mignolo, W. (2000). *Local histories/global designs: Coloniality, subaltern knowledges, and border thinking*. Princeton University Press.

Otheguy, R., García, O., & Reid, W. (2015). Clarifying translanguaging and deconstructing named languages: A perspective from linguistics. *Applied Linguistics Review, 6*(3), 281–307. https://doi.org/10.1515/applirev-2015-0014

Pennycook, A. (2024). *Language assemblages*. Cambridge University Press.

Privette, C., & Saechao, K. (2024). Black languaging IS translanguaging: We not just talking bout it, we bout it bout it! *Perspectives of the ASHA Special Interest Groups, 10*(1), 64–73. https://doi.org/10.1044/2024_PERSP-23-00297

Robin, K. (2002). *Freedom dreams: The Black radical imagination*. Beacon Press.

Saeedi, S., & Richardson, E. (2020). A Black Lives Matter and critical race theory-informed critique of code-switching pedagogy. In V. Kinloch, T. Burkhard, & C. Penn (Eds.), *Race, justice, and activism in literacy instruction* (pp. 147–161). Teachers College Press.

Santos, B. de S. (2007). Beyond abyssal thinking: From global lines to ecologies of knowledges. *Review (Fernand Braudel Center)*, *30*(1), 45–89.

Santos, B. de S. (2018). *The end of the cognitive empire: The coming of age of epistemologies of the South*. Duke University Press.

Seltzer, K., & García, O. (2020). Broadening the view: Taking up a translanguaging pedagogy with all language-minoritized students. In Z. Tian, L. Aghai, P. Sayer, & J. Schissel (Eds.), *Envisioning TESOL through a translanguaging lens* (pp. 23–42). Springer.

Smith, L. T. (2005). Building a research agenda for Indigenous epistemologies and education. *Anthropology & Education Quarterly*, *36*(1), 93–95.

Wynter, S. (2003). Unsettling the coloniality of being/power/truth/freedom: Towards the human, after Man, its overrepresentation—an argument. *CR: The New Centennial Review*, *3*(3), 257–337.

Chapter Three

Still Playing in the Dark: Whiteness in the Literary Imagination of Children's and Young Adult Literature Teaching

Gloria Ladson-Billings

Toni Morrison (1992) argues that literary critics have been silent about the "Africanist" presence in nineteenth- and twentieth-century literature. However, Morrison suggests that this presence functions dialectically in literature and in the social imagination of White authors and readers (p. 278). Morrison suggests that writers position readers as "White" by using "serviceable" representations of "the Black." More pointedly, Morrison argues that race as it is used in America holds more power and sovereignty today than ever before. In this chapter, I assert that Morrison's notions are enacted in the way that teachers (both inservice and preservice) teach literature, particularly literature with explicitly racial themes.

In *Playing in the Dark: Whiteness and the Literary Imagination* (1992), Morrison prevailed on her literary criticism talents to address the persistent silences in literary criticism around issues of race and racism. Morrison's book is an expansion of her provocative article, "Unspeakable Things Unspoken" that appeared in the *Michigan Quarterly* (1989). In both the *Michigan Quarterly* article and *Playing in the Dark,* Morrison argued that the Western literary canon, so long regarded as a set of texts written by White men to inform us of the human condition, was replete with instances of what she termed the "Africanist" presence. According to King (1995), "Morrison deciphers the way that race, in the form of invented 'Africanism,' functions dialectically in literature and in the social imagination of White authors and readers" (p. 278). Morrison suggests that writers position readers as "White" by using "serviceable" representations of "the Black." More pointedly, Morrison argues that race as it is used in America holds more power and sovereignty today than ever before. She points out that:

> Race has become metaphorical—a way of referring to and disguising forces, events, classes, and expressions of social decay and economic division far more threatening to the body politic than biological "race" ever was. Expensively kept, economically unsound, a spurious and useless political asset in election campaigns, racism is as healthy today as it was during the Enlightenment. It seems that it has a utility far beyond economy, beyond the sequestering of classes from one another, and has assumed a metaphorical life so completely embedded in daily discourse that it is perhaps more necessary and more on display than ever before. I am prepared to be corrected on this point insofar as it misrepresents the shelf life of racism in social and political behavior. But I remain convinced that the metaphorical and metaphysical uses of race occupy definitive places in American literature, in the "national" character, and ought to be a major concern of the literary scholarship that tries to know it. (p. 63)

To support her argument, Morrison develops a line of analysis that interrogates literary classics by Mark Twain, Edgar Allan Poe, Herman Melville, Willa Cather, and William Faulkner. Morrison asserts that these authors use literary devices to deal with the "fact of blackness" (Fanon, 1967), but the world of literary criticism ignores the existence of race and racialized discourses (Ladson-Billings, 2000). Taxel (1997) asserts that:

> Morrison addresses the "studied indifference" in most literary criticism to issues of race in the construction of what is deemed "American." She explains the telling "paucity of critical material on this large and compelling subject" by noting that "in matters of race, silence and evasion have historically ruled literary discourse. . . ." Most troubling to Morrison is the denial of the importance of race in a "wholly racialized society" where there "is no escape from racially inflected language." (p. 423)

In turning to the subject of children's literature, Taxel (1997) argues that more recent moves toward multiculturalism have created a backlash against a political correctness in children's literature. Taxel (1997) challenges the liberal concerns that claims of cultural authenticity have overridden quality literature. This debate about who is qualified to tell whose story is not the focus of this discussion; rather, this chapter focuses on how teachers fail to pay attention to the racialized themes that are embedded in a variety of children's and young adult literature. Harris (1996) agrees that the major journals of criticism and discussion of children's literature also fail to engage in substantive discussion about race and culture.

I want to argue that Morrison's notion of racial evasion in literary discourse is similarly deployed in the world of children's and young adult literature. To be sure, children's and young adult literature has improved over the last half-century. More books are written by and about people of color. People of color show up in children's and young adult texts of all kinds. However, the *teaching* of these texts, like the discourses of literary criticism in adult texts, maintains an obvious silence about race and racism—even when the books themselves are overtly racial or explore racial themes.

My warrants for this argument come from examinations of teaching (by both preservice and inservice teachers) of a selection of well-known and (for the most part) well-regarded children's and young adult texts. Further, I argue that White teachers avoid race talk of any kind because of their dysconscious racism (King, 1991) and the potential of conversations about race to yield unintended consequences. Dysconscious, according to King (1991), is "an uncritical habit of mind (including perceptions, attitudes, assumptions, and beliefs) that justifies inequity and exploitation by accepting the existing order of things as given" (p. 135). I begin my argument with a look at a controversial children's literature incident.

Happy to Be Nappy?

ELA teacher Ruth Sherman found herself in the midst of a firestorm created by her decision to teach Carolivia Herron's book,

Nappy Hair. While I would not consider this text an exemplary one, the incident does illustrate the point I want to make about the volatility of race in schools and classrooms. I also want to address the silences and evasions around race and children's (and young adult) literature. Ms. Sherman is a young White woman who chose to teach in the Bushwick section of Brooklyn where she "was going to turn things around [and], really make a difference" (Leyden, 1998, p. A3). In addition to Ms. Sherman's youthful idealism (that can be accompanied by arrogance), there is a naïveté about race and race relations in this story. Ms. Sherman claims that she chose the book as "a tool [she] used on teaching self-esteem and pride" (Norris). Ms. Sherman claimed to be unaware of the derogatory and racially charged aspect of the term "nappy hair" and was stunned by the furor her using the book caused.

> Them some willful intentional naps you got all over your head.
> ***Sure enough.***
> Your hair intended to be nappy.
> ***Indeed it did.***
>
> I mean combing your hair . . .
> ***Yep.***
> . . . is like scrunching through the New Mexico desert in brogans in the heat of summer.
> ***That's the way.*** (Herron, p. 6)

Within a week, the story of how some angry Black parents' intimidation forced Ms. Sherman to leave the school was on every print and broadcast news service. What was missing from the news analysis of the incident was the fact that Ms. Sherman's White privilege reinscribed the racially subordinate status that the Black children in her classroom held. As one parent remarked, "It had to be because she's White, if she were a Black teacher teaching that book, it wouldn't have been no problem" (Norris, p. 4).

The reason it "wouldn't have been no problem" is that a Black teacher would likely have experienced the challenge of having "nappy hair" in a society obsessed with long straight hair. Just as no one appreciates being called overweight by an emaciated runway model, few if any Black people would tolerate being told they had nappy hair by a White person. But the *Nappy Hair* incident is an unusual one. It received widespread media coverage and left no room for serious interrogation of the ways that race is a persistent undercurrent in the lives of our children. Instead, the *Nappy Hair* incident became the story of the "poor, vulnerable, White teacher" versus the "big, bad angry Black parents." The news media presumes a White audience that sympathizes with a White teacher trying to civilize the savage Black and Latino children.

I chose this incident as the kind of extreme reaction that teachers point to in order to avoid talking about race and racism. Clearly, no teacher wants to be attacked by angry parents. But, the *Nappy Hair* incident is simultaneously about teachers' lack of knowledge of a community and assumptions of low self-esteem and the way teachers submerged in a discourse of sameness and colorblindness wander ignorantly into racially charged situations.

From *The Snowy Day* to *Niña Bonita*

The big splash of *Nappy Hair* is far from the daily exercise of playing in the dark that students experience in classrooms throughout the nation. So, I would like to start with a set of rather familiar, and I might add, excellent children's and young adult literature works. My critique then is not about the texts themselves but rather about the way they are taught in most classrooms. Thus, my analysis here is to look at the way teachers—both inservice and preservice—fail to take up the racial themes that permeate these texts. Like the literary critics to whom Morrison refers, teachers turn a blind eye to the way race configures texts.

One of the first texts to insert race as a problematized subject is *The Snowy Day* by Ezra Jack Keats. Keats was the first White author to offer a Black child as the central character in a children's book. However, this central character, Peter, is rarely presented as a raced subject. As I perused the web, I located a site a first-grade teacher developed on two of Keats's books—one was *The Snowy Day*. Of the ten or so representations of Peter on this website, only one child drew Peter as a Black child. This raceless (Fordham, 1988) rendering is quite common, not just because young children fail to assign a race to their drawings but because teachers fail to assign a race to Peter. Even discussions of the text fail to ask the question, "What do you notice about the boy in this story?" According to his biography, Keats's use of the Black child in the text is deliberate, yet teachers treat it as irrelevant and incidental.

In 1962, Keats worked on a book featuring a little boy named Peter. Peter was inspired by an article Keats had clipped from *Life* magazine in 1940:

> Then began an experience that turned my life around—working on a book with a black kid as hero. None of the manuscripts I'd been illustrating featured any black kids—except for token blacks in the background. My book would have him there simply because he should have been there all along. Years before I had cut from a magazine a strip of photos of a little black boy. I often put them on my studio walls before I'd begun to illustrate children's books. I just loved looking at him. This was the child who would be the hero of my book. (de Grummond, *Children's Literature Collection*, n.d.)

The point that Keats makes about Peter belonging in the text all along should provide an opening for teachers to begin asking questions such as, "Why do you think this book is the first picturebook in the US to feature a Black child as the central character?" "What do you think people thought when they first saw this book in 1962?" "What difference does it make that Keats chose a Black boy to be his main character?" These are questions that young children can consider and discuss with teacher guidance. Such a discussion can begin to pry open the silences that so completely clamp shut classroom discourse about race and racism.

In another book, Christopher Paul Curtis's *The Watsons Go to Birmingham—1963* (1995), racial themes emerge after students have had an opportunity to meet the Watson family—Dad and his quirky car, Mom, big brother Byron, middle child Kenny, and baby sister Joetta. Kenny narrates their rather ordinary lives in Flint, Michigan. The typical sibling rivalries emerge, and big brother Byron's teenage struggles force the family to seek a solution to keep him out of trouble. They decide to take him to stay with relatives in Birmingham, Alabama. While there, the horrific bombing of the Sixteenth Street Baptist Church occurs.

The experience traumatizes Kenny deeply and offers the reader a glimpse into the psychic costs of racism.

> I had been disappearing but Momma really didn't need to worry, I wasn't going anywhere. I'd just been going behind the couch for a little while every day. There was a big enough space between the couch and the wall for me to squeeze in back there and just sit in a little ball. It was quiet and dark and still back there. (p. 193)

I witnessed a group of preservice teachers using this text and was curious as to how they planned to teach it. Surprisingly, these prospective teachers felt the most difficult aspect of the book was the Black mother's disciplinary techniques.

> Momma lit a match and grabbed Byron by the wrist and said, "Put your finger out." . . . Momma's horrible snake-woman voice came out again and said, "If you ever . . ." The match got closer to Byron's skinny finger . . . "play with—no, if you ever look at . . ." Byron's hand was shaking and he was crying like a big baby . . . "another match in this house. . . ." The match was getting closer and closer, and I knew Byron could feel the heat. ". . . I will personally, by myself . . . I will burn not just one finger, I will burn your entire hand, then send you to the juvenile home." (pp. 73–74)

The racial ecology into which the entire text is submerged was hardly mentioned by these soon-to-be teachers. Thus, we can count on them treating the church bombing as a tragic and unfortunate incident without making it a part of the larger fabric of American life in the early 1960s. Where critical race theorists (Bell, 1992; Crenshaw, 1988; Delgado, 1995) would argue that racism is normal, not aberrant in US life, our students see it as a series of isolated incidents. This book provides teachers with a wonderful opportunity to delve into the historical record and help students understand some of the troubled racial past that made a book like *The Watsons* possible. As an adult reader of this book, I had a feeling of trepidation from the moment I started reading the words "Birmingham" and "1963." I knew at some point the book would involve the church bombing and the death of the four little Black girls. The evening I finished the book, I found myself standing in the shower crying uncontrollably. Like Kenny, the trauma of racism was something that wounded me deeply, and it was a piece of children's literature that made me face it.

Clearly teachers will not have the same experience with this text as I did. But teachers can share the historical context to help students understand how taking a trip to Birmingham in 1963 was not a simple family outing for a Black family. Teachers also can ask their students to interview family members (parents, grandparents, aunts, uncles) and neighbors about what they remember about life in 1963.

One of the more difficult books I have seen teachers attempt to grapple with is Sharon Flake's *The Skin I'm In* (1998). In it, the author presents the within-group racial dynamic of color consciousness. A colleague and I presented this book to a group of teachers participating in a research group workshop. None of the White teachers thought it was an appropriate book to teach. However, several of the African American teachers teaching in urban classrooms believed that they could and would teach the text. Over the course of the year, we observed two of the African American teachers use the book. The book delves into the world of internalized racism and self-hatred.

> He stared at me half the year. I thought he saw what everybody else saw. Skinny, poor, black Maleeka. But Caleb saw something different. . . . He wrote me poems and letters. . . . He walked me to class. . . . Charlese and them laughed when Caleb and I walked by. They'd stuck out their legs and tried to trip me. . . . Somebody said I had hair so nappy I needed a rake to comb it. (p. 13)

Dealing with *The Skin I'm In* requires the teachers to take up the problem of White standards of beauty and the internalized racism that people of color, particularly African American girls, confront every day. While most of the teachers shied away from *The Skin I'm In*, they were more eager to teach Jerry Spinelli's (1990) *Maniac Magee,* in which a young boy is a kind of "every person" who bridges two communities divided by race by employing a color-blind strategy:

> Maniac kept trying, but he still couldn't see it, this color business. He didn't figure he was white any more than the East Enders were black. He looked himself over pretty hard and came up with at least seven different shades and colors right on his own skin, not one of them being what he would call white (except for his eyeballs, which weren't any whiter than the eyeballs of kids in the East End). (p. 58)

Maniac offered teachers a way to seem to deal with issues of race by reinforcing discourses of sameness and colorblindness. They, too, could assert that they don't see it while simultaneously working under the society's racial regime.

In Ann Warren Turner's *Nettie's Trip South* (1987), readers are confronted by the stark reality of slavery through the eyes of a child. Ronald Himler's charcoal illustrations set the tone for a painful and provocative story of conscience. In a teachers' workshop, a presenter shared this story through a series of overhead reproductions of the pages. No sooner had her presentation ended then one of the teachers in the audience spoke up. "I would never use that book in my classroom." When the presenter asked why, the audience member indicated that the story was too sad and depressing for her (White, upper-middle class) students to read. Several other teachers agreed that the book was "inappropriate" for young children. Thus, long-term Black corporate suffering is submerged to ameliorate White individual temporary pain. Turner (1987) deliberately leaves the reader with a sense of uneasiness and uncertainty when her narrator concludes by saying she is plagued with bad dreams after the experience of seeing people in chattel slavery. This text is a wonderful way to initiate discussion about the moral dimensions of the slavery question because it does not focus on the pathetic condition of slaves but rather on the ethics of a society that would permit slavery. The narrator recognizes the slaves' humanity and questions that of Whites who endorse and accept slavery as the natural order of things.

In Marybeth Lorbiecki's *Sister Anne's Hands* (2000), a second grader confronts the individual and collective racism surrounding the appointment of an African American nun as her new teacher. When Sister Anne comes to teach in a small-town parochial school in the 1960s, she brings fun and spirit to Anna Zabrocky's second-grade classroom, but Sister Anne is Black ("Her skin was darker than any person's I'd ever known"), and her presence makes Anna confront racism in her community and in herself. When the nun reaches out to touch Anna's cheek, the White child dodges the brown hand "as if it were hot." Then someone sends a hate note to Sister Anne's classroom, and she teaches the children about segregation and persecution, about "Whites Only" barriers, and the struggle for civil rights.

I have seen this book taught in two classrooms—with an African American teacher in an all-Black classroom in Kansas City and with a White teacher in a predominately White classroom in Madison. In the Madison classroom, the discussion about the book focused on how the children were "mean" to Sister Anne but learned an important lesson about how to treat people. There was no discussion of the tension in the community and the questioning of Sister Anne's competence because of her race. There was no discussion of the visceral reaction that Anna had to the nun's color. In the Kansas City second-grade classroom, a number of the children cried at the end of the story. They related incidents when people treated them the way Sister Anne was treated. The teacher introduced the word "racism," explaining what it meant and that it continued today. Several children asked the teacher to reread the story. In this classroom, the issues of race and racism were foregrounded because the students and the teacher related to the experiences, and the teachable moment demanded that they be addressed.

In Faith Ringgold's (1991) *Tar Beach*, Cassie tells the story of her family's summer nights on the roof of their New York apartment building. However, amid the family's good times is the story of the father's exclusion from the trade union despite his construction skills. Ringgold introduces the notion of "grandfather clauses" that allow White workers to earn preferences over many generations. She also introduces the notion of mixed race identities:

> Daddy took me to see the new union building he is working on.
>
> He can walk on steel girders high up in the sky and not fall. They call him the Cat.
>
> But still he can't join the union because Grandpa wasn't a member.

> Well, Daddy is going to own that building, 'cause I'm gonna fly over it and give it to him. Then it won't matter that he's not in their old union, or whether he's colored or a half-breed Indian, like they say. (Ringgold, 1991, pp. 11–14)

Ringgold attached vivid borders from her award-winning quilts to each page of the book, and typically classroom discussions and subsequent activities on this text focus on the artwork. One widely circulated internet lesson on this book suggests the following objectives in teaching this text:

- To introduce the artist Faith Ringgold and her story *Tar Beach.*
- To discuss the closeness of family and wishes for the future.
- To focus on a work of art created out of paint and fabric rather than paint and paper.
- To explore pattern by overlapping color and design.
- To foster cooperation within the class dynamic by creating both individual and small work.

Once again, we see how even explicit references to race and racism get submerged by the colorblind scripts enlisted by most teachers.

Two texts about juvenile justice offer powerful opportunities to talk about race and racism. Louis Sachar's *Holes* (1999) and Walter Dean Myers's *Monster* (1999) both tell tales about adolescent boys faced with incarceration. *Holes* is the more fanciful tale (released as a Disney movie), but both have racial overtones and undertones that could be explored in the classroom. From *Holes* we have this passage:

> Stanley kept his mouth shut most of the time. He didn't talk too much to any of the boys, afraid that he might say the wrong thing. They called him Caveman and all that, but he couldn't forget that they were dangerous, too. . . . Stanley was thankful that there were no racial problems. X-Ray, Armpit, and Zero were black. He, Squid, and Zigzag were white. Magnet was Hispanic. On the lake there were all the same reddish brown color—the color of dirt. (Sachar, p.84)

Monster is more overtly steeped in issues of race and the justice system. However, the prevailing approach to teaching it is to isolate the main character, Steve Harmon, from the racial inequities of the justice system and the larger society. Instead, most students experience this book as a story of the individual. Myers deliberately plays with the readers' penchant to assume an African American teenage boy's guilt, yet the teachers charged with examining those assumptions regularly fail to do so. My preservice teachers focus on the original way the book is written. The book discussion is often about Steve's journal and his screenplay. Teachers rarely engage in conversations about how the author recognizes that we will be easily led to believe in Steve's guilt, and such beliefs follow a racial script that is repeated over and over in our newspapers and news broadcasts. Steve's screenplay begins in the following way:

> FADE IN: INTERIOR: Early morning in CELL BLOCK D, MANHATTAN DETENTION CENTER. Camera goes slowly down grim, gray corridor. There are sounds of inmates yelling from cell to cell; much of it is obscene. Most of the voices are clearly Black or Hispanic. Camera stops and slowly turns toward a cell. (Meyers, p. 7)

This early description of the detention center sets the stage for the action. The narrator creates a familiar image for the reader—a jail or prison filled with people of color. Immediately, teachers can interrogate students' beliefs and attitudes about who is incarcerated and why. Teachers also can help students recognize the way the author makes use of cultural scripts by monitoring newspapers and news broadcasts to show the congruence between Myers's work of fiction and the daily representation of Black and Latino youth.

Two books that many teachers seem to avoid teaching altogether are *From the Notebooks of Melanin Sun* (1995) and *If You Come Softly* (2000), both by Jacqueline Woodson. Woodson takes on difficult and complex social issues in all of her books. *Melanin Sun* is the story of an African American teenage boy who lives alone with his mother. The book's major tension appears when Melanin Sun, named for the dark pigment of his skin, learns that his mother is involved in a lesbian relationship with a White woman. Melanin is conflicted over whether it is the discovery of his mother's sexual orientation or the fact that her partner is White that troubles him:

> Behind me, I heard Mama telling me to stop punching the walls, stop putting holes in the walls. But our house was filled with holes now and she'd put the biggest one right through the roof—a big giant hole that let in all of this darkness . . . she had the nerve to say, "Stop punching holes." Holding on to my arms, trying to hold me back or up because I felt like I was going to fall right over every time I thought about what it meant that she's a dyke—a big bulldagger who kisses on other women.
>
> "You're a dyke! A dyke! A dyke! You and that stupid white lady. Nobody .That's why my father disappeared and even the ugly guys didn't come back. Nobody."
>
> . . . she was holding tight to my wrists so I couldn't break away. "Let me go, Mama! Just let me go!" But at the same time I was falling right onto her chest and blubbering like a baby because I knew everybody was going to know. Everyone. Then I was begging her, crying and begging. "Please Mama. Please Mama be anything. But *please* don't be a dyke." (pp. 64–65)

He works hard to hide his mother's relationship from his best buddies. Although I regularly assign this book to preservice students, they often report that they do not think they can teach it. The immediate objection is to the sexuality issue. However, when I probe students about the race issue they insist that race is not a central issue in the story. They remark, "It's just about a middle school boy—any middle school boy." They fail to acknowledge the way race interacts with gender and sexuality to produce different responses for teenagers of color.

In *If You Come Softly* (2000), Woodson deals with the interracial relationship between a Black teenaged boy, Jeremiah, and a White teenaged girl, Ellie. The author minimizes the status differential by drawing her Black male character as the son of two relatively famous and well-educated artists.

> This evening, his mama was wearing jeans and a T-shirt with Vassar printed across the front. She had gone there, had studied literature and film. The summer after she graduated, she took a film course at NYU that his father was teaching. She had heard of him—had even seen a couple of his movies. They dated a long time before they married. I wanted to make sure he was the right man, his mother used to say. (p. 35)

His girlfriend is from an upper-middle class family that has begrudgingly accepted their adult daughter's lesbian partnership. Again, Woodson deliberately complicates the story by forcing readers to confront racism and heterosexism.

> "Don't you want to hear about the ceremony?"
>
> I laughed. "No. Lost interest. Anyway I need to talk to you about something."
>
> "Me and Stacey are having a commitment ceremony."
>
> Stacey was Anne's girlfriend. They had been together almost four years. When Anne first came out, Marion hit the roof. But by then Anne was already living in San Francisco, so there wasn't a whole lot Marion could do. Anne had told me stories about parents who threw their kids out of the house or snatched them out of college.
>
> "What are you guys committing to?"
>
> "Not what, silly. Whom. We're committing to each other." (pp. 51–52)

The two friends attend a private prep school where Jeremiah is a star basketball player. He is aware that most of the students (and perhaps the teachers also) assume that he is attending the school on a basketball scholarship. However, his parents' status and resources, which he downplays, allow him to attend the school as a tuition-paying student. An interesting turn in the story occurs when Ellie tells her lesbian sister about her crush on Jeremiah:

> Anne was quiet for a moment. "Tell me what's special about him."
>
> . . . Anne laughed. "I bet I'd like him. Anybody who makes something inside my stable baby sister go crazy must be amazing."
>
> "He's taller than me," I said. "He has locks and these bright brown eyes—"
>
> "Locks?"
>
> "His hair, you know."
>
> "Ugh. That's kind of a bummer."
>
> "Why?"
>
> "I don't like white guys with locks. I mean—it's so obviously an appropriation—"
>
> "He's *black*, Anne."
>
> She didn't say anything. I could feel the air between us getting weird. Maybe a minute passed. Maybe two. (pp. 54–55)

The book's tragic ending forces readers to confront race and racism. They must ask how race factors into the way the circumstances unfold. Once again, most of my students have declined to teach this book.

A final book I have introduced to students is *Niña Bonita* by Ana Maria Machado (1996). I introduce my students to the Spanish language version of the book. The book is the story of a little white rabbit that finds a little Black girl, Niña, strikingly beautiful. In fact, the rabbit thinks Niña's blackness is so beautiful that the rabbit would like to become black. The story is about the various strategies the rabbit tries to turn black. It is not until the rabbit learns that Niña's grandmother married a Black man that the rabbit figures out the genetic connection to Blackness. Almost no book available to US students makes the black aesthetic the norm. Because *Niña Bonita* is out of print, I do not expect that students will use it. However, in our in-class discussions, students accept the book as a "cute" story that would be "perfect for building self-esteem." They do not take up the novelty of making blackness the desired quality or how students would possibly react to this idea.

Everything Can't Be about Race

A typical response that teachers have to the claim that they maintain persistent silences about race is that we can't make everything be about race. Like the larger society, many teachers believe that discussions about race foster racism. Instead, they seem more comfortable pretending that the classroom is a colorblind community. What they actually do is what Butler (1997) refers to as repetition of regulatory identities, knowledge, and practices. Thus, certain identities are privileged while others are marginalized, and we begin to associate certain groups with certain identities, e.g., Whiteness with Americanness (Kumashiro, 2002), dropouts with Blackness. Teachers often put that repetition to use when, as Britzman (1998) argues, they search for learning that affirms their identities, experiences, perspectives, and values. Winant (2001) is eloquent in explaining why we must engage in serious and analytic talk about race:

> Race has been fundamental in global politics and culture for half a millennium. It continues to signify and structure social life not only experientially and locally, but nationally and globally. Race is present everywhere: it is evident in the distribution of resources and power, and in the desires and fears of individuals from Alberta to Zimbabwe. Race has shaped the modern economy and nation-state. It has permeated all available social identities, cultural forms, and systems of signification. Infinitely incarnated in institutions and personality, etched on the human body, racial phenomena affect the thought, experience, and accomplishments of human individuals and collectivities in many familiar ways and in a host of unconscious patterns as well. (p. 1)

Winant's words suggest that, indeed, it is *all* about race. If a major problem facing schools is that some students are achieving while others are not and the divide is a racial one, then race is the issue. If advanced placement classes rarely enroll African American students while categorical programs such as "Title I" or special education almost always enroll them, then the issue is about race. If suspension, expulsion, and dropout rates among African American students far exceed those of White students, then it is about race. If White teachers leave schools that have a majority of Black students (Freeman, Scafidi, & Sjoquist, 2002), and Black students are more likely to be taught by teachers who are either not certified or possess fewer advanced degrees (Ansell & McCabe, 2003), then the issue is race.

My argument has been that children's and young adult literature authors and illustrators *have* taken up race as a relevant issue in students' lives. They have used race in both explicit and implicit ways. Yet teachers have denied and rejected the opportunity to explore race and racial themes. Make no mistake: teachers do and will talk about "cultural differences," but these conversations are about our various unique characteristics that make us all special and our common characteristics that make us all the same. Rarely are there conversations about how race makes some of us less able to lay claim to full humanity. Rarely are there conversations about the constructed and arbitrary nature of race. And certainly, there are no critical race theory (Bell, 1992) conversations about racism that argue its permanence and its intimate relationship with capitalism. Teachers' race talk is among themselves in coded and secret conversations about families, resources, and ability. Talk in the teachers' lounge focuses on the way "those kids" and "those people" and "Title 1 kids" behave or learn.

The increasing number of children's and adult literature that is infused with race and racial themes makes teachers' decisions to ignore these themes active decisions to avoid engaging in an antiracist pedagogy. I need to be clear that teachers do this avoidance with the full authority and sanction of their administrators and the wider school community. The decision to not take up race and racial themes is the safe decision. One such argument, about taking up these themes, is that "we don't want White children to feel guilty." It is interesting to note that we rarely consider how the ongoing silences about race and racism are harmful to children—both White and those of color.

The comfortable celebration of diversity that has become routine in our schools and classrooms will never dislodge the persistent and deeply entrenched racial ideology that subsumes our lives.

Those teachers, Black, Latino, Native American, Asian American, and White, who do challenge the prevailing regimes of truth (Foucault, 1972) do so with limited support and at some peril. Typically, such teachers work with networks of antiracist and progressive educators beyond their schools and districts. They sometimes do this work in secret or by deploying a variety of subversive techniques (e.g., drama, simulations, guest speakers) that allow them enough room to move beyond the conventional treatment of such texts.

The powerful and lovely books written by Walter Dean Myers, Virginia Hamilton, the McKissacks, Mildred Taylor, Jacqueline Woodson, Christopher Paul Curtis, and others are not enough to interrupt the pedagogy of whiteness that positions the school, the curriculum, and the classroom as a space of privilege for those who can leverage White identities. Thus, students, regardless of their racial identities, are asked to be (conceptually) White (King, 1995). Despite our attempts to "multiculturalize" the curriculum, we find ourselves still playing in the dark.

References

About Ezra Jack Keats. (n.d.). de Grummond Children's Literature Collection. Retrieved from https://www.degrummond.org/about-ezra-jack-keats#:~:text=%22Then%20began%20an%20experience%20that,have%20been%20there%20all%20along.

Ansell, S., & McCabe, M. (2003). Off target: Ensuring qualified teachers. *Education Week*, 22(17), 57–59.

Bell, D. (1992). *Faces at the bottom of the well*. Basic Books.

Britzman, D. (1998). *Lost subjects, contested objects: Toward a psychoanalytic inquiry of learning*. State University of New York Press.

Butler, J. (1997). *Excitable speech: a politics of the performative*. Routledge.

Crenshaw, K. (1988). Race, reform, and retrenchment: Transformation and legitimation in antidiscrimination law. *Harvard Law Review*, *101*(7), 1331–1387.

Curtis, C. P. (1995). *The Watsons go to Birmingham—1963*. Delacorte Press.

Delgado, R. (Ed.). (1995). *Critical race theory: The cutting edge*. Temple University Press.

Fanon, F. (1967). *Black skin, white masks*. Grove Press.

Flake, S. (1998). *The skin I'm in*. Hyperion.

Fordham, S. (1988). Racelessness as a factor in Black students' school success: Pragmatic strategy or Pyrrhic victory? *Harvard Educational Review*, *58*(1), 54–84.

Foucault, M. (1972). *The archaeology of knowledge* (A. M. Sheridan Smith, Trans.). Harper & Row.

Freeman, C., Scafidi, B., & Sjoquist, D. (2002). *Racial segregation in Georgia public schools, 1994–2001: Trends, causes and impact on teacher quality*. Georgia State University.

Harris, V. (1996). Continuing dilemmas, debates, and delights in multicultural literature. *The New Advocate*, 9(2), 107–122.

Keats, E. J. (1962). *The snowy day*. Viking Press.

King, J. (1991). Dysconscious racism: Ideology, identity, and the miseducation of teachers. *The Journal of Negro Education*, *60*(2), 133–146.

King, J. (1995). Culture-centered knowledge: Black studies, curriculum transformation, and social action. In J. Banks & C. Banks (Eds.), *Handbook of research on multicultural education* (pp. 265–290). Macmillan.

Kumashiro, K. (2002). Against repetition: Addressing resistance to anti-oppressive change in the practices of learning, teaching, supervising, and researching. *Harvard Educational Review*, *72*(1), 67–92.

Ladson-Billings, G. (2000). Racialized discourses and ethnic epistemologies. In N. Denzin & Y. Lincoln (Eds.), *Handbook of qualitative research* (2nd ed., pp. 257–277). SAGE.

Leyden, L. (1998, December 2). Story hour didn't have a happy ending: N.Y. teacher runs into a racial divide with black author's "nappy hair." *The Washington Post.*

Lorbiecki, M. (2000). *Sister Anne's hands* (K. W. Popp, Illus.). Puffin Books.

Machado, A. M. (1996). *Niña Bonita* (R. Faría, Illus.). Kane Miller Books.

Morrison, T. (1989). Unspeakable things unspoken: The Afro-American presence in American literature. *Michigan Quarterly Review*, *28*(1), 9–34.

Morrison, T. (1992). *Playing in the dark: Whiteness and the literary imagination.* Harvard University Press.

Myers, W. D. (1999). *Monster.* HarperCollins.

Norris, M. (1998, December 4). *Nappy hair flap: Parents' outrage drives teacher from school.* ABC News. http://more.abcnews.go.com:80/onair/DailyNews/wnt981204_nappyhair.html

Ringgold, F. (1991). *Tar Beach.* Crown Publishers.

Sachar, L. (1999). *Holes.* Farrar, Straus & Giroux.

Spinelli, J. (1990). *Maniac Magee.* Harper Trophy.

Taxel, J. (1997). Multicultural literature and the politics of reaction. *Teachers College Record*, *98*(3), 417–448.

Turner, A. W. (1987). *Nettie's trip south.* Simon & Schuster.

Winant, H. (2001). *The world is a ghetto: Race and democracy since World War II.* Basic Books.

Woodson, J. (1995). *From the notebooks of Melanin Sun.* Scholastic.

Woodson, J. (2000). *If you come softly.* Puffin.

CHAPTER FOUR

Turning Back Time: Toward Critical Multilingual Approaches to English Language Arts

SABINE LITTLE
JENNIFER ROWSELL

Introduction

In this chapter, we examine the trajectory of critical English education through multilingual research studies we have conducted over the years to show how conceptual turns have given us a space to disrupt narrower definitions of language learning. This chapter moves across two decades of conceptual turns in language and literacy research, drawing together conceptual threads to reimagine multilingual and language research across English education contexts. Foregrounding theoretical turns through vignettes from our own research, we hope to show the promise of taking a long view of the ideas and practices that have strongly influenced literacy scholarship and praxis. The chapter tours the various turns with research examples and ends with a social justice lens on language research and practice.

The Multimodal and Multiliteracies Turns

In the early 2000s, the multimodal and multiliteracies conceptual turns took place in response to the increasingly interactive nature of texts and communication. With the ascendance of digital texts and technologies as central to communication, it became increasingly important to document how literacy changed with new and more diverse modes of expression and representation. Multimodality and multiliteracies evolved from systemic functional linguistics (Halliday, 1973) and social semiotics (Hodge & Kress, 1988) as ways to describe and theorize how readers and writers moved across words, pictures, moving images, and hypertextual elements of print and digital texts. A crucial year in their evolution was 1996, when a group of linguists, semioticians, critical theorists, and literacy researchers gathered in the United States to codevelop a reimagined framework for new text genres. The New London Group (1996), as they came to be known, moved multimodality and multiliteracies as key concepts into literacy, offering scholars a theory of literacy pedagogies premised on design and multimodality and linguistic diversity, equity, and social justice. Multimodality is a term applied to multiple modes of representation and communication present in contemporary forms of communication (Kress, 1997; 2003). The multimodal turn in multilingual research (Kenner, 2004) opened language teaching to research perspectives that move beyond words to include multiple text genres and media.

Within multilingual research, the multimodal turn gave multilingual researchers ways to examine how bilingual and multilingual learners apply different modes effectively, creatively, and fluidly across linguistic systems and how, often, this modal switching is invisible and marginalized in school (Flewitt, 2008; Kenner, 2004; Lancaster, 2003; Pahl, 1999). Language learners so often rely on visuals, moving images, and non-linguistic modes and cues to understand texts. Take, for example, procedural texts like a manual or instructions that have visuals to explain how to do something. Modes (e.g., words, pictures, social media, etc.) have specific affordances, and text users exhibiting fluency appreciate and understand the meaning potential of varied text affordances. Fluency is a reader's ability to efficiently, thoroughly, and accurately read a text. Think for a moment about blue text in an email that a reader taps to move into another text. Meaning potential does not solely reside on language and words but also on a facility with multiple modes for text comprehension. Multimodality allowed literacy and language researchers to move beyond words alone to interpret and theorize multilingual contexts (Kress, 1997).

Multiliteracies, in contrast, argues that design drives communication systems, informing how we make meaning: "As curriculum is a design for social futures, we need to introduce the notion of pedagogy as Design. As educators we need to discuss and to debate the overall shape of that design as we supplement literacy pedagogy in the ways suggested by the notion of Multiliteracies" (Cope & Kalantzis, 2000, p. 19). A key difference between multimodality and multiliteracies is that multiliteracies informs teaching and learning through a specific framework premised on the notion of design, redesign, and available design.

To illustrate multimodality and multiliteracies, Jennifer and Amelie Lemieux (Lemieux & Rowsell, 2019) conducted a coding study in 2017 in a Year 4 classroom with eighteen students (seven multilingual students) that was part of a larger Social Sciences and Humanities Research Council of Canada grant entitled Maker Literacies. The focus of the coding project was to play with language by working across print-based texts that students then coded in Scratch. Scratch is a visual programming language that gives users/designers the capacity to create multimodal stories through animations and images strung together into a story narrative. Using block coding, Scratch combines blocks to create animations. Amelie and Jennifer sat with language learners who moved across linguistic systems like Urdu or Mandarin into English while designing texts. Students designed stories based off their drawings or cutouts or a collage that they moved into block coding in Scratch. Figure 1 shows Rishu and Mark (pseudonyms) developing a storyline together in Scratch.

Within this classroom moment, a bilingual speaker and a monolingual speaker sit side-by-side to design across texts with modes building on each other. The students worked together to produce a simple story with very little language, relying very much on the affordances of colors, shapes, images, and block code. This simple example of composing a Scratch composition illustrates how multilingual learners leverage multiple modes of representation and communication to create texts.

FIGURE 1. *Coding across print-digital texts, multilingual learning across representational modes.*

The Digital Turn

Multilingualism and digital literacies have been explored from a range of theoretical perspectives to rethink what language education can be in contemporary times (Chik, 2015). Digital multilingual research studies push for what we might think of as more nuanced perspectives on digital literacy that complicate the old wine in new bottles syndrome (Lankshear & Knobel, 2003). The old wine in new bottles syndrome alludes to ways that "longstanding school language routines have a new technology tacked on here or there without in any way changing the substance of the practice" (Lankshear & Knobel, 2003, p. 5). Think of an e-reader that simply has written text on a tablet without the meaning and expressive potential of pictures, sounds, or moving images. Bringing multilingual research into digital spaces invites new constellations of skills, practices, and understandings about language that are semiotic, fluid, and invite design-based understandings. How do print multilingual practices differ from digital ones? There is multilingual research that recognizes what Lemke calls the multiplicative potential of modes (Lemke, 2002). D'Warte (2014), in her research, interprets ways that children forge new linguistic practices on technologies that invite dynamic play and participation with modes across visual, interactive texts.

Linguistic systems very often combine or blend with visuals, sounds, moving images, and the inherent logic of digital texts. Think about the hypertext (colored text moving to another often entirely different text and tab) example from earlier, which is a multimodal signifier that sits outside of language. There are also converged texts like YouTube that converge moving-image texts with conversation threads within the interface on a screen. Someone watching YouTube may be listening to a short video in Mandarin with a familiar English song in the background and with Asian culturally infused images (i.e., colors, images, and icons that signal a given culture). Reflecting on text orientations from left to right or right to left, visuals, colors, and so on, it is clear that multimodality has always played a role in language teaching and research. A key difference between multilingualism in print versus digital text genres is that digital texts invite more embodied, sensory, immersive, and machine-led language practices (Rowsell, 2025). As Chik (2015) notes, popular culture has been a way into multilingual teaching because of the pervasive use of transmodal logic.

In exploring a young child's multilingual development, Sabine and Kexin Cheng (Little & Cheng, 2024) write about the experiences of three-year-old Feifei, who grows up trilingual in England, speaking English, Mandarin, and Bahasa Indonesia. Through the use of mediagrams (Lexander & Androutsopoulos, 2021), we explored how Feifei's use of touchscreens was impacted by her multilingualism and her parents' willingness to interact with her in her multiple languages. With Mandarin and English being far more "present" through apps, Feifei's use of Bahasa Indonesia is mainly through communication tools such as talking with her grandmother or communicating about a game with her mother, whereas English and Mandarin are directly represented in the technology she consumes and interacts with, facilitating encounters with written as well as oral language.

The Temporal Turn

Time matters in language acquisition, with research around the concept of a critical period hypothesis for language learning being continually expanded and refined for more than fifty years (see Chiswick & Miller, 2008; Krashen, 1973; Penfield & Roberts, 1959). At the same time, research focused around migration and generational changes has problematized the notion of first- and second-generation immigrants, instead arriving at a more nuanced definition (Rumbaut, 2004) based on the amount of formal education an arriving person has yet to complete. These two research narratives, when woven together, highlight a complex time-driven consideration for multilingual parents and their children: How much time will there be to learn the societal or heritage language, but also, how much potential language loss or language shift (Fishman, 1991; Little, 2023) will occur in the heritage language over time?

With children spending a significant amount of time in school, understanding opportunities for supporting and valuing multilingual development becomes a vital component in holistically supporting children. One example helpful in exploring children's multilingual and multiliterate development over an extended period of time can be found in the rivers of reading methodology (Cliff Hodges, 2010; Little, 2024)—the methodology supports children in creating a chronological artifact that explores important encounters with literary texts, regardless of format or language. In her research, Sabine explored seven children's (eight to thirteen years old) rivers of reading, conducting three interviews per family, with the child-created river of reading falling between the second and third interview. In understanding what children and young people might deem "important" enough to include in their "river," she was able to understand the role that different languages, texts, and people play in children's lives. Her research indicates that multilingual children's reasonings are highly varied and are linked to narratives around language learning and acquisition, migrational journeys, and social and emotional connections to family members and friends abroad, as well as standard "likes" and "dislikes" (Little,

2024). The metaphor of the river, beginning at a source (analogous to birth) and then continuing with branches, confluences, etc., enables children to construct, with parental input, a complex multimodal artifact that explores engagement with text-based sources (see Figure 2).

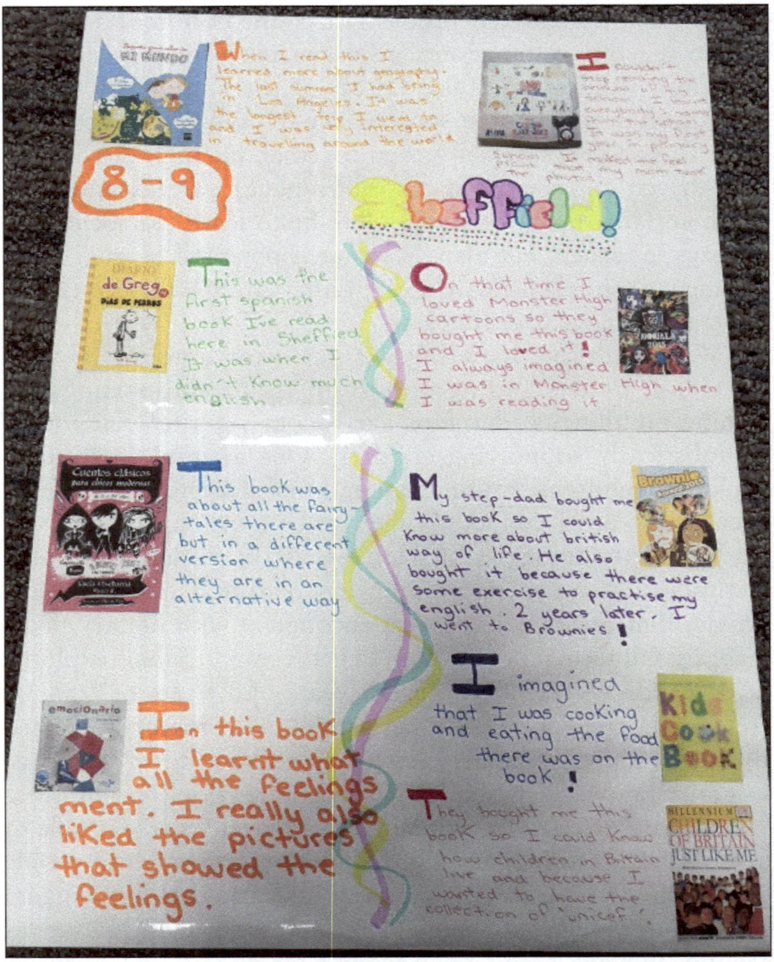

FIGURE 2. *A partial River of Reading, highlighting a temporary "split" between the child's two languages, which later disappears.*

The river of reading artifact not only gives families the opportunity to discuss how different languages are used within the family over time, but it also enables teachers to access children's funds of identity (Esteban-Guitart, 2012), facilitating a more nuanced and responsive understanding of children's multilingual development.

The Spatial Turn

The spatial turn in literacy and language research marked a movement into the role of spaces in how learners practice and experience moving across linguistic systems. Gutiérrez (2008) applied third space theory to describe collective spaces where diverse language learners interrupt deficit perspectives, share their stories, dreams, and cultural knowledge, in an educational environment that supports and extends students' communicative repertoires as they redefine their sense of self and "the world as it could be" (p. 158). We find this type of research on multilingual contexts generative because it captures a sense of collective linguistic practices in places.

Methodologically, third space theory offers an opportunity to conduct research into a family's multilingual experiences, creating a third space (Bhabha, 1994) or fusion of horizons (Gadamer, 1989) between children and adults to facilitate children's agency and control over research. In Little and Little (2022), Sabine and her son (aged 6.5 years at the start of a 2.5-year-long autoethnographical study and aged twelve when the paper was published) jointly explore their experiences of parent and child, respectively. Here, the third space affords the chance to sensitively and meaningfully explore different experiences, highlighting common ground and differences through communication.

At a more literal level, dedicating physical space to multilingual resources in public spheres, including schools and libraries, is part of a holistic approach to supporting multilingual children's language and identity development. In researching the impact of a multilingual children's library on families' sense of identity and belonging in relation to the city the library was situated in, Sabine and Rebecca Murray found that parents valued having "their" language visible and accessible, the dedication of "space" being viewed as a signal of support and inclusion (Little, 2025; Little & Murray, 2024). This space is, of course, also metaphorical: In dedicating physical space, the message is that multilingual children have a literal "right to take up space" (Lefebvre, 1996).

The Posthuman Turn

There has been an increasing acknowledgment of nonhuman qualities to language and literacy learning by accounting for objects, technologies, and media (Pennycook, 2017). This research is known as posthumanism and sociomateriality, and it is helpful to explain the ways that language speakers engage in language practices with nonhuman matter. Posthumanism broadens researchers' perspectives so that they think about how people, as humans, are fully entangled with the agentive forces such as technologies, media, and nature. With posthumanism coming into literacy and language research, scholars begin to see how people, things, ideas, and the ecologies within us and around us are inseparable; they interconnect and intersect in often unpredictable ways (Pennycook, 2017). An example of research situated within a materialist paradigm is the notion of artifactual literacies (Pahl & Rowsell, 2010) that focuses on artifacts as signaling identities and as laden with stories and contexts as well as with an increased focus on modes, materials, and technologies. There are constant interactions between humans and objects, and objects are sometimes technologies but not always—sometimes they are the stuff that surrounds us as part of the environment, the natural environment as well as mundane, everyday objects (Kuby et al., 2015; Pahl & Rowsell, 2010).

Scholars like Candace Kuby (2013) interpret how individuals and matter/things coexist, co-construct, co-become across contexts. What posthuman research has done for multilingual researchers is to open spaces to examine how human and nonhuman assemblages intra-act across time and space (Pennycook, 2017). Materialist and posthumanist scholars (Barad, 2007) account for how entangled people are with objects and texts that surround them. Rather than regarding material objects that we use as passive or inert, researchers apply posthumanism and new materiality to multilingual research to show how objects are performative agents. Through a posthumanist lens, artifacts and other nonhuman resources become active participants in language assemblages (Pennycook & Otsuji, 2017).

An example of ways that a posthumanist lens can be applied in multilingual learning contexts is a high school study in 2018 called Face Value that Jennifer, Peter Vietgen, and an English and media teacher conducted with twenty Year 12 students as a part of their English and media class (Rowsell, 2020). Most of the students were English speakers, but one student had recently arrived from China with very little English proficiency. The research involved creating a self-portrait out of arts and crafts materials. After taking a conceptual selfie, students then designed a self-portrait out of a myriad of supplies. What you see below (Figure 3) is Menting's (pseudonym) self-portrait made from yarn glued onto canvas.

FIGURE 3. *Menting's self-portrait, materialising linguistic and cultural diversities in mixed media.*

The Affect Turn

As language and literacy scholars are discovering, the affective turn holds untapped potential for exploring emotional and affective intensities and atmospheres that saturate classrooms (and the spaces beyond), that touch us in unexpected ways, and that prompt us to consider other ways of observing and documenting language and literacy research. The affect turn in literacy and language research (Ehret & Rowsell, 2021) marked a movement away from a focus on modes of representation and communication to more of a lived, nonrepresentational perspective on how people practice literacy and language.

Ahmed (2015) describes affective intensities as collective sensibilities "crucial to the very constitution of the physical and the social as objects" so that emotions "allow the individual and the social to be delineated as if they are objects" (p. 10). Emotions can spread, moving through the movement or circulation of objects. To consider language an assemblage means viewing all the semiotic resources at play, interacting, "generating different forms of synergy for meaning making" (Canagarajah, 2018, p. 4), leading to the production of meanings and knowledge.

Research by literacy scholars like Lewis and Tierney (2013) gave the field of literacy and multilingualism ways to explore emotion as an action, as mediated by language, and how language, in turn, can mobilize emotion in a racially and ethnically diverse high school setting. Such work moves beyond an account of design principles, affordances, and constraints and instead moves closely into the embodied dimensions of language. As well, Leander and Boldt's (2013) seminal article pushed scholars in literacy studies to move into felt experiences when engaging with media and multimodal texts. Such conceptual work explores youth identities, investigating emotionally saturated multimodal literacy-related activities that youth engage in all the time. In Leander and Boldt's (2013) article, they detail and theorize several hours in middle schooler Lee's day at home with a friend. Leander and Boldt describe digital play, physical movements, gestures, drawing, writing, and then more moving—in other words, Lee's meaning-making is "in the body," drawing out emotions, materialities, and different timescales. Ehret's research, too, paved new ground with an affect turn that invites researchers to think of literacy practices as relational and filled with affective intensities (2018). Researching in hospitals and secondary schools with young people, Ehret showed the ways that fluency in language and literacy emerges from the ways that young people feel and experience texts that they value and invest in, and this cannot be interpreted by literacy and language researchers without explicit accounts of affect.

In a 2018 research project that Jennifer and Julianne Burgess conducted called Resettled Literacies (Burgess & Rowsell, 2020), they spent two months in a welcome center in Niagara, giving ten different multimodal workshops on the notion of resettlement. Participants were aged from twenty-five to seventy-five and created soundscapes, short animated texts, and artifact activities. Thinking and composing with affect became a strong theme throughout the research project and particularly the notion of experiencing language through affect. Take Figure 4 below, which is a Storybird text by a student in her late twenties.

This particular text materializes transcultural moments that come alive through emotion, nostalgia, and affective intensities brought forth during teaching. There was a felt force she showed when she talked about this Storybird-produced text that moved beyond words and learning English to relationality and occupying a space in a new context.

FIGURE 4. *Sumaya's Storybird artifact about her grandmother's view at home composing narratives across emotional landscapes.*

Connections with Critical English Education

The properties of critical English education are not easy to put your finger on; criticality is something experienced and felt. Being a critical English educator demands acknowledging linguistic, modal, affective, temporal, spatial complexities—respecting and sitting within them. Critical English teaching and learning is not confined to a certain kind of text written in a particular language with a specific register. Rather, critical English education pedagogies display what Perry (2023) calls "pluriversal literacies"—the many different meaning-making practices that people use to interact and communicate across time and place. Traditional English education does not match this kind of definition and framing. Classic schooled English pedagogies assume that there is one way to learn a text—in one language through one mode in one setting. We hope that our brief historical tour of key turns has built a picture of the great potential of critical, disruptive, pluriversal English education for generations to come.

This chapter shows that there is much to learn from conceptual turns that can help multilingual learners in our English language arts teaching. We hope that the chapter offers a useful lens through which to explore the theoretical and practical concerns impacting research over the past decade or so. However, in conclusion, a final "turn," although it is not typically thus defined, must shape our future research and endeavors. The various turns highlighted in this chapter must be used to critically highlight inequalities—not just the inequalities facing many multilingual learners themselves (Cunningham & Little, 2022) but also inequalities across different languages. Whereas some multilingual learners—typically those speaking languages that are widely recognized or those that can be found on the national curriculum as "modern foreign languages"—are advantaged (through the availability of technology, apps, printed resources, research, etc.), others remain less visible, less supported, less "validated" in the eyes of learners and their families. Hints of this are visible in Feifei's use of apps and games, where two of her languages (English and Mandarin) are supported much more than her third one (Bahasa Indonesia), and in the difficulties the multilingual children's library encountered when it came to providing books across Sheffield's most spoken languages, not all of which have a rich publishing industry (Little & Murray, 2024). In our ongoing research, then, we must be aware of not only our increasing numbers of multilingual learners but also of the underlying privilege experienced by some but not by others. The multilingual turn, in and of itself, has a social justice element, working hard to make multilingualism visible, relevant, and supported. As we move forward through the various turns, our understanding of social justice becomes ever more nuanced, looking at raciolinguistics and deficit discourses around language (Cushing, Georgiou, & Karatsareas, 2021). Our closing argument, then, in a volume dedicated to criticality in English education, is that in today's world, it is impossible to be a critical researcher and remain solely focused on English in classrooms full of learners who bring with them multilingual assets and who will live, move, and work in a multilingual world.

References

Ahmed, S. (2015). *The cultural politics of emotion* (2nd ed.). Routledge.

Barad, K. (2007). *Meeting the universe halfway: Quantum physics and the entanglement of matter and meaning*. Duke University Press.

Bhabha, H. K. (1994). *The location of culture*. Routledge.

Burgess, J., & Rowsell, J. (2020). Transcultural-affective flows and multimodal engagements: Reimagining pedagogy and assessment with adult language learners. *Language and Education, 34*(2), 173–191. https://doi.org/10.1080/09500782.2020.1720226

Canagarajah, S. (2018). Materializing "competence": Perspectives from international STEM scholars. *The Modern Language Journal, 102*(2), 268–291.

Chik, A. (2015). Popular culture, digital worlds and second language learners. In J. Rowsell & K. Pahl (Eds.), *The Routledge handbook of literacy studies* (pp. 339–353). Routledge.

Chiswick, B. R., & Miller, P. W. (2008). A test of the critical period hypothesis for language learning. *Journal of Multilingual and Multicultural Development*, *29*(1), 16–29.

Cliff Hodges, G. (2010). Rivers of reading: Using critical incident collages to learn about adolescent readers and their readership. *English in Education, 44*(3), 181–200.

Cope, B., & Kalantzis, M. (2000). *Multiliteracies: Literacy learning and the design of social futures.* Routledge.

Cunningham, C., & Little, S. (2022). "Inert benevolence" towards languages beyond English in the discourses of English primary school teachers. *Linguistics and Education*, *78,* Article 101122. https://doi.org/10.1016/j.linged.2022.101122

Cushing I., Georgiou, A., & Karatsareas, P. (2021). Where two worlds meet: Language policing in mainstream and complementary schools in England. *International Journal of Bilingual Education and Bilingualism*, *27*(9), 1182–1198. https://doi.org/10.1080/13670050.2021.1933894

D'Warte, J. (2014). Exploring linguistic repertoires: Multiple language use and multimodal literacy activity in five classrooms. *Australian Journal of Language and Literacy*, *37*(1), 21–30.

Ehret, C. (2018). Moments of teaching and learning in a children's hospital: Affects, textures, and temporalities. *Anthropology & Education Quarterly*, *49*(1), 53–71.

Ehret, C., & Rowsell, J. (2021). Teaching through the moment: Affect and literacy in uncertain times. *Literacy Today, 38*(5), 16–18.

Esteban-Guitart, M. (2012). Towards a multimethodological approach to identification of funds of identity, small stories and master narratives. *Narrative Inquiry,* 22(1), 173–180.

Fishman, J. A. (1991). *Reversing language shift: Theoretical and empirical foundations of assistance to threatened languages.* Multilingual Matters.

Flewitt, R. (2008). Multimodal literacies. In J. Marsh & E. Hallet (Eds.), *Desirable literacies: Approaches to language and literacy in the early years* (pp. 122–139). SAGE.

Gadamer, H. G. (1989). *Truth and method* (2nd ed.). Continuum.

Gutiérrez, K. D. (2008). Developing a sociocritical literacy in the Third Space. *Reading Research Quarterly, 43*(2), 148–164.

Halliday, M. K. (1973). *Explorations in the functions of language*. Edward Arnold.

Hodge, R., & Kress, G. (1988). *Social semiotics*. John Wiley & Sons.

Kenner, C. (2004). *Becoming biliterate: Young children learning different writing systems*. Trentham Books.

Krashen, S. (1973). Lateralization, language learning, and the critical period: Some new evidence. *Language and Learning, 23*(1), 63–74.

Kress, G. (1997). *Before writing: Rethinking the paths to literacy*. Routledge.

Kress, G. (2003). *Literacy in the new media age*. Routledge.

Kuby, C. R. (2013). *Critical literacy in the early childhood classroom: Unpacking histories, unlearning privilege*. Teachers College Press.

Kuby, C. R., Gutshall Rucker, T., & Kirchhofer, J. M. (2015). "Go be a writer": Intra-activity with materials, time and space in literacy learning. *Journal of Early Childhood Literacy, 15*(3), 394–419.

Lancaster, L. (2003). Beginning at the beginning: How a young child constructs time multimodally. In C. Jewitt & G. Kress (Eds.), *Multimodal literacy* (pp. 107–122). Peter Lang.

Lankshear, C., & Knobel, M. (2003). *New literacies: Changing knowledge and classroom learning*. Open University Press.

Leander, K. M., & Boldt, G. M. (2013). Rereading "A pedagogy of multiliteracies": Bodies, texts, and emergence. *Journal of Literacy Research, 45*(1), 22–46.

Lefebvre, H. (1996). *Writings on cities* (E. Kofman & E. Lebas, Eds.). Wiley-Blackwell.

Lemieux, A., & Rowsell, J. (2019). Taking a wide-angled view of contemporary digital literacy. In O. Erstad, R. Flewitt, B. Kümmerling-Meibauer, & Í. S. Pires Pereira (Eds.), *The Routledge handbook of digital literacies in early childhood* (pp. 453–463). Routledge.

Lemke, J. (2002). Travels in hypermodality. *Visual Communication, 1*(3), 299–325.

Lewis, C., & Tierney, J. D. (2013). Mobilizing emotion in an urban classroom: Producing identities and transforming signs in a race-related discussion. *Linguistics and Education, 24*(3), 289–304.

Lexander, K. V., & Androutsopoulos, J. (2021). Working with mediagrams: A methodology for collaborative research on mediational repertoires in multilingual families. *Journal of Multilingual and Multicultural Development, 42*(1), 1–18.

Little, S. (2023). "Half of who you are": Parent and child reflections on the emotional experiences of reversing familial language shift. *International Journal of Bilingualism, 27*(2), 217–231.

Little, S. (2024). Rivers of multilingual reading: Exploring biliteracy experiences among 8–13-year old heritage language readers. *Journal of Multilingual and Multicultural Development, 45*(2), 323–336. https://doi.org/10.1080/01434632.2021.1882472

Little, S. (2025). "There's a sense of pride": The multilingual children's library as perezhivanie. *Public Library Quarterly*. https://doi.org/10.1080/01616846.2024.2447977

Little, S., & Cheng, K. (2024). Digital funds of identity: Understanding a young child's plurilingual development through mediagrams. *Innovation in Language Learning and Teaching, 18*(3), 208–222, https://doi.org/10.1080/17501229.2023.2276952

Little, S., & Little, T. (2022). An un/familiar space: Children and parents as collaborators in autoethnographic family research. *Qualitative Research, 22*(4), 632–648.

Little, S., & Murray, R. (2024). The multilingual children's library as physical and metaphorical "space" within the community: Practical and emotional considerations. *Journal of Librarianship and Information Science, 56*(1), 131–144. https://doi.org/10.1177/09610006221133837

New London Group. (1996). A pedagogy of multiliteracies: Designing social futures. *Harvard Educational Review, 66*(1), 60–92.

Pahl, K. (1999). *Transformations: Meaning making in nursery education*. Trentham Books.

Pahl, K., & Rowsell, J. (2010) *Artifactual literacies: every object tells a story*. Teachers College Press.

Pahl, K., Rowsell, J., Collier, D., Pool, S., Rasool, Z., & Trzecak, T. (2020). *Living literacies: Literacy for social change*. The MIT Press.

Penfield, W., & Roberts, L. (1959). *Speech and brain mechanisms*. Princeton University Press.

Pennycook, A. (2017). *Posthumanist applied linguistics*. Routledge.

Pennycook, A., & Otsuji, E. (2017). Fish, phone cards and semiotic assemblages in two Bangladeshi shops in Sydney and Tokyo. *Social Semiotics, 27*(4), 434–450.

Perry, M. (2023). *Pluriversal literacies for sustainable futures: When words are not enough*. Routledge.

Rowsell, J. (2020). "How emotional do I make it?" Making a stance in multimodal compositions. *Journal of Adolescent & Adult Literacy, 63*(6), 627–637. https://doi.org/10.1002/jaal.1034

Rowsell, J. (2025). *The comfort of screens: Literacy in postdigital times*. Cambridge University Press.

Rumbaut, R. G. (2004). Ages, life stages, and generational cohorts: Decomposing the immigrant first and second generations in the United States. *International Migration Review, 38*(3), 1160–1205.

Chapter Five

Histories and Futures Matter in Critical English Education

Maisha T. Winn

Preparing my return to English language arts (ELA) methods teaching after a seven-year hiatus, I looked through teaching journals chronicling my experiences as a ninth- and tenth-grade literature teacher in Northern California. Those journal entries focused less on well-executed lesson plans and units than on my deepening relationships with students and attempts to cultivate joy while navigating difficult classroom moments and patterns. I dove back into entries and memories of approaching the assistant principal regarding whether some of my hardest working Black and Latinx students could receive "college-prep" credit for their coursework, in this class designated "non-college prep," and being told that the school was unable to accommodate my request. Of having to return to these students and attempt to explain this decision without understanding it myself. Of discovering the one resource in the school book-closet written by a Black author—Richard Wright's *Black Boy*—and being so excited to integrate it into the syllabus until one of my Black students sought me out to ask why every Black protagonist they discovered through school had to be depressing.

This revelation became one of the themes and larger inquiry projects our classroom community grappled with that academic year. I came across reflections from Friday community literacy events to which I invited local poets, writers, government workers, students from a nearby law school, and anyone willing to share with my students, "What does literacy mean to you and how does it show up in your everyday life?" Many Fridays, I would walk into my classroom to find friends of current students asking if they could participate that day because they had been told how fun and fascinating these sessions were. With reluctance, I had to turn them away due to school policy.

These stories affirm what I believed then and now: Teaching through literature is at least as much about the relationships and community one cultivates as it is about the curriculum. While I did not have, then, the discursive tools I would subsequently acquire in graduate school as a language, literacy, and culture researcher to analyze my experiences as a classroom teacher, it was definitely by leading classrooms at the elementary and high school levels that the seeds of my research were planted. Then and now, I understood a critical English education as focused learning that seeks to humanize and historicize—to borrow from Kris Gutiérrez—the diverse readers, writers, thinkers, and "doers" in our classrooms (Gutiérrez, 2008). Critical English education is equally concerned with teachers and their ability to leverage writing, reading, and engaging with literature as opportunities to/for transformation in and beyond the classroom. This chapter traces the trajectory of my thinking around critical English education and repositions critical English education as an act of transformative justice and possibility.

English Teachers as "Practitioners of the Craft"

I have spent the last two decades learning from and with African American writers, readers, thinkers, and "doers of the word," examining spaces they have excavated to support their literate and literary trajectories. This work has taken me into Black bookstores, cafes that double as cultural centers, youth detention centers, after-school programs, elective writing classes, and restorative justice circles in classrooms and in communities. Over time, I shifted from attempting to understand the culture of these spaces, which I refer to as "participatory literacy communities" (PLCs), to learning from and with these communities about how to identify and leverage salient characteristics to design more equitable and justice-seeking educational practices and institutions (Fisher, 2003; Winn, 2018; Winn & Winn, 2021). My projects have coalesced around the historical traditions of multiply marginalized people creating their own institutions within institutions—when communities have only had partial access to or been excluded altogether from high-quality, rigorous educational environments.

Over the years, I have reimagined and introduced several terms that guide my thinking around critical English education. Doing ethnographic research with student poets in a Bronx alternative high school, I referred to these students' ELA teacher, Papa Joe, as a "practitioner of the craft." Papa Joe did not merely assign reading and writing; he was a reader and writer making his own process transparent to his students (Fisher, 2007). Papa Joe and his co-teachers, Amy and Roland, modeled reading community participation, constantly bringing each other books during class, and exchanging and sharing their own writing in ways that demonstrated vulnerability and humanity and growth to their students, who also offered feedback and ideas. These and other practitioners of the craft engage in—and share—literate practices *beyond* the classroom. A practitioner of the craft is likely making their way through different literary genres on their nightstand, keeping journals to explore new lenses and various aspects of themselves, and joyfully engaging with an author event at a local bookstore, participating in a reading group, or being a writer or poet themselves.

As I journeyed with Papa Joe to understand "performing literacy" as a pathway through which young people can develop literate identities, I began using another term in my work (Fishman et al., 2015): "Worthy witness" was how Papa Joe referred to my approach as a researcher exploring and offering theoretical and methodological intervention for literacy scholars in school communities. Together, we identified four phases of a worthy witness approach: admission, declaration, revelation, and confidentiality. Admission refers to how researchers enter the site/community. Typically, this process can be top down from the viewpoint of youth who may be in classrooms or communities where the work is being done.

In Papa Joe's class, students were engaged in a discussion about the value (or lack thereof) of having a researcher in their space, creating a culture of collaboration and youth agency. Declaration draws from the researcher's positionality or reflexivity: Who is the researcher beyond titles and affiliations and what are the parts of a researcher's identity that the community wants to learn more about? Revelation, according to Papa Joe, referred to the auspicious moment where the learning community's goals and the researcher's goals begin to merge, creating robust learning opportunities for all stakeholders. And, finally, confidentiality is supporting youth who share their stories about their experiences in education institutions and beyond, knowing you will carry these stories with great integrity while actively resisting "damage-centered" research (Tuck, 2009). These phases, and the approach overall, continue to emerge as relevant to pursuits and revisits of critical English education (Winn & Ubiles, 2011), and scholars have identified worthy witnessing as a valuable approach for examining and transforming the "communicative repertoires" of youth (Martinez et al., 2017), as a "critical epistemological framework" (Caraballo et al., 2017), and understanding teachers' "raciolinguistic literacies" (Seltzer & de los Ríos, 2018). Worthy witnessing can take place anywhere educators who are "practitioners of the craft" partner with researchers in intentional ways to discover what they can learn from and with each other as teaching and learning happen.

Worthy witnesses can be primary teachers, co-teachers, support teachers, librarians, researchers who believe in researching with communities, parent volunteers, and others who participate in the classroom as a valuable resource of ideas to teachers. In addition to my time with Papa Joe, Amy, and Roland, the Power Writers showed me (and provided evidence) that educators can seek to be humanizing, transformative, and rigorous. The Power Writers, a collective of youth poets in the Bronx, New York, who participated in a co-curricular course at their high school, were young writers learning together to "catch words" (improve their vocabulary); "sing" their writing (focus on the power of voice); and "read and feed" value (both give feedback and share their work). I note with interest and gratitude the enduring impact the Power Writers had on young learners: A decade after the initial study, former student-participants self-reported that aspects of their adult lives continued to be guided by mindset work and practices they had cultivated in class (Winn, 2016). For me, too, learning from and with the Power Writers informed my thinking about what it means to be in a "lifetime circle" and how to prioritize restorative and transformative approaches in and through the teaching of ELA.

From Critical to Transformative

My multisite ethnography of the Power Writers provided me with a foundation for worthy witnessing in a range of literacy teaching and learning contexts. A key takeaway was the compelling nature and power of a team of educators working toward a common goal, bringing their own stories and histories to their teaching and being in conversation with their students' lived experiences. I first started imagining the intersections of critical English education and restorative justice through the lens of Mary Rose O'Reilley's work imagining the "peaceable classroom" (O'Reilley, 1984; 1993). At the height of the Vietnam War, when O'Reilly was a graduate student in the Midwest, Ihab Hassan posed the question: "I wonder if it is possible to teach literature in such a way that people stop killing each other?" I could relate to O'Reilley's reflection when she writes "the question has stayed with me and from time to time assailed my conscious" as it continues to haunt me as I seek to make the teaching of English relevant (O'Reilley, 1984, p. 109). When I did revisit the question, I reframed it more broadly: How might we teach every discipline so that people stop killing? English? Math? Social Studies? Art? Science? This was a baseline for my emerging concept of restorative English education, which I later called transformative justice English education.

Realizing I had wrongly omitted the word "justice" from early iterations of that work, I corrected myself by positioning "justice" as rightly central to English education teaching. Restorative justice is a paradigm, shifting interpersonal and system dynamics and cultural norms toward inclusive and humanizing relational practices for building and sustaining community and, as needed, for addressing harm and wrongdoing. Restorative justice colleague-leaders within and beyond the domain of education then challenged me to consider some of the limitations in the notion of "restorative," which suggests a return to a desired prior state. Yet many writers, readers, poets, performers, teachers, and students whom I had observed and interviewed did not find their literary voices within the confines of the classrooms of their pasts. The word "restorative" did not capture the desires of people and groups who had experienced their formal learning environments as restrictive spaces, where there was more focus on disciplining the body than cultivating the mind, let alone pursuits of joy and liberation.

Transitioning from "restorative" to "transformative" was largely informed by my time with a collective of teaching artists in the Southeast who taught playmaking and acting to student artists in youth detention centers. Witnessing these student artists reclaim aspects of their identities as playwrights, performers, artists, and writers required a new lens through which I viewed a critical English education. Too many of the student artists I met started with a normal school day, only to have an in-school incident lead to arrest and subsequent incarceration. It was humbling to note that what these student artists—mostly African American girls—wanted most was to connect with positive people and to have space to express themselves. Playmaking and performing provided an opportunity for a particular kind of restorative justice; however, girls in the program needed more substantial change in their life beyond the program (Winn, 2011).

These experiences begged the question if the notion of restorative went far enough. The 2015 National Conference on Community and Restorative Justice was the first critical space where I heard restorative justice theorists and practitioners challenge restorative justice discourse. In sum, many young people did not have healthy relationships to the place called "school" or with the people inside. Some of these discussions and debates begged the question, what if restoration and being restorative—which implies that there is something worthy of returning to—should be replaced with "transformative" to signal the need for a radical overhaul of the system. I think about this when people ask me why "critical" is added to English education: It simply gives us an opportunity to expand the canon, speak to a range of stakeholders, and—finally—take into consideration what students, their families, and communities already know.

Looking Back to Look Ahead: Histories and Futures Matter in Critical English Education

In contemplating the future of critical English education, it will be important for the field to consult historical models for this work. Our challenge and opportunity are to consult out-of-school teaching and learning communities as well as grassroots movements. Parents, educators, and students from a range of communities have engaged in movement building, institution building, and organizing that we can learn from as we imagine how to leverage the teaching of writing, literature, discussion, and debate for equitable learning communities, including Latinx struggles for education (Marquez, 2020) and Black/Asian solidarity work (Wong, 2023). To be sure, I have been engaged in what I call historiography for the future—a methodological intervention seeking to reclaim untapped histories of Black parents, educators specifically from the Black Arts Movement (1965–1975) who designed Independent Black Institutions (IBIs), which often housed schools, publishing companies and typesetting services, food cooperatives or eateries, and intergenerational learning opportunities for the community. Historiography for the future examines the relationship between contemporary signals of change—or a datapoint with potential to grow in scale and point people in the direction of a particular future—with historical signals. Historical signals reposition history as innovation, especially in the case of non-dominant communities who had to be solution oriented when denied access to mainstream institutions or denied access to equitable opportunities in such institutions. Elsewhere, I argue that IBIs left maps of the future of Black education through their many publications, including pamphlets, booklets, brochures, newspapers, journals, and magazines (Winn, 2025). Parents, educators, and everyday people during the Black Arts Movement—the cultural wing of the Black Power Movement, typically situated between 1965 and 1975—launched initiatives to establish independent preK–12 schools for Black children.

The primary source documents some of these IBIs left behind demonstrate that a key focus was to ensure that each generation saw the value in reading, writing, and doing. All too often, the idea of innovation and the future are intertwined with new directions and technologies. However, restorative justice theorist Mimi Kim reminds us that sometimes innovation involves reaching back and considering some of the practices of indigenous communities, social movements, and grassroots efforts to reclaim and reimagine (Roberts, Kim, & Maruna, 2024). As I imagine the next decade of critical English education, I ask: What are the different ways non-dominant communities have engaged in literate and literary practices? What institutions did they create, nurture, and sustain even in the absence of formal buildings? How can we harness the power of past innovations and efforts to cultivate a reading, writing, and thinking culture on the contours of schools and English classrooms? New directions for research and practice will need to consult history and seek out historical signals for where to go next.

References

Caraballo, L., Lozenski, B. D., Lyiscott, J. J., & Morrell, E. (2017). YPAR and critical epistemologies: Rethinking education research. *Review of Research in Education, 41*, 311–336.

Fisher, M. T. (2003). *Choosing literacy: African diaspora participatory literacy communities* [Unpublished doctoral dissertation]. University of California, Berkeley.

Fisher, M. T. (2007). *Writing in rhythm: Spoken word poetry in urban classrooms*. Teachers College Press.

Fishman, J., Lunsford, A., McGregor, B., & Otuteye, M. (2005). Performing writing, performing literacy. *College Composition & Communication, 57*(2), 224–252.

Gutiérrez, K. D. (2008). Language and literacies as civil rights. In S. Greene (Ed.), *Literacy as a civil right: Reclaiming social justice in literacy teaching and learning* (pp. 169–184). Peter Lang.

Marquez, L. (2020). *La gente: Struggles for empowerment and community self-determination in Sacramento*. University of Arizona Press.

Martinez, D. C., Zitlali Morales, P., & Aldana, U. S. (2017). Leveraging students' communicative repertoires as a tool for equitable learning. *Review of Research in Education, 41*(1), 477–499.

O'Reilley, M. R. (1984). The peaceable classroom. *College English, 46*(2), 103–112.

O'Reilley, M. R. (1993). *The peaceable classroom.* Heinemann.

Roberts, D., Kim, M., & Maruna S. (2024). *How to share and transfer innovations in justice across silos* [Panel discussion]. Justice Innovations Summit 2024, University of Hawai'i Mānoa.

Seltzer, K., & de los Ríos, C. V. (2018). Translating theory to practice: Exploring teachers' raciolinguistic literacies in secondary English classrooms. *English Education, 51*(1), 49–79.

Tuck, E. (2009). Suspending damage: A letter to communities. *Harvard Educational Review, 79*(3), 409–427.

Winn, M. T. (2011). *Girl time: Literacy, justice, and the school-to-prison pipeline.* Teachers College Press.

Winn, M. T. (2016). *Still* writing in rhythm: Youth poets at work. *Urban Education, 54*(1), 89–125. http://uex.sagepub.com/content/early/2016/04/08/0042085916641174.abstract

Winn, M. T. (2018). *Justice on both sides: Transforming education through restorative justice.* Harvard Education Press.

Winn, M. T. (2025). *Futuring Black lives: Independent Black institutions and the literary imagination.* Vanderbilt University Press.

Winn, M. T., & Ubiles, J. R. (2011). Worthy witnessing: Collaborative research in urban classrooms. In A. Ball & C. Tyson (Eds.), *Studying diversity in teacher education* (pp. 295–308). Rowman & Littlefield.

Winn, M. T., & Winn, L. T. (Eds.). (2021). *Restorative justice in education: Transforming teaching and* learning through the disciplines. Harvard Education Press.

Wong, C. P. (2023, September). Power matters: Some personal notes for educators on restorative and transformative justice [Paper]. University of California, Davis: Transformative Justice in Education Center.

Chapter Six

Embracing Complexity with Critical Hope: Toward Intergenerational Inquiry in English Education

Limarys Caraballo

A voice from the dark called out,
'The poets must give us
imagination of peace, to oust the intense, familiar
imagination of disaster. Peace, not only
the absence of war.'
But peace, like a poem,
is not there ahead of itself,
can't be imagined before it is made,
can't be known except
in the words of its making,
grammar of justice,
syntax of mutual aid.
—Denise Levertov, from "Making Peace," 1987

I am on my second cup of coffee of the day, sitting in an office with shelves of books, dozens of cherished student projects and professional artifacts, and memories from almost three decades of teaching. I look over my notes, make a few edits on this chapter, write a few sentences, delete them, and return to the news. Abandoning my revision, I turn to my journal instead, determined to bear worthy witness, rendering vignettes that document the interactions with those closest to me[1]—amid a constant stream of opinion pieces and social posts, no one feels heard. I wonder what experiences and engagements in English language arts, as we would imagine or desire it, might nurture those "poets" who, as Denise Levertov muses, might offer an "imagination of peace" that can "oust the intense, familiar imagination of disaster" and instead foster critical hope.

Once again, educators are on the front lines where youth and communities are questioning and seeking answers. Academic institutions across the spectrum must once again hold in balance the importance of authentic discourse while protecting the vulnerable. Within the past several years, global and local crises such as the coronavirus pandemic and mass gun violence, Black and Brown lives have birthed new coalitions against racism, homophobia, and xenophobia while polarizing discourses about race, immigration, gender, and language have bred uncertainty about what should and should not be taught in classrooms and schools. Fellow scholars have addressed the ways in which recent crises have exposed and exacerbated inequities in society (Roy, 2020), calling for a "hard reset" in education that holds all stakeholders accountable in rethinking institutional and academic practices that further marginalize nondominant communities (Ladson-Billings, 2021), while a vocal few control public discourse about what is wrong or lacking in education. Many seem mired in a paralyzing paradox, where silence enables further injustice or violence, yet taking a stand can feel polarizing. Solidarities seem elusive when they are most needed.

What is the role of a critical English education in such contexts? How has English education embraced, resisted, or built upon the many ideological, practical, and theoretical legacies in the field? What might we desire into being? In any area of study, curricula and pedagogy are informed by major debates and shifts in the fields, such as the push and pull of disciplinary objectives, professional roles, and societal expectations. In English education, this complexity is exacerbated by questions such as those posed by Allan Luke (2004) almost two decades ago in "The Trouble with English," written at the dawn of the new millennium: "What might it mean to teach and to profess English in a multilingual and multicultural, heteroglossic and multi-mediated world where it is alternatively seen as threat and promise, deficit and capital?" (p. 85). Contemporaneous with Luke's essay, Morrell (2005) argued that critical English education is "explicit about the role of language and literacy in conveying meaning and in promoting or disrupting existing power relations" while also fostering the skills for students to "deconstruct dominant texts" as well as "create their own critical texts that can be used in the struggle for social justice" (p. 313). Being explicit about how languages and literacies can function in our struggle to dismantle oppression remains of utmost importance, particularly in relation to how digital and multimodal literacies currently function in an increasingly fraught sociopolitical context—one in which the media used to democratize knowledge, foster solidarity, and promote social action—where they are being very effectively leveraged to proliferate tribalism, extremism, and polarization.

As we reimagine what lies ahead in critical English education, we must theorize across these various areas, considering simultaneously what counts as English education and for what purposes as well as who can/does/should engage in this project and in what ways. Drawing from existing vision-driven scholarship and my own collaborative and participatory research with youth and educators, I have been thinking about these questions in terms of the *what* and *why* of a critical English education in relation to our ever-shifting sociopolitical realities, as well as the *who* and *how*. Addressing the complex interrelatedness of various positions and positionalities, as well as multiple perspectives across contexts, invites a situated and dynamic conceptualization of English education that builds with and across critical and inclusive curriculums, multimodalities, collaborative inquiries, and reflexive praxes. In light of what may seem like irreconcilable tensions in our society, I consider how we might grapple with these conflicting demands and interests in schools and communities in humanizing and empathic ways (Mirra, 2018). In this chapter, I discuss possibilities for transformative approaches in our discipline that lean into complexity, reimagining curriculum and pedagogies theoretically as well as personally and relationally. Building upon a *curriculum-as-assemblage* stance[2] that incites educators and researchers to embrace the current and future complexity of our field, I make a case for a deep engagement with praxis in curriculum and pedagogy in ways that foster intergenerational and relational approaches to English and literacies education (Caraballo, 2023). Drawing from participatory critical youth epistemologies and autoethnographic inquiry, I propose the *self-in-context* as a conceptual framework for praxis that centers joyful and vision-driven, humanizing futures forged *with*, rather than *for*, youth and communities (Caraballo & Gomez, 2025; hooks, 1994; Muhammad, 2020).

Embracing Complexity: English Education *as* Assemblage(s)

In the wake of multiple and overlapping global and local crises related to racialized violence and transphobia, terrorizing extremism, and nationalistic polarization pertaining to climate, immigration, gender, and language, many educators are fatigued, uncertain about how to approach difficult topics with their students and with little consensus in the field about how they might do so. Fervent tribalism and a contentious political climate therefore threaten to extinguish public discourse at a time when it is most needed, with many individuals retreating to their respective ideological corners (Kahne et al., 2025).

While educators have access to research and resources representing a broad spectrum of perspectives, ranging from the need for critical thinking and conflict resolution skills to justice-oriented anticolonial epistemologies, to address controversial topics with students (Milwicki et al., 2023; Schieble et al., 2020), anecdotal evidence suggests that these types of conversations are not happening in many classrooms, where many teachers face battles over censorship or respond to emerging crises with limited autonomy or support. Youth are often exposed to extreme rhetoric and misinformation on social media in a "post-truth" society (Peters, 2017), and educators are increasingly vulnerable in many school districts throughout the United States (Pratt, 2024). The growing tension surrounding students' being "brainwashed" and "groomed," driven by baseless claims about critical race theory and other conspiracy theories and misinformation promoted via some news outlets and social media, represent some of the most toxic propaganda in a "post-truth" era (Oleksiyenko & Jackson, 2020).

Social psychology and cognitive research offer partial explanations to the resistance to opposing views and the prevalence of "echo chambers" across the ideological spectrum, where people may struggle with questions that challenge their sense of themselves and their loved ones. For example, according to theories of *motivated cognition*, individuals may resort to various strategies to rationalize or dispel information to mitigate their discomfort or may avoid situations or information that exacerbates this cognitive dissonance "rather than seek accuracy or engage with information that seems to contradict their view of themselves and members of their social groups" (Banks, 2021, p. 12; Madan, 2017). At its core, however, is deeply damaging discourse that breeds polarization, including doublespeak around "wokeness" as limiting "freedom of speech," which masks white supremacist agendas and foments culture wars between people with different perspectives (Gentile, 2019). The rise of populism and highly organized conservative lobbies have led to policies and emboldened hegemonic racist, heteronormative, and xenophobic discourses to an extent that leaves many youth and their communities disenfranchised, deteriorating public trust in democracy (Love, 2023).

In societies where public discourse is steeped in beliefs and attitudes rooted in egalitarianism, where an illusory meritocracy is romanticized and revered, there is a seemingly unnavigable divide between the reality of educational institutions that function as racist and oppressive gatekeepers in society and those who view them as legitimate paths to self-actualization and social mobility. The planned curriculum is often in the crosshairs of these tensions pertaining to what knowledge and skills are prioritized and valued in any subject and for which students (Anyon, 1980). In English education, whose origin scholars date to the late nineteenth century (Applebee, 1974; Kliebard, 2004), the boundaries that circumscribe what counts as curriculum (or not) are particularly complex in a discipline that can be as narrow and persistent as it is endlessly expansive and dynamic (Applebee, 2008; LaBrant, 1951; Thomas & Goering, 2017). We might think about the future of curriculum in English and literacies education by considering *both* how curriculum is intertwined with interdisciplinary debates in the field and discipline and is also very local and personal, enacted in specific sociopolitical contexts that impact the lives of students as well as teachers.

In this sense, conceptualizing *curriculum-as-assemblage* as a heuristic device compels us to consider the interrelatedness between distinct aspects that inform English language arts specifically and in education more broadly, such as what texts are valued, how writing is taught, and whose knowledge counts. As DeLanda (2016) theorizes in his reading of Giles Deleuze and Felix Guattari (1987), essential to assemblage theory is the understanding that "the parts that are fitted together are not uniform either in nature or origin, and . . . the assemblage actively links these parts together by establishing relations between them" (p. 2). In part, the examination of kinds of relations between/among the parts tells us more about both the parts and the composite whole. Emphasizing the field's consensus that English curricula consists of much more than texts to be read or literacy skills to be mastered, I use DeLanda's conceptualization of Deleuzian assemblage as a lens that renders visible multiple underlying assumptions and expectations, literacy models, and discourses of achievement that are implicit in the production of English as an academic subject. I argue that curriculum is produced at the intersection of multiple desires, struggles, and purposes—both explicit and implicit—in classrooms, in the discipline of English, and in society. In any given context, a curriculum assemblage is an organic, self-organizing composite of the various discourses, purposes, desires, and struggles in the cultural worlds of classrooms. Both the local and the global are produced and shaped by the field's history and traditions, past and present actors, and current debates, concerns, interests, and agendas (e.g., Applebee, 2008; Caraballo, 2018; Johnson, 2018; Luke, 2004; Morrell, 2005; Nelms, 2011; Smagorinsky, 2002; Zaino, 2021).

According to Pinar and colleagues (1995), "curriculum is a highly symbolic concept . . . [It] becomes the site on which the generations struggle to define themselves and the world" (pp. 847–848). While curriculum has historically contributed to the gatekeeping and sorting of youth as well as perpetuating the status quo (Anyon, 1980; Hurn, 1993; Kliebard, 2004), it has also been transformative, leading to "existential possibilities of multiple kinds" that "extend and deepen" what we think about others and ourselves (Greene, 1993) and how we express ourselves in aesthetic, multimodal, and speculative ways (Coleman, 2021; Pyndyck et al., 2022; New London Group, 1996; Thomas, 2017). Yet curriculum has also been known to mark, often by omission, the literacies and identities that are excluded—such as what Eisner (1985) described as the null curriculum and Britzman (1989) referred to as "all that is not selected as well as all that occurs but remains unnamed and unacknowledged" (p. 149). For decades, critics have maintained that English curricula often straddle the border between the standards and benchmarks imposed by school, district, and state policies (National Governors Association Center for Best Practices and Council of Chief State School Officers, 2011; Lipman, 2004; Zumwalt, 2004), as exemplified by the now-decommissioned Engage NY framework aligned to the CCSS (Haydel & Carmichael, 2015).

English language arts (ELA) curricula have been—and will arguably continue to be—defined, invoked, or imagined in the midst of tensions in the structures of schooling, the liberal arts, and the fields of English and literacies education. Like Gramsci's (1971) doctrine of hegemony, which explained how the nondominant are persuaded to accept the norms and belief systems of the dominant class, European American epistemological traditions (Ladson-Billings, 2000) are inseparable from the story of schooling, past and present. Furthermore, schools are embedded in assumptions about childhood and adolescence, such as developmental discourses in progressive education, that have both historically paved the way for innovations and also reified existing structures (Kliebard, 2004). While theories of child and adolescent development have been instrumental in the rationale for public school reform since the Progressive Era, Lesko argues that these discourses of adolescence have also largely cast youth as not adults at the cusp of "evolutionary arrival in an enlightened state after a lengthy period of backwardness" (2012, p. 2). From a critical youth lens, interrogating the positionalities from which all stakeholders conceptualize and engage in English education can facilitate thinking across multiple sociopolitical and disciplinary boundaries.

For example, Zaino (2021) examined the knowledge systems that have informed enactments in the field of English education over time. Using discourse analysis to examine the "continuities and discontinuities" in English education from the late nineteenth to the mid-twentieth centuries, she argued that "discourses grounded in liberal humanism and social sciences have shaped enduring (and often competing) norms in the field" (p. 10). In 1893, the Committee of Ten issued foundational humanistic guidelines for English instruction that centered literary analysis, composition, rhetoric, and grammar as key to instilling the mental discipline and refinement of reason required for postsecondary education. In the first half of the twentieth century, the National Council of Teachers of English (NCTE) promoted curricula and approaches to instruction in the newly termed "language arts" that were increasingly informed by developmental theories in the social sciences (Kliebard, 2004).

In the same vein, persistent assumptions may prevent deeply transformative (re)visions in English education. For example, Smagorinsky (2002) observed, when revisiting the popular *growth through English* model of the 1970s—highly regarded for its role in centering the legitimacy of learners' individual growth and concerns as counter to the tyranny of skills and cultural heritage curricula—it still left unexamined how a personal growth model overlooked our collective responsibility for others' wellbeing:

> For those who embrace the growth model and student-centered curriculum it implies, the great challenge is to encourage individuals to reconstruct the curriculum toward personal ends, while also growing as socially responsible citizens of a respectful and democratic society. (p. 26)

This approach also presents the historically humanistic goals of self-expression, literary appreciation, and cultural literacy components of the subject that become increasingly manifest as students enter secondary studies (Applebee, 1974; Kliebard, 2004). Finally, it reflects broader expectations about higher education and career readiness as shaped by social, political, and economic discourses about individual success, democratic participation, and national progress (Au & Raphael, 2000; Mirra & Garcia, 2021). The curriculum offers students and teachers "a worldview that is implied or explicitly taught through the texts, activities, sequences, and other dimensions of learning" that are included or excluded (Burroughs & Smagorinsky, 2009, p. 180). Furthermore, while Fairclough (1992) asserted that readers have the capacity to critique, transform, or resist the subject positions that texts construct, readers are often further constrained by internalized norms and "academic" conventions.

Therefore, while the prominence of developmentalism in progressive education during the early twentieth century was useful in recognizing and addressing some of youth's needs and priorities in schooling, it also helped to solidify a conception of adolescence as "not quite adulthood," reifying the hierarchy of adult purposes, desires, and expectations as the most valid and desirable for the human subject and the most productive in/for society. Despite their seeming contradictions, these norms shared desires and investments in epistemologies that privilege particular ideals about "humanities" education. Relatedly, educators' approaches to curriculum that focus on "best practices" (Zemelman et al., 2005)—whether driven by these disciplinary legacies, or high-stakes standardization, assessment, or motivated by anti-deficit resource pedagogies—all have the potential to essentialize if not situated in the particular contexts in which students learn. As Ladson-Billings (2014) argued, "Teachers undertaking culturally informed pedagogies take on the dual responsibility of external performance assessments as well as community- and student-driven learning" (p. 83; Paris & Alim, 2014). Enacting curriculum as part of a critical educational project in the midst of this dual responsibility is especially challenging without a conceptual framework that engages both educators and youth in negotiating these tensions (Conner et al., 2023). A *curriculum-as-assemblage* stance catalyzes a decentering of mainstream knowledge, and creates dialogic spaces for other knowledges, literacies, and identities to enter into Pinar's (2004) and other reconceptualists' notion of curriculum as "complicated conversation." A *curriculum-as-assemblage* stance challenges us to consider how curriculum and pedagogy are enacted and experienced in particular classrooms and schools and as enactments of curricula writ large in K–12 schooling as well as in postgraduate teaching and teacher preparation.

An English Education Assemblage: Disciplinary Legacies, Discourses, and Possible Directions

Aligned with practice approaches that center curriculum as it is enacted and experienced by students and teachers, several contemporary areas of research and scholarship in English and literacies education offer more expansive perspectives of a critical English education toward more inclusive social futures (Kinloch, 2023; Morrell, 2005; New London Group, 1996). Transgressing the boundaries of mainstream English curricula, which often privilege a Western canon (whether explicitly or implicitly) and essayist forms of literacies, can amplify the voices of students who are usually muted in schools and classrooms due to any combination of intersectional marginalized identities and positionings related to race, dis/ability, gender or sexual orientation, religion, citizenship status, and many more (see Kelly, 2023a, and Schey, 2023, among others). Discourses about equity, effort, and colorblindness (e.g., Caraballo, 2014) that are rooted in liberal humanism and social science produce certain versions of ELA that are rhizomatically interrelated and overlapping and invoke particular selves-in-practice in classroom contexts. Conceptualizing *English-as-assemblage*, a composite assembled from these versions, renders visible a multiplicity of positionalities that are simultaneously available in the classroom as teachers and students enact the curriculum. More importantly, making explicit the intersections of multiple identities, contexts, and discourses in curricula more broadly interrupts the illusion of neutrality and objectivity embedded in the conventions of the discipline, especially as they are enacted in particular English classrooms.

Constructing and Negotiating Identities in the Figured World of English Education

Given the situated nature of curriculum as experienced at the intimate classroom level, assemblage and practice theories are both useful in helping us recognize how multiple external as well as local discourses and identities interact simultaneously. In the tradition of social constructivism (Vygotsky, 1978), Erickson and Shultz (1992) argued for the need to highlight students' individual and collective experiences in the discourse on curriculum because it is "within such experience that learning about self and the world takes place" (p. 466). Yet that learning about the self and the world involves dynamic interactions of/with expectations, desires, and purposes. The assemblage is thus a heuristic for the multiplicity of factors that inform how students and teachers experience the enacted curriculum. An assemblage of curriculum, as Feely (2019) advises, "should not be understood as a fixed entity because it is always in a process of becoming" (p. 179).

To illustrate the dynamic interactions between/among identities, literacies, discourses, and curriculum, I draw upon Deleuze and Guattari's (1987) notion of *machinic assemblages.* A curriculum is formed as an "organic, self-organising, desiring, and always *becoming*" machine (Semetsky, 2006, p. xiii, emphasis added), like a dynamic collage in which each part or entity has a role or conveys a unique idea yet takes on other meanings as part of the larger whole. Assuming a *curriculum-as-assemblage* stance can be generative in reimagining a critical English education by challenging all stakeholders to consider the interrelatedness and simultaneous intra-action of multiple factors that inform and shape how education is enacted and experienced in shifting contexts. Unlike a collage, an assemblage is not static: "[a]n assemblage is precisely this increase in the dimensions of a multiplicity that necessarily changes in nature as it expands its connections" (Deleuze & Guattari, 1987, p. 8). Rather than a "fixed or static" set of representations and relations, assemblages depict a "constantly shifting set of relations" (Walkerdine, 2007, p. 33).

In keeping with a practice theory approach, conceptualizing *curriculum-as-assemblage* accentuates the emergent properties of not only the texts selected and assessments implemented but also educators' and students' identities and how they are interrelated with, and irreducible from (DeLanda, 2016), enactments of teaching and learning. The enacted curriculum (Snyder et al., 1992) is defined as that which results from the interaction between the planned curriculum (Zumwalt, 2007) and the students and teachers who experience and enact it in the figured world of the classroom. Bartlett and Holland (2002) extended a practice approach to literacy studies by "specifying the space of literacy practice" and examining the "locally operant figured world of literacy" (p. 12). Similarly, I argue that the enacted curriculum co-creates a socially produced and culturally constructed figured world. The figured world of the classroom has a limited "range of meaningful acts . . . in a particular institution" (Holland et al., p. 52), such as using a range of grades for excellent or poor performance and rubrics for appropriate participation, and within broader discourses in the discipline and in society.

Considering the origins of English education in both the humanities and social sciences, Zaino (2021) challenges us to "reexamine history so that we can unearth clandestine literacy legacies that have produced and been produced by other discursive formations" (p. 11), such as critical race counternarratives (Johnson, 2018), intersectional queer literacies pedagogies (Blackburn, 2003; Schey, 2023), and Indigenous ways of knowing (Eagle Shield et al., 2021). Such reexamination has the power to reconceptualize our field via the centering of what may have historically been framed as tending to the margins.

Several recent studies and frameworks demonstrate such reexamination. For example, a critical language awareness (CLA) approach does not pertain only to the teaching of English as a new language. Rather, it questions "the inequities inherent in social norms tied to language use," thus promoting research and action that can transform "the social order through deepening awareness of the processes of language use" (Metz, 2023, p. 60). Such an approach encompasses research and scholarship representing varied language ideologies, theories, and practices; for example, translanguaging bears an increasing significance for English classrooms by redefining how we think about the way bilingual and multilingual people communicate, as having "one interrelated linguistic-semiotic repertoire from which they draw features to express themselves, make meaning, engage critically and creatively in the world, and communicate with others" (de los Ríos & Seltzer, 2023, p. 221).

Similarly, Johnson's (2018) critical race English education (CREE) framework, in which he theorizes humanizing curricula and pedagogies to counter anti-Blackness in English classrooms, builds on a critical autoethnographic study of his experiences during the #BlackLivesMatter movement in ways that all educators can take up in their own classrooms, with proper support for their own self-excavation (Price-Dennis & Sealey-Ruiz, 2021). Smith (2022) addresses the intersectionality of race and gender by centering humanizing pedagogies that draw on arts-based approaches, applicable in multiple contexts. In the same vein, Baker-Bell's (2020) justice- and vision-driven approach to Black language has the potential not only to foster humanizing learning environments for Black students but also to transform English language arts (ELA) pedagogies and curriculum, broadly conceived.

Many more "otherwise" discursive formations continue to flourish in nondominant communities, as exemplified by fugitive literacy practices (Lee, 2020; Ohito, 2020), speculative literacies (Coleman, 2021; Garcia & Mirra, 2021; Thomas, 2017), and the posthumanist theorizing of curriculum (Friedrich et al., 2022). I posit that many of the transgressive and transformative properties of these literacies in nondominant communities emerge from their interrelatedness with multiple identities, formations, discourses, and experiences, wherein a stance that is informed by assemblage theories and rooted in critical autoethnography can provide a conceptual and theoretical framing that we may build from and across multiple approaches to foster collaborative, intergenerational reimaginings of critical English education in the years to come. However, the challenging nexus of ideology, theory, and praxis has historically thwarted many efforts to sustain transformative approaches for many students and educators, often in the most underserved schools that are subject to greater surveillance and pathologizing policies. Despite important shifts in teaching paradigms and critical approaches to English and literacies education over the past century or so (Applebee, 1974; Bloome & Kinzer, 1998; Morrell, 2005; Price-Dennis & Sealey-Ruiz, 2021), policies such as No Child Left Behind, Race to the Top, and the Common Core State Standards have contributed to many students' continued experience of ELA curricula that privilege skills and canons established in long-past decades (Caraballo, 2018; Gurl et al., 2016). Currently, growing polarization about most debates in education—about everything ranging from the science of reading to decolonizing histories, as well as policy mandates and censorship debates—presents formidable barriers to enactments of curricula and pedagogies such as those described above. How might we develop a stance that supports leaning into complexity, negotiating our own lived experiences and educational goals in the service of inclusion and justice?

A *curriculum-as-assemblage* stance challenges us to consider how curriculum and pedagogy are enacted and experienced in particular classrooms and schools and as enactments of curricula writ large in K–12 schooling as well as in postgraduate teaching and teacher preparation. In the next sections, I discuss the self-in-context as one way to frame such an intergenerational inquiry stance in praxis. The self-in-context framework, which originated in an autoethnographic examination of collaborative research with youth, is designed to situate students' as well as educators' multiple identities-in-practice in the contexts where they live and learn (Caraballo & Soleimany, 2018), a necessary first step toward negotiating the intersecting discourses, identities, and practices that shape our social, cultural, and political worlds (Caraballo, 2014, 2016, 2019, 2023).

The Self-in-Context: Intergenerational Inquiry as Critical Epistemology and Method

Given the multiplicity of dynamics described above, youth and adults construct and negotiate multiple identities and positionalities within the social contexts of their classrooms, schools, and communities. Practice and assemblage theories can therefore support greater critical meta-awareness of how we are positioned within the contexts in which we teach and learn (e.g., Caraballo 2019; Gurl et al., 2016). Wills and colleagues' (2004) notion of "particularity" is directly linked to the importance of intersections; they maintain that instructional practice involves more than cultural knowledge about students' backgrounds—teachers should "learn about the details of their students' lives in particular" and "adapt general principles to local circumstances" (p. 179). Such knowledge is insufficient, however, if it does not disrupt mainstream knowledge or inform instructional practice in ways that do not just recognize but also sustain students' multiple cultural identities and literacies (Paris, 2012). Conceptualizing *curriculum-as-assemblage* thus necessitates an inquiry stance (Cochran-Smith, 1999) that transgresses disciplinary boundaries and reimagines educators as well as youth as researchers and curriculum theorists.

In my own ethnographic research with middle and high school students, I have sought to render visible the frequently overlooked interactions and negotiations that impact students' experiences (Caraballo, 2011, 2014, 2016, 2019). Despite the hegemonic function of some mainstream discourses related to literary analysis and written communication, for example, students' literacy practices demonstrate how they carve out spaces in which to construct and reconstruct versions of themselves in and beyond classrooms (Kelly, 2023b). In examining students' consumption and creation of texts as they negotiate the space between their home/cultural communities and the figured world English classrooms, liminal spaces between worlds become evident. Students continuously, and intuitively, construct identities around intersections in relation to these experiences. Such a situated analysis documents students' style-shifting demands, desires, and struggles in an increasingly dynamic society.

Like Tuck (2010), who ultimately diverges from Deleuze to present a desire that is "about longing, about a present that is enriched by both the past and the future" and "the textured acumen and hope" (p. 644), I continue to examine how critical autoethnographic methods, as described above, can shift paradigms, working toward generative spaces in which educators and researchers are invited to engage in interdisciplinary and intergenerational dialogue and critical analysis with youth about key social and educational issues (Caraballo & Filipiak, 2021; Lyiscott et al., 2021; Yeom et al., 2020). For example, in an article that I coauthored with Elma Rahman (a middle school English teacher and my former student in the secondary English education program), we drew on elements of critical autoethnography to examine the intersection of her identities as a Muslim woman and as an educator when she experienced microaggressions in her teaching career. According to Camangian (2010), "autoethnography is a method of learning about and understanding experience in order to benefit self, society, community, and culture" (p. 184). The move from the self to "collective consideration is important to foster interpersonal communication and intercultural compassion" (p. 184) and is especially and most urgently important in contexts where people from very different backgrounds learn with and from each other. Using autoethnography to position ourselves and others with/in broader assemblages of curriculum render visible some key "points of departure toward thinking about relations among self, other, and curriculum" (Jewett, 2008, p. 6). However, in most mainstream schools, there are rarely sanctioned or structured opportunities for this kind of engagement between adults and youth because educators and students have been socialized into particular hierarchies that dictate what knowledge and skills count and who is positioned as a knower and/or leader (Kelly & Sawyer, 2019). Many of our lived experiences, norms in teacher education and administration, discourses of achievement, and the roles associated with these discourses position adults primarily as authority figures who impart knowledge—and this dynamic is so deeply embedded in education that even after decades of student-centered contemporary schools, educators typically assume responsibility for determining what students' needs are, and children as well as adolescents are framed as unprepared to make decisions about consequential matters (Beach, 2022; Lesko, 2012; Zaino, 2021). While adults must certainly remain accountable and have considerable life experience, expertise, and professional knowledge to bring to bear in educational spaces, it is important to recognize that some developmentalist assumptions function in ways that silence youth perspectives and discourage dialogue and collaboration, making it difficult to work toward deeper and more authentic intergenerational learning and world building (Mirra & Garcia, 2021). If educators see themselves primarily as the authority figures and gatekeepers, that limits the social imagination of everyone involved. Seeing ourselves differently and embracing self-examination and self-interrogation is a necessary step to even begin to imagine new possible structures in *third spaces* that invite thinking and engaging otherwise (Bhaba, 1994; Gutiérrez, 2008).

In this sense, the context for critical participation fostered in figured worlds of youth participatory action research (YPAR) and other youth-engaged third spaces challenges us to refine and redefine and reimagine those boundaries (Cammarota & Fine, 2008; Caraballo & Lyiscott, 2018; Caraballo et al., 2017; Mirra et al., 2015). The "otherwise" curricula and pedagogies engendered via YPAR can offer a sense of what is possible. What is a brave third space—where critical and multimodal literacies emerge as peer-to-peer *and* youth-adult conversations that lead to shared understandings, civil discourse, comfort zones being challenged—also becomes an immersive and impact-driven context for innovative social futures (Filipiak et al., 2015; New London Group, 1996) and speculative literacies (Ohito, 2020). Several YPAR collectives and initiatives, whether part of a school initiative or a cocurricular partnership expanding relationships, are sustained for a decade or more (Kelly, 2023b; Rubin, 2012). A growing corpus of YPAR scholarship documents the collective agency, multimodal literacies, and brave third spaces that are sustained in these engagements, such as the pedagogy of collegiality practiced by the Youth Radio Collective (Chávez & Soep, 2005) and the speculative civic literacies (Mirra & Garcia, 2020) that are arguably driven by the desires of educators as well as students who have reimagined together their learning spaces in and beyond classrooms.

Similarly, in Cyphers for Justice (CFJ), our work as youth and adult allies has challenged our collective to explore how we negotiate the inevitable hierarchies of power in which our intergenerational work is embedded (Lyiscott et al., 2021). By making explicit how all stakeholders in educational spaces are actors who shape and are shaped by multiple and overlapping discourses, we have co-developed inquiries that bridge theory and practice in curriculum, pedagogy, and teacher education, providing a platform for educators to simultaneously enact and examine their reflexive praxes (Lyiscott et al., 2023). In a YPAR collective such as CFJ, youth are engaged in relational work through our discovering new ways of being together, of co-constructing knowledge, and connecting to each other through our multiple and varied literacy practices of caring for one another (Filipiak & Caraballo, 2023). Everything we create together is bound up in our relationships with one another. The ethos of YPAR, grounded in critical youth epistemologies, participatory inquiry, and action research (Caraballo et al., 2017), catalyzes the rethinking of youth as well as adult positionalities and disrupts the curricula and pedagogies that we might enact in classrooms. As part of our research with/in in Cyphers for Justice, we consider intergenerational work as that which seeks to disrupt hierarchies between learners and educators by considering intersecting and interrelated desires, purposes, and goals—all of which are deeply connected to the identities that we construct and negotiate in these spaces. How might these engagements inform our positioning with/in a *curriculum-as-assemblage* stance toward a critical English education?

As discussed above, autoethnographic inquiry invites the examination of identities constructed and negotiated in the context of practice, in academic and nonacademic spaces, for youth as well as adult allies. Each space has a different intersection of identities in which we have to negotiate those different spaces and the different cultural worlds that we are engaging in, and with whom. A *curriculum-as-assemblage* stance depends on continuous reflexive inquiry and the interrogation of positionalities in order to transform our pedagogies in increasingly complex local and global contexts, yet the demands of standardization and accountability in teacher preparation and professional development, among other pressures, have not been conducive to such fluid conceptions of critical teacher learning (Caraballo & Gomez, 2025; Lucero et al., 2025).

Developing the first iteration of the self-in-context framework, therefore, was an interactive and organic process. Working with Sahar, one of the adult allies in CFJ who was also a student teacher in the secondary English teacher preparation program, to analyze her experiences, she and I developed a conceptual framework inspired by an ethic of care in teacher education and the idea of the *cypher*, keeping in mind that a cypher is a cultural practice that came from the innovation and literacies of Black and Brown youth (Caraballo & Soleimany, 2019; Lyiscott, 2019). The cypher became a metaphor for a transformative pedagogy that disrupted those traditional divisions between teachers and students, becoming a means to problematize existing issues in classrooms and helping us create a space where participants can question and reimagine their own positions (Lyiscott, 2019).

There is something inherently disruptive in the ethos and pathos of the cypher, which leads to productive discomfort. Sitting or standing in a circle, interrogating a complex social problem, we gathered together thinking about issues without predetermined solutions. We were intentional about engaging in that space without falling, or actively trying not to fall into our traditional roles because *how* to engage in a cypher also requires a degree of vulnerability and comfort in who we are and who we are constantly becoming, and that is not typical in schools. As adults as well as youth, we aimed to be present with our whole selves in order to fully participate in the cypher (Lyiscott et al., 2023).

In this sense, the teacher and/or student "self" can be examined as part of a dynamic assemblage of discourses, expectations, norms, relationships, among other considerations, that Sahar and I explored. The figure below, adapted from our framework, illustrates the recursive framing of three dimensions that we conceptualized as the *self-in-context*. The *internal* refers to individual work in examining and reconsidering our perspectives and assumptions, especially when we are working with students with backgrounds different from ours and/or in classrooms where students come from diverse contexts.

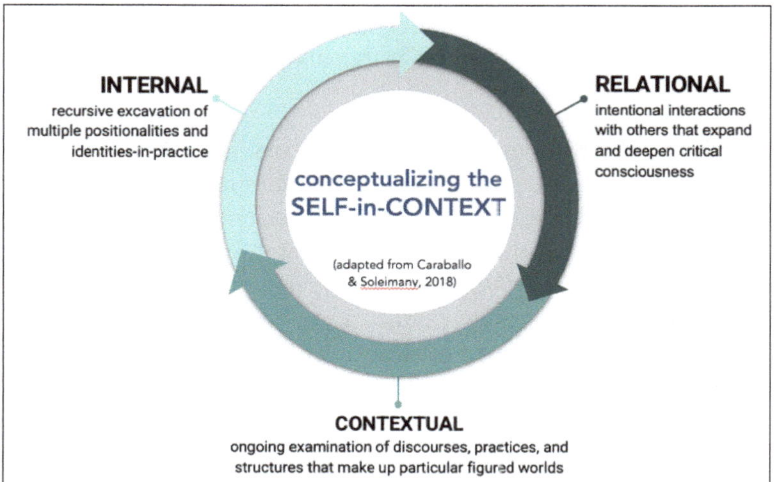

FIGURE 1. *Practice and assemblage theories inform this conceptual framework for examining the self-in-context via critical autoethnography (first published in Caraballo, 2023).*

This kind of self-reflection can deepen students' and teachers' critical awareness and *relational* understanding, as in interactions with students and among peers, as well as in making curricular and pedagogical decisions. These relational dynamics are rendered visible when our students reflect on their relationships with their families, friends, and communities and when we as educators reflect on our relationships as well.

A third important and interrelated element is *contextual*, referring to the context in which these interactions take place. Recognizing the opportunities and obstacles that we face individually and collectively is one way to broaden a critical understanding of how systems of oppression function as barriers and how individual and collective agency can be amplified. A safer and more inclusive classroom culture would need to be co-constructed; when students and educators' assumptions, perspectives, and commitments are made visible (rather than obscured by the desire to be "objective" or "neutral"), deepening our understanding of our identities, home cultures, and lived experiences can disrupt traditional barriers to learning.

> Transformational and revolutionary teaching cannot take place unless teachers are prepared and willing to create classroom environments where students are encouraged to ask questions about the human condition, reflect on their lived experiences, and even interrogate the very power structures that surreptitiously work to marginalize them. (Caraballo & Soleimany, 2019, p. 17)

In this sense, the challenge to educators is to build beyond constraints to design curriculum in pursuit of meaningful inquiry. We can do this via methods that build students' critical thinking and media literacy skills and that also foster openness to dialogue with those who may hold different perspectives. Approaching this complexity via teacher education and development from a continuous stance toward critical teacher learning is one way to begin to address the vulnerability that educators experience in practice, where taking risks with curriculum may feel like their jobs are at stake (Caraballo & Gomez, 2025).

Beyond questions about what counts as an English curriculum and how students experience it, a *curriculum-as-assemblage* stance compels all educators and researchers to engage with the nuances of how our professional and academic roles inform, and are shaped by, the field itself. It compels the interrogation of assumptions in English, literacies, and the social sciences (including anthropology and cultural studies). It catalyzes a theory-into-practice approach to the knowledge centered in the field and how students and teachers negotiate their own complex classroom and community contexts.

Toward Intergenerational Relationality: "Assembling" a Critical English Education

Tuck (2010) grapples with Deleuze and Guattari's conception of desire as "not an absence—not something that is blocked or missing, so therefore wanting. It is not a hole, not a gap, not a lacking, but an exponentially growing assemblage" (p. 639). I think of the curriculum as a desiring machine, catalytic and self-propelling in the midst of the tensions defining the field and the myriad roles educators and researchers assume with/in English education over time. In this growing assemblage, another area of challenge stems from the polarized sociopolitical context that informs assumptions about teacher preparation and professional development and also limits access to the profession in communities of color (Carter Andrews et al., 2021; Gurl et al., 2016). Because the teaching force continues to be predominantly white and middle-class (Carter Andrews et al., 2021; Zumwalt & Craig, 2005), many teachers' experiences and beliefs about education are often disconnected from minoritized students' experiences and needs. This disconnect between students and teachers is exacerbated by curricular trends based on best practices, as discussed above, and atheoretical approaches to "on-the-job" training for new teachers (Zeichner, 2014) or restrictive mandates that may restrict teachers to implementing scripted curricula and prescriptive approaches rather than supporting their autonomy as experts in their field and collaborators with their students and their communities. Yet approaching curriculum as a series of multiple and dynamic assemblages pertaining to what we teach, who is teaching, and for what purposes can provide a lens to see and grapple with the overlapping challenges ahead.

As educators and researchers, we can draw from critical autoethnography to examine our own selves-in-context by interrogating how our positionalities inform our commitments to teaching and the youth entrusted to us. Building from such a dynamic reflexivity, we can begin to reconceptualize curricula in ways that support the identities and literacies of minoritized and marginalized students in and beyond schools and classrooms in ways that are actually situated in our own figured worlds. To do so is to center critical consciousness and culturally responsive and sustaining pedagogies as integral to the local contexts and communities that we are all situated in, as well as broader social justice agendas in academic contexts (Paris & Alim, 2014).

Approaching *curriculum-as-assemblage* prepares us to embrace complexity, and challenges all stakeholders to transgress existing boundaries and engage in the co-construction of critical knowledges in English education and beyond, making visible the curricular enactments that position English education as nonlinear and multidimensional as a composite of multiple interests and ways of knowing, reading, and writing the world. I argue that a *curriculum-as-assemblage* stance offers all who engage with the disciplines of English and literacies a way of thinking about and operationalizing how context matters—and how the context of an academic space is shaped and regulated by visible and tangible things like course objectives and classroom rules, but also by how figured worlds are shaped and produced by multiple discourses and actors in schools and society at large.

Rather than arguing for particular solutions to the tensions in English and education, I propose that a *curriculum-as-assemblage* stance toward teaching and learning challenges English educators and researchers to engage in ongoing inquiry and curricular provocations—centering themselves, their students, their communities, and their situated academic figured worlds. Considering how critical English education is informed by and embedded within situated contexts, and embracing the complexity of these relations in current times, cannot happen in a vacuum. Such a stance is contingent upon our own ongoing self-excavation (Sealy-Ruiz, 2022), as well as a growing and dynamic understanding of how our positionalities inform the relationships we build upon as we teach and learn. Using the self-in-context to frame our reflexive collaborative praxis with youth, an ongoing interrogation of our relational learning, can provide much-needed mutual inspiration, care, and sustenance in the community during complex and uncertain times. Such an approach is also necessary for critical discourse in a participatory democracy, part of a call to critical English educators seeking to confront injustice and fill in the gaps in cultural knowledge that media and political discourses about marginalized communities often perpetuate. Developing these critical literacies is crucial to amplifying vision-driven efforts toward antiracism, transphobia, xenophobia, and other forms of exclusion, harm, oppression, and polarization that may otherwise remain unaddressed in schools and communities. And recognizing the dynamic nature of the profession, preparing teachers to thrive as they serve *all* students in an ever-shifting educational assemblage—as well as nurturing the critical dispositions needed to critique and resist its limitations—will always be transformative curriculum work. While the path forward may be uncertain, educators and youth can lean into this complexity together, sustained by critical hope.

Notes

1. See Winn & Ubiles (2011) for a discussion of a writing class in which Joe Ubiles fosters youth power writer's use of poetry to provide "worthy witness" to the strengths of their communities.

2. An earlier version of this chapter was published as Caraballo, L. (2023). Curriculum-as-assemblage: Transgressive (re)imaginings in English and literacies. *Research in the Teaching of English, 58*(1), 81–104.

References

Anyon, J. (1980). Social class and the hidden curriculum of work. *Journal of Education, 162*(1), 67–92. https://www.jstor.org/stable/42741976

Applebee, A. N. (1974). *Tradition and reform in the teaching of English: A history.* National Council of Teachers of English.

Applebee, A. N. (2008). *Curriculum as conversation: Transforming traditions of teaching and learning*. University of Chicago Press.

Au, K. H., & Raphael, T. E. (2000). Equity and literacy in the next millennium. *Reading Research Quarterly, 35*(1), 170–188. https://www.jstor.org/stable/748294

Baker-Bell, A. (2020). *Linguistic justice: Black language, literacy, identity, and pedagogy*. Routledge.

Banks, A. M. (2021). *Civic education in the age of mass migration: Implications for theory and practice*. Teachers College Press.

Bartlett, L., & Holland, D. (2002). Theorizing the space of literacy practices. *Ways of Knowing Journal*, 2(1), 10–22.

Beach, R. (2022). *Drawing on students' worlds in the ELA classroom: Toward critical engagement and deep learning*. Routledge.

Blackburn, M. (2003). Exploring literacy performances and power dynamics at The Loft: Queer youth reading the world and the word. *Research in the Teaching of English, 37*(4), 467–490.

Bloome, D., & Kinzer, C. K. (1998). Hard times and cosmetics: Changes in literacy instruction. *Peabody Journal of Education, 73*(3–4), 341–375. http://www.jstor.org/stable/1493211

Britzman, D. P. (1989). Who has the floor? Curriculum, teaching, and the English student teacher's struggle for voice. *Curriculum Inquiry, 19*(2), 143–162. https://doi.org/10.2307/1179406

Burroughs, R., & Smagorinsky, P. (2009). The secondary English curriculum and adolescent literacy. In L. Christenbury, R. Bomer, & P. Smagorinsky (Eds.), *Handbook of adolescent literacy research* (pp. 170–182). Guilford Press.

Camangian, P. (2010). Starting with self: Teaching autoethnography to foster critically caring literacies. *Research in the Teaching of English, 45*(2), 179–204.

Caraballo, L. (2011). Theorizing identities in a "just(ly)" contested terrain: Practice theories of identity amid critical-poststructural debates on curriculum and achievement. *Journal of Curriculum and Pedagogy, 8*(2), 155–177. https://doi.org/10.1080/15505170.2011.624939

Caraballo, L. (2014). The student as assemblage of success: Constructing multiple identities amidst classed, gendered, and raced discourses of achievement. *Curriculum and Teaching Dialogue, 16*(1–2), 103–124.

Caraballo, L. (2016). Students' critical meta-awareness in a figured world of achievement: Toward a culturally sustaining stance in curriculum, pedagogy, and research. *Urban Education, 52*(5), 585–609. https://doi.org/10.1177/0042085915623344

Caraballo, L. (2018). Multiple literacies as culturally sustaining pedagogy in English language arts. In A. T. Costigan (Ed.), *An authentic English language arts curriculum: Finding your way in a standards-driven context* (pp. 156–183). Routledge.

Caraballo, L. (2019). Being "loud": Identities-in-practice in a figured world of achievement. *American Educational Research Journal, 56*(4), 1281–1317. https://doi.org/10.3102%2F0002831218816059

Caraballo, L. (2023). Curriculum-as-assemblage: Transgressive (re)imaginings in English and literacies. *Research in the Teaching of English, 58*(1), 81–104.

Caraballo, L., & Filipiak, D. (2021). Building futures: Youth researchers and critical college-going literacies. *Review of Education, Pedagogy, and Cultural Studies, 42*(5), 427–450. https://doi.org/10.1080/10714413.2021.1874852

Caraballo, L., & Gomez, C. (2025). Talking the walk, walking the talk: Identity and inquiry in critical teacher learning. *Urban Education*. Advance online publication. https://doi.org/10.1177/00420859251359257

Caraballo, L., Lozenski, B., Lyiscott, J., & Morrell, E. (2017). YPAR and critical epistemologies: Rethinking education research. *Review of Research in Education, 41*(1), 311–336. https://doi.org/10.3102/0091732X16686948

Caraballo, L., & Lyiscott, J. (2018). Collaborative inquiry: Youth, social action, and critical qualitative research. *Action Research, 18*(2), 194–211. https://doi.org/10.1177%2F1476750317752819

Caraballo, L., & Soleimany, S. (2019). In the name of (pedagogical) love: A conceptual framework for transformative teaching grounded in critical youth research. *The Urban Review, 51*(1), 81–100. https://doi.org/10.1007/s11256-018-0486-5

Carter Andrews, D. J., He, Y., Marciano, J. E., Richmond, G., & Salazar, M. (2021). Decentering Whiteness in teacher education: Addressing the questions of who, with whom, and how. *Journal of Teacher Education, 72*(2), 134–137. https://doi.org/10.1177/0022487120987966

Chávez, V., & Soep, E. (2005). Youth radio and the pedagogy of collegiality. *Harvard Educational Review, 75*(4), 409–434. https://doi.org/10.17763/haer.75.4.827u365446030386

Cochran-Smith, M., & Lytle, S. (1999). Relationships of knowledge and practice: Teacher learning in communities. *Review of Research in Education, 24*(1), 249–305.

Coleman, J. J. (2021). Restorying with the ancestors: Historically rooted speculative composing practices and alternative rhetorics of queer futurity. *Written Communication, 38*(4), 512–543. https://doi.org/10.1177/07410883211028230

Conner, J. O., Goldstein, M., Mammen, J., Hernandez, J., Phillippo, K., Pope, D., & Davidson, S. (2023). What students and teachers do to build positive reciprocal relationships: A study co-led by youth and adult researchers. *American Journal of Education, 129*(4), 449–479. https://doi.org/10.1086/725585

de los Ríos, C., & Seltzer, K. (2023). Translanguaging. In L. M. Barker, D. Gorlewski, J. Gorlewski, & C. M. Miller (Eds.), *Encyclopedia of English language arts education: A critical perspective* (pp. 226–233). Brill.

DeLanda, M. (2016). *Assemblage theory*. Edinburgh University Press.

Deleuze, G., & Guattari, F. (1987). *A thousand plateaus: Capitalism and schizophrenia*. University of Minnesota Press.

Eagle Shield, A., Munson, M. M., & San Pedro, T. (2021). Dreams, healing, and listening to learn: Educational movements in the everyday. *Equity & Excellence in Education, 54*(1), 39–49. https://doi.org/10.1080/10665684.2020.1863881

Eisner, E. (1985). *The educational imagination*. Macmillan.

Erickson, F., & Shultz, J. (1992). Students' experience of curriculum. In P. W. Jackson (Ed.), *Handbook of research on curriculum: A project of the American Educational Research Association* (pp. 465–485). Macmillan.

Fairclough, N. (1992). *Discourse and social change*. Polity Press.

Feely, M. (2019). Assemblage analysis: An experimental new-materialist method for analysing narrative data. *Qualitative Research, 20*(2), 174–193. https://doi.org/10.1177/1468794119830641

Filipiak, D., & Caraballo, L. (2023). Exploring (r)evolutionary college-going literacies with immigrant youth in a youth participatory action research (YPAR) seminar. *English Teaching: Practice & Critique, 22*(3), 349–367. https://doi.org/10.1108/ETPC-10-2022-0160

Friedrich, D., Corson, J., & Hollman, D. (Eds.). (2021). *Pop culture and curriculum, assemble! Exploring the limits of curricular humanism through pop culture.* Dio Press.

Garcia, A., & Mirra, N. (2021). Writing toward justice: Youth speculative civic literacies in online policy discourse. *Urban Education, 56*(4), 640–669. https://doi.org/10.1177/0042085920953881

Gentile, J. (2019, June). Vaginal veritas: Thoughts on misogyny, psychoanalysis, and democracy. *ROOM: A Sketchbook for Analytic Action*, 6.19. https://analytic-room.com/essays/vaginal-veritas-by-jill-gentile/

Gramsci, A. (1971). *Selections from the prison notebooks.* Lawrence & Wishart.

Greene, M. (1993). The passions of pluralism: Multiculturalism and the expanding community. *Educational Researcher, 22*(1), 13–18.

Gurl, T., Caraballo, L., Grey, L., Gunn, J., Gerwin, D., & Bembenutty, H. (2016). *Policy, professionalization, privatization, and performance assessment: Affordances and constraints for teacher education programs.* Springer.

Gutiérrez, K. D., & Rogoff, B. (2003). Cultural ways of learning: Individual traits or repertoires of practice. *Educational Researcher, 32*(5), 19–25. https://doi.org/10.3102/0013189X032005019

Haydel, E., & Carmichael, S. B. (2015). *Uncommonly engaging? A review of the EngageNY English language arts common core curriculum.* Thomas B. Fordham Institute.

Holland, D., Lachicotte, W., Jr., Skinner, D., & Cain, C. (1998). *Identity and agency in cultural worlds.* Harvard University Press.

hooks, b. (1994). *Teaching to transgress: Education as the practice of freedom.* Routledge.

Hurn, C. J. (1993). *The limits and possibilities of schooling: An introduction to the sociology of education.* Allyn & Bacon.

Jewett, L. (2008). *A delicate dance: Autoethnography, curriculum, and the semblance of intimacy.* Peter Lang.

Johnson, L. L. (2018). Where do we go from here? Toward a critical race English education. *Research in the Teaching of English, 53*(2), 102–124.

Kahne, J., Rogers, J., & Kwako, A. (2025). The new politics of education and the pursuit of a diverse democracy. *AERA Open, 11*(1). https://doi.org/10.1177/23328584241311819

Kelly, L. L. (2023a). *Teaching with hip hop in the 7–12 grade classroom: A guide to supporting students' critical development through popular texts* (1st ed.). Routledge. https://doi.org/10.4324/9781003293767

Kelly, L. L. (2023b). "It's what we're about": Youth epistemologies in the design of social and educational futures. *Equity & Excellence in Education, 56*(3), 323–336. https://doi.org/10.1080/10665684.2023.2187897

Kelly, L. L., & Sawyer, D. C., III. (2019). "When keeping it real goes wrong": Enacting critical pedagogies of hip-hop in mainstream schools. *IASPM Journal, 9*(2), 6–21. https://doi.org/10.5429/2079-3871(2019)v9i2.2en

Kinloch, V. (2023). Equity, justice, and antiracist teaching: Who will join this? *Research in the Teaching of English, 57*(3), 314–321.

Kliebard, H. M. (2004). *The struggle for the American curriculum: 1893–1958* (3rd ed.). Routledge.

LaBrant, L. (1951). *We teach English*. Harcourt, Brace and Company.

Ladson-Billings, G. (2000). Racialized discourses and ethnic epistemologies. In N. K. Denzin & Y. S. Lincoln (Eds.), *Handbook of qualitative research* (2nd ed., pp. 257–278). SAGE.

Ladson-Billings, G. (2014). Culturally relevant pedagogy 2.0: AKA the remix. *Harvard Educational Review, 84*(1), 74–84. https://doi.org/10.17763/haer.84.1.p2rj131485484751

Ladson-Billings, G. (2021). I'm here for the hard re-set: Post-pandemic pedagogy to preserve our culture. *Equity & Excellence in Education, 54*(1), 68–78. https://doi.org/10.1080/10665684.2020.1863883

Lee, C. D. (2007). *Culture, literacy, and learning: Taking bloom in the midst of the whirlwind*. Teachers College Press.

Lee, C. D. (2020). A new generation of fugitive scholarship. *English Education, 52*(3), 180–185.

Lesko, N. (2012). *Act your age!: A cultural construction of adolescence* (2nd ed.). Routledge.

Levertov, D. (1987). *Selected poems.* Bloodaxe Books.

Lipman, P. (2004). *High stakes education.* Routledge.

Love, B. L. (2023). *Punished for dreaming: How school reform harms Black children and how we heal* (1st ed.). St. Martin's Press.

Lucero, A., Schieble, M., Vetter A., & Zaino, K. (2025). Expanding sites of opportunity for critical teacher learning in urban education. *Urban Education.* Advance online publication. https://doi.org/10.1177/00420859251359255

Luke, A. (2004). At last: The trouble with English. *Research in the Teaching of English, 39*(1), 85–95. https://www.jstor.org/stable/40171653

Lyiscott, J. J. (2019). *Black appetite. White food. Issues of race, voice, and justice within and beyond the classroom.* Routledge.

Lyiscott, J. J., Caraballo, L., Filipiak, D., Riina-Ferrie, J., Yeom, M., & Lee, M. A. (2021). Cyphers for justice: Learning from the wisdom of intergenerational inquiry with youth. *Review of Education, Pedagogy, and Cultural Studies, 42*(5), 363–383.

Lyiscott, J., de los Ríos, C. V., & Clark, C. H. (2023). Case studies of effective learning climates for civic reasoning and discussion. *The Annals of the American Academy of Political and Social Science, 705*(1), 138–155. https://doi.org/10.1177/00027162231178627

Madan, C. (2017). Motivated cognition: Effects of reward, emotion, and other motivational factors across a variety of cognitive domains. *Collabra: Psychology, 3*(1), Article 24. https://doi.org/https://doi.org/10.1525/collabra.111

Metz, M. (2023). Critical language awareness. In L. M. Barker, D. Gorlewski, J. Gorlewski, & C. M. Miller (Eds.), *Encyclopedia of English language arts education: A critical perspective* (pp. 60–66). Brill.

Milwicki, A., Carey, M. H., & Wiinikka-Lydon, J. (2023, April 17). *"Never again" starts with education.* Learning for Justice. https://www.learningforjustice.org/magazine/never-again-starts-with-education

Mirra, N. (2018). *Educating for empathy: Literacy learning and civic engagement.* Teachers College Press.

Mirra, N., Filipiak, D., & Garcia, A. (2015). Revolutionizing inquiry in urban English classrooms: Pursuing voice and justice through youth participatory action research. *English Journal, 105*(2), 49–57.

Mirra, N., & Garcia, A. (2020). "I hesitate but I do have hope": Youth speculative civic literacies for troubled times. *Harvard Educational Review, 90*(2), 295–321.

Mirra, N., & Garcia, A. (2021). In search of the meaning and purpose of 21st-century literacy learning: A critical review of research and practice. *Reading Research Quarterly, 56*(3), 463–496.

Mirra, N., Garcia, A., & Morrell, E. (2015). *Doing youth participatory action research: Transforming inquiry with researchers, educators, and students*. Routledge.

Morrell, E. (2005). Critical English education. *English Education, 37*(4), 312–321.

Morrell, E. (2008). Six summers of YPAR: Learning, action, and change in urban education. In J. Cammarota & M. Fine (Eds.), *Revolutionizing education: Youth participatory action research in motion* (pp. 155–187). Routledge.

Muhammad, G. E. (2020). *Cultivating genius: An equity framework for culturally and historically responsive literacy*. Scholastic.

National Governors Association Center for Best Practices and Council of Chief State School Officers. (2010). *Common Core State Standards for English language arts & literacy in history/social studies, science, and technical subjects*. https://corestandards.org/wp-content/uploads/2023/09/ELA_Standards1.pdf

Nelms, B. F. (2011). Celebration and conversation, consensus and dissent: What NCTE means to me. *The English Journal, 101*(1), 26–32. http://www.jstor.org/stable/23047842

New London Group. (1996). A pedagogy of multiliteracies: Designing social futures. *Harvard Educational Review, 66*(1), 60–92.

Ohito, E. O. (2020). "The creative aspect woke me up": Awakening to multimodal essay composition as a fugitive literacy practice. *English Education, 52*(3), 186–222.

Oleksiyenko, A. V., & Jackson, L. (2020). Freedom of speech, freedom to teach, freedom to learn: The crisis of higher education in the post-truth era. *Educational Philosophy and Theory, 53*(11), 1057–1062. https://doi.org/10.1080/00131857.2020.1773800

Paris, D. (2012). Culturally sustaining pedagogy: A needed change in stance, terminology, and practice. *Educational Researcher, 41*(3), 93–97. https://doi.org/10.3102/0013189X12441244

Paris, D., & Alim, H. S. (2014). What are we seeking to sustain through culturally sustaining pedagogy? A loving critique forward. *Harvard Educational Review, 84*(1), 85–100.

Peters, M. A. (2017). Education in a post-truth world. *Educational Philosophy and Theory, 49*(6), 563–566. https://doi.org/10.1080/00131857.2016.1264114

Pinar, W. (2004). *What is curriculum theory?* Lawrence Earlbaum Associates.

Pinar, W., Reynolds, W., Slattery, P., & Taubman, P. (1995). Understanding curriculum as autobiographical/biographical text. In W. Pinar, W. Reynolds, P. Slattery, & P. Taubman (Eds.), *Understanding curriculum: An introduction to the study of historical and contemporary curriculum discourses* (pp. 515–566). Peter Lang.

Pindyck, M., Vinz, R., Liu, D., & Wittchow, A. (2022). *A poetry pedagogy for teachers: Reorienting classroom literacy practices*. Bloomsbury Publishing.

Pratt, T. (2024, July 3). Georgia lawsuit challenges anti-LGBTQ+ book bans over "real harms." *The Guardian*. https://www.theguardian.com/us-news/article/2024/jul/03/georgia-lawsuit-book-bans

Price-Dennis, D., & Sealey-Ruiz, Y. (2021). *Advancing racial literacies in teacher education: Activism for equity in digital spaces*. Teachers College Press.

Roy, A. (2020, April 3). The pandemic is a portal. *Financial Times*. https://www.ft.com/content/10d8f5e8-74eb-11ea-95fe-fcd274e920ca

Rubin, B. C. (2012). *Making citizens: Transforming civic learning for diverse social studies classrooms*. Routledge.

Schey, R. (2023). Literacy (dis)orientations in a secondary classroom: Possibilities and limits of an intersectional LGBTQ+-inclusive curriculum. *Reading Research Quarterly, 58*(1), 25–43.

Schieble, M., Vetter, A., & Martin, K. (2020). *Classroom talk for social change: Critical conversations in English language arts*. Teachers College Press.

Sealey-Ruiz, Y. (2022). An archaeology of self for our times: Another talk to teachers. *English Journal, 111*(5), 21–26.

Semetsky, I. (2006). *Deleuze, education, and becoming*. Sense Publishers.

Skerrett, A., & Smagorinsky, P. (2023). *Teaching literacy in troubled times*. Corwin Press.

Smagorinsky, P. (2002). "Growth through English" revisited. *The English Journal, 91*(6), 23–29. https://doi.org/10.2307/821812

Smith, D. (2022) *Transformational sanctuaries in the middle level ELA classroom: Creating truth spaces for Black girls*. Routledge.

Snyder, J., Bolin, F., & Zumwalt, K. (1992). Curriculum implementation. In P. W. Jackson (Ed.), *Handbook of research on curriculum* (pp. 402–435). Macmillan.

Thomas, E. E. (2020). *The dark fantastic: Race and the imagination from Harry Potter to the Hunger Games*. New York University Press.

Thomas, P. L., & Goering, C. (2017). Speaking truth to power: Revisiting Lou LaBrant's *We teach English* (1951): Debating whole-class novel instruction, and more. *The English Journal, 107*(2), 88–90.

Tuck, E. (2010). Breaking up with Deleuze: Desire and valuing the irreconcilable. *International Journal of Qualitative Studies in Education, 23*(5), 635–650. https://doi.org/10.1080/09518398.2010.500633

Vygotsky, L. S. (1978). Interaction between learning and development. In M. Cole, V. John Steiner, S. Scribner, & E. Souberman (Eds.), *Mind in society: The development of higher psychological processes* (pp. 79–91). Harvard University Press.

Walkerdine, V. (2007). *Children, gender, video games: Towards a relational approach to multimedia*. Palgrave Macmillan.

Wills, J. S., Lintz, A., & Mehan, H. (2004). Ethnographic studies of multicultural education in U.S. classrooms and schools. In J. A. Banks & C. A. M. Banks (Eds.), *Handbook of research on multicultural education* (2nd ed., pp. 163–183). Jossey-Bass.

Winn, M. F., & Ubiles, J. R. (2011). Worthy witnessing: Collaborative research in urban classrooms. In A. Ball & C. Tyson (Eds.), *Studying diversity in teacher education* (pp. 295–308). Rowman & Littlefield.

Yeom, M., Caraballo, L., Tsang, G., Larkin, J., & Comrie, J. (2020). Reimagining impact: Storying youth research, arts, and activism. *Review of Education, Pedagogy, and Cultural Studies, 42*(5), 482–503. https://doi.org/10.1080/10714413.2021.1874850

Zaino, K. (2021). Liberal humanism, social science, and the discursive legacy of the "human" in English education. *Theory, Research, and Action in Urban Education (TRAUE)*, *6*(1).

Zeichner, K. (2014). The struggle for the soul of teaching and teacher education in the USA. *Journal of Education for Teaching: International research and pedagogy*, *40*(5), 551–568. https://doi.org/10.1080/02607476.2014.956544

Zemelman, S., Daniels, H., & Hyde, A. (2005). *Best practice: Today's standards for teaching and learning in America's schools* (3rd ed.). Heinemann.

Zumwalt, K. K. (2004). Choosing to make a difference. In A. T. Costigan, M. S. Crocco, & K. K. Zumwalt (Eds.), *Learning to teach in an age of accountability* (pp. 247–262). Lawrence Erlbaum & Associates.

Zumwalt, K. (2007). The misunderstood curriculum. In D. T. Hansen, M. E. Driscoll, & R. V. Arcilla (Eds.), *A life in classrooms: Philip W. Jackson and the practice of education* (pp. 122–134). Teachers College Press.

Zumwalt, K. K., & Craig, E. (2005). Teachers' characteristics: Research on the demographic profile. In M. Cochran-Smith & K. Zeichner (Eds.), *Studying teacher education: The report of the AERA Panel on Research and Teacher Education* (pp. 111–156). Lawrence Erlbaum Associates.

Chapter Seven

Booming Ballads: Corrido Poetics in the Critical English Classroom

Cati de los Ríos

As Mexican regional music newcomers like Yahritza y Su Esencia, Eslabon Armado, and Peso Pluma—who primarily sing Mexican ballads known as corridos—continue to rise to Billboard Top 100 lists and even peak at #1 on Billboard Global 200 (Romo, 2023), these commercialized cultural sounds are not new. On the contrary, corridos are among Mexico's oldest literary genres and a consequential form of "life writing" (Alviso, 2024) in what has been known as "Greater Mexico" (Paredes, 1958). Chicano folklorist Américo Paredes coined the term "Greater Mexico" to refer to "all the areas inhabited by people of Mexican culture—not only within the present limits of the Republic of Mexico but in the United States as well—in a cultural rather than a political sense" (Paredes, 1976, p. xiv). Despite their long history, there has been a surge in the renovation of corridos by young people who have recreated these age-old Mexican regional sounds into a genre that fits their urban, rural, and suburban worlds on both sides of the border (de los Ríos, 2022, 2023). Romo (2023) noted that this new generation of regional Mexican musicians, or the "Gen Z spin to traditional Mexican music" have both modernized and elevated the historically racialized genres of guitar-, accordion-, and horn-driven music into the cultural mainstream.

Corridos, as narrative folk ballads (Paredes, 1958), are often interwoven into the cultural and linguistic fabric of Mexican-origin children's literacy worlds (de los Ríos, 2018, 2019) and among the literary inheritances of children raised in Mexican immigrant Spanish-dominant households (de los Ríos & Portillo,

2021). These ballads are frequently a form of marking significant events in both public and home life. For example, my abuela Cati, a multi-instrumentalist and folklorista in her own right, would play her guitar and sing corridos (border ballads) and románticas (romance ballads) to her grandchildren every year on their birthdays. These literacy events (Heath, 1983) were forms of commonplace oracy and multimodal performance in my Mexican immigrant household.

Theorists of children's literacy and literature have provided numerous studies of how genres like fairy tales (Tatar, 2009) and folk songs like corridos (de los Ríos, 2018) can stay in children's memories as incentives for further reading, study, writing, and engagement (Heath, 2018). This chapter briefly historicizes the corrido as an adolescent critical literacy practice and then highlights youth's important corrido poetics that critical English classrooms (Morrell, 2005) can leverage and build upon, particularly through critical translanguaging approaches to writing (de los Ríos et al., 2021; García et al., 2017). Morrell (2005) noted that critical English classrooms encourage "practitioners to draw upon the everyday language and literacy practices of adolescents to make connections with academic literacies and to work toward empowered identity development and social transformation" (p. 313), and this includes students' translingual literacies and critical textual practices with corridos (de los Ríos, 2018). Housed within an ethos of critical English education (Morrell, 2005), corridistas (balladeers) have long seen reading and writing as social and political practices deeply rooted in one's cultural, community, and familial contexts, emphasizing literacy as a tool for social change and self-determination (Paredes, 1958).

Situating Corrido Poetics

The corrido has been defined as a type of "dissident folklore" (Saldívar, 1997) and an "epic-lyric-narrative genre" that is "based on musical phrases organized in four parts that tells of events that powerfully move the sensibilities of the masses" (Mendoza, 1954, p. ix). The corrido has been defined mostly as "an anonymous folk song narrative composed in octosyllabic quatrains and sung to a tune typically in ternary rhythm and in 3/4 or 6/8 meter. The quatrains are usually structured in an a b c b rhyme pattern and the entire narrative may be framed with formulaic openings and closings" (Limón 1984, pp. 11–12 as cited in R. Saldívar, 1990, p. 27).

The corrido tradition has often been understood as a counter-hegemonic discourse practice of historically marginalized communities. Because the corrido is narrative, reflexive, and poetic in technique, it readily lends itself as an instrument for analysis of larger sociopolitical experiences in secondary literacy classrooms, particularly with emergent bilinguals (de los Ríos et al., 2021).

Similar to the editorial section of a local newspaper, the corrido addresses a socially significant topic, presenting key points in a rhythmic and concise manner (Chew Sánchez, 2006). It often interprets these points through a critical moral perspective, offers social commentary, and may propose future solutions (Griffith & Fernández, 1988). However, the unique aspect of the corrido is its focus on the experiences of poor, working-class, and marginalized groups (Harpole, 1980; Paredes, 1958). From this perspective, social issues are not only documented but also analyzed and interpreted. In a world where ordinary people have limited economic and political power, cultural forms like the corrido serve as a vital means of amplifying the voices and experiences of the general population (Saldívar, 1997).

Corridos have typically followed a standard structure that includes: (1) the balladeer's announcement that they will be singing a corrido; (2) the date, place, and name(s) of the main protagonist(s); (3) the actions of the protagonist(s); (4) the main message of the corrido; (5) the despedida, or special farewell verse; and (6) the farewell of the person singing the corrido (Harpole, 1980). The corridos as a foundational oral tradition are songs that survived generations without written language or mass media (Griffith & Fernández, 1988). In addition to documenting historical events, natural disasters, and social conflict, corridos can be considered poetics and a way to document both individual and collective human endeavors (Saldívar, 1990). Richard Bauman and Charles L. Briggs define poetics as "the artful use of language in the conduct of social life" (1990, p. 79). In my work with adolescent corridistas (de los Ríos, 2018), corrido poetics as a critical literacy practice capture some of the ways that young people continue to take up this culturally anchored composition for creative exchange, life writing, and social critique (de los Ríos et al., 2022). I've documented how young people write corridos about a loved one, a death in the family, an injustice in their community, and for cross-racial solidarity (de los Ríos, 2018; de los Ríos et al., 2021; de los Ríos et al., 2022). Critical literacy, according to Morrell (2008), "is necessary not only for the critical navigation of hegemonic discourses . . . [but] is also essential to the redefining of the self and the transformation of oppressive social structures and relations of production" (p. 5).

Contemporary corridos, particularly the most evocative ones, "draw their power from their resemblance to and resonance with what is perceived as true and real, that is, the difficulties and injustices of life faced by Mexican Americans and other Latinx populations in the United States" (Avisu, 2024, p. 29). While there continues to be concerns about the appropriateness, hyper-masculinist, and gendered dynamics of modernized corridos (Cantero, 2021; de los Ríos, 2019), they remain an important counterculture among many transnational young people and a lens through which youth articulate their lives, hopes, and futures. As Winn (2018) stated regarding taking the concerns of youth of color seriously, "whether we will listen with filters of correctness and appropriateness or embody stances that support their goals for articulating their dreams, ideas, and intentions" (p. 221). It is precisely for this reason that critical English educators must continue to orient themselves to the popular cultural knowledge of young people, including those of transnational and immigrant backgrounds.

Why Engage Critical Corrido Poetics in the Critical English Classroom?

Teachers in urban, suburban, and rural schools are experiencing changing demography and a growth of immigrant, transnational students, including those labeled as "English language learners" (Educational Statistics, 2019). As the enrollment of students of color and racialized bi/multilingual continues to rise, teachers across contexts must meet the challenge and find ways to forge meaningful relationships with young people who come from different cultures and speak languages other than English, while also supporting these students to develop robust academic skills. Part of this work requires that educators expand notions of what constitutes literature, academic texts, and the greater canon in their English classrooms. A critical English classroom also advocates for a shift in textual pedagogy, consumption, and creation (Morrell, 2005). It necessitates that teachers learn more about their students' everyday practices with music, songwriting, poetry, and popular culture in languages other than English and find ways to incorporate those everyday literacy practices into their classrooms.

Corridos are a political art form fusing balladry, storytelling, political education, and music to explore rich narratives of human endeavor (de los Ríos et al., 2022). Regional Mexican music is increasingly popular among transnational, immigrant, and racialized youth populations due to its power to engender strong community feelings and reflection that span languages, vernaculars, and sounds. As racialized sounds (Kun, 2005), Mexican regional music like corridos allows its audience to forge cultural and multimodal self-understanding while living through politically adverse periods and unwelcoming environments (Simonett, 2000). Moreover, Gee (2003) contends that "learning is not just a matter of what goes on inside people's heads but is fully embedded in (situated within) a material, social and cultural world" (p. 8). In other words, literacy transcends notions of print-centricity; rather, it can more properly be thought of as a semiotic domain: "any set of practices that recruits one or more modalities (e.g., oral or written language, images, equations, symbols, sounds, gestures, graphs, artifacts, etc.) to communicate distinctive types of meanings" (Gee, 2003, p. 18).

Mexican-origin bilingual students labeled "English learners" have long been framed as deficient in the dominant literature as defined by traditional metrics like standardized tests. My ethnographic research on corrido pedagogy in literacy classrooms, in harmony with other sociocultural, critical, and translingual scholars, has worked to craft the linguistic skills and dexterity of young people classified as "English learners" through their writing, performance, and oratorical practices with corridos and as a legitimate way of knowing and being in the world (de los Ríos, 2023). As a researcher, in examining under-studied cultural practices from the point of view of the Mexican-heritage youth participants, I have heeded Gutiérrez and colleagues' entreaty to document "people's history of involvement in practices of the cultural community" (Gutiérrez et al., 2009, p. 219) and center those skills in literacy classrooms. With Mexican regional music being among the fastest growing genres (Davies, 2024), incorporating corrido writing pedagogy in the classroom can foster "sites for expressive conversations" and allow youth to participate in "the poetics of everyday life" (Limón, 2012, p. 134).

"La Pandemia" as a Booming Ballad in the Classroom

As a high school English language development (ELD) and Chicanx/Latinx studies teacher, I regularly incorporated corridos into my classrooms. I used the Kennedy Center's free online[1] curricular resources for incorporating the teaching of corridos in English and social studies classrooms. These resources help to scaffold the analysis of corridos to gain a sense of their traditional written form, analyze the rhetorical devices, and then encourage students to write their own original ballads. As a teacher educator, I have continued to suggest these curricular materials to teachers while also encouraging the pairing of older corridos noted in the Kennedy Center's webpage with more recent corridos from popular culture. A regional Mexican band that has resonated with young people, specifically transnational and bi/multilingual students of color, is Fuerza Regida. Originally from San Bernardino, California, Fuerza Regida is a quintet mostly known for their party anthems and are hugely popular, unique, and endlessly creative.

Their song "La Pandemia/The Pandemic" reflects on the time when most of the world entered lockdown, and it encourages their listeners to have patience and keep working for a better future. It's entirely in Spanish but with English words sprinkled in and reflective of this band's discourse style. When studying corridos, you can ask students questions about the narrative structure, historical context, protagonists, themes, musical elements, and cultural impact. For example:

1. Who are the main characters in the corrido?
2. What is the central conflict of the ballad?
3. What social issues or injustices are addressed in the corrido?
4. What literary devices are present in the corrido?
5. What are the potential limitations or biases in the way corridos portray history?
6. How does the music contribute to the story being told?

Attempts to support emergent bilingual students in writing and classroom discussions often utilize sentence stems and frames since they can be generative offerings to support students in entering into conversations (Rodríguez-Mojica & Briceño, 2018). In my work with teachers of emergent bilinguals, some have examined the rhetorical devices in the ballad, and others have used several of these lines as sentence and/or stanza starters where they encourage their students to create their own ballads reflecting on their experiences and learning during the COVID-19 pandemic. For example,

Excerpt of Re-Writing Pandemia Corrido Activity

It's raining outside
And I remember ________________
Taking off ____________________
And now everything changed, a pandemic arrived and here I am

Outside is another world
The _________ are empty, __________
People at home ______________________
But not even a few months ago, everyone____________________

<table>
<tr><th>“Pandemia” (2020)</th><th>“Pandemic” (2020)</th></tr>
<tr><td>De los corridos originales
Y pura Fuerza Regida, viejo
Otro pedo

Afuera está lloviendo
Y recuerdo buenos tiempos y escenarios
Despegando vuelos en diferente estado
Y ahora todo cambió, una pandemia salió y aquí estoy

Afuera es otro mundo
Las calles están vacías, no es seguro
La gente en su casa y sin trabajo
Pero ni hace unos meses, todos querían más vacación

Muchos piensan que es una conspiración
Otros dicen que es culpa de los buenos
Pero todos estamos en la misma puta situación

Pura Lumbre Music
Rancho Humilde
Street, ma’
Otro pedo

Hay que aguantar la tormenta
Como dice el dicho: “después se viene la calma”
Mente bien positiva, sigo chambeando
Nunca agaches la cabeza ni pa’ verte los zapatos

Quizás, mañana, todo se acabará
Y todo regrese la normalidad
Por lo tanto, ansioso espero pronto volver a volar</td><td>One of the original ballads
Pure Fuerza Regida
Another one/problem

It’s raining outside
And I remember good times and sceneries
Taking off on flights in different states
And now everything changed, a pandemic arrived and here I am

Outside is another world
The streets are empty, it’s not safe
People at home and without work
But not even a few months ago, everyone wanted more vacation

Many think it’s a conspiracy
Others say it’s the fault of the good guys
But we are all in this same f**king situation

Pure fire music
Humble ranch (records)
Street, ma’
Another one/problem

You have to endure the storm
As the saying goes: “then comes the calm”
Very positive mindset, I keep working
Never lower your head even to look at your shoes

Maybe tomorrow it will all be over
And everything returns to normal
There, I eagerly hope to fly again soon</td></tr>
</table>

Students, particularly those that are still adding English to their linguistic repertoires, can reflect on their strengths and struggles during the pandemic shutdown while engaging this textual production activity.

Conclusion

By documenting students' cultural experiences and practices with corridos, we can learn how their modes of expression are often enactments of alternative worlds. It is important for students to see that corridistas, or balladeers, have long worked to make their points of view and arguments heard in ways that pertain to communicative domains beyond spoken language. Reading and writing corridos and studying cultural expressivity, which is expressly multimodal in language use, highlight the importance of alternative worlds like disrupting hegemonic naming processes by pointing to their colonial roots and documenting how they have been used to police minoritized communities, including emergent bilingual communities.

Pahl (2014) highlighted the importance of aesthetics and the creation of meaning in students' writing, particularly emphasizing the work of Hull and Nelson (2005), who argued that at the heart of developing such skills is artistic creative practice. Hull and Nelson noted that practice "promotes an understanding of textual meaning-making as a fluid, context-dependent, intertextual, and fundamentally design-oriented process" (p. 219). This perspective should also apply to the writing of adolescents, many of whom engage in various forms of storytelling (de los Ríos & Molina, 2020; García & Morrell, 2013; Mirra et al., 2018) through their multimodal activities, which often go unrecognized in classrooms.

Engaging corrido poetics in critical English classrooms further builds upon the connections between the literacies associated with young people's participation with popular culture and the work of secondary English classrooms (Morrell, 2005, 2008). The corrido is a literary and musical genre that can lead to alternative routes for the construction of consequential stories. Lastly, as literary texts, corridos can be used to scaffold literary terms and concepts and ultimately foster literary interpretations that are situated in the social, cultural, and political lives of students.

Notes

1. The Kennedy Center, "Traditional Mexican Corridos": https://www.kennedy-center.org/education/resources-for-educators/classroom-resources/lessons-and-activities/lessons/9-12/form-and-theme-in-traditional-mexican-corridos/

References

Alviso, R. (2024). With a pencil in their hand: The corrido as life writing. In M. J. Villasenor & C. J. Fernandez (Eds.), *The Routledge handbook of Latinx life writing* (1st ed., pp. 22–35). Routledge.

Bauman, R., & Briggs, C. (1990). Poetics and performance as critical perspectives on language and social life. *Annual Review of Anthropology, 19*, 59–88.

Chew Sánchez, M. I. (2006). *Corridos in migrant memory.* University of New Mexico Press.

Davies, C. (2024, July 18). Latin music takes the lead as the U.S.'s fastest-growing genre. *Los Angeles Times.* https://www.latimes.com/delos/story/2024-07-18/latin-music-growth-us-musica-mexicana-fuerza-regida-peso-pluma#:~:text=Latin%20music%20takes%20the%20lead

de los Ríos, C. V. (2018). Toward a *corridista* consciousness: Learning from one transnational youth's critical reading, writing, and performance of Mexican corridos. *Reading Research Quarterly, 53*(4), 455–471. https://doi.org/10.1002/rrq.210

de los Ríos, C. V. (2019). "Los músicos": Mexican corridos, the aural border, and the evocative musical renderings of transnational youth. *Harvard Educational Review, 89*(2), 177–200.

de los Ríos, C. V. (2022). Guitarras on the rise: Framing youth sierreño bands as translingual ingenuity. *Reading Research Quarterly, 57*(2), 691–706. https://doi.org/10.1002/rrq.433

de los Ríos, C. V. (2023). Delinking to learn from youth expressive practitioners of the everyday: A commentary on "Undoing competence: Coloniality, homogeneity, and the overrepresentation of Whiteness in applied linguistics." *Language Learning, 73*(S2), 308–311. https://doi.org/10.1111/lang.12539

de los Ríos, C. V. (2024). "Al sonido del huehuetl": Situating danza azteca as family translingual prayer and civic engagement. *Journal of Language, Identity, and Education*, *23*(3), 355–367. https://doi.org/10.1080/15348458.2024.2324281

de los Ríos, C. V., & Molina, A. (2020). Literacies of refuge: "Pidiendo posada" as ritual of justice. *Journal of Literacy Research*, *52*(1), 32–54. https://doi.org/10.1177/1086296X19897840

de los Ríos, C. V., Portillo, Y., & Cantero, B. (2022). Critical worldmaking through balladry: Youth corrido literacies as a lived civic poetic. *Journal of Adolescent & Adult Literacy, 66*(2), 55–59. https://doi.org/10.1002/JAAL.1251

de los Ríos, C. V., & Seltzer, K. (2017). Translanguaging, coloniality, and English classrooms: An exploration of two bicoastal urban classrooms. *Research in the Teaching of English*, *52*(1), 55–76.

de los Ríos, C. V., Seltzer, K., & Molina, A. (2021). "Juntos somos fuertes": Writing participatory corridos of solidarity through a critical translingual approach. *Applied Linguistics, 42*(6), 1070–1082. https://doi.org/10.1093/applin/amab026

Garcia, A., & Morrell, E. (2013). City youth and the pedagogy of participatory media. *Learning, Media and Technology, 38*(2), 123–127. https://doi.org/10.1080/17439884.2013.782040

García, O., Johnson, S., & Seltzer, K. (2017). *The translanguaging classroom: Leveraging student bilingualism for learning*. Caslon.

García, O., & Otheguy, R. (2020). Plurilingualism and translanguaging: Commonalities and divergences. *International Journal of Bilingual Education and Bilingualism*, *23*(1), 17–35. https://doi.org/10.1080/13670050.2019.1598932

García, O., & Li, W. (2014). *Translanguaging: Language, bilingualism and education*. Palgrave Macmillan.

Gee, J. P. (2003). *What video games have to teach us about learning and literacy*. Palgrave Macmillan.

Griffith, J. S., & Fernández, C. (1988). Mexican horse races and cultural values: The case of *Los corridos del Merino*. *Western Folklore, 47*(2), 129–151.

Gutiérrez, K., Zitlali Morales, P., & Martinez, D. (2009). Re-mediating literacy: Culture, difference, and learning for students from nondominant communities. *Review of Research in Education*, *33*(1), 212–245.

Heath, S. B. (1983). *Ways with words: Language, life, and work in communities and classrooms.* Cambridge University Press.

Heath, S. B. (2018). Finding life in literacy. *Literacy Research: Theory, Method, and Practice, 67*(1), 147–163.

Hull, G. A., & Nelson, M. E. (2005). Locating the semiotic power of multimodality. *Written Communication, 22*(2), 224–261.

Kun, J. (2005). *Audiotopia: Music, race, and America.* University of California Press.

Limón, J. (2012). *Américo Paredes: Culture and critique.* University of Texas Press.

Mendoza, V. T. (1954). *El corrido mexicano.* Fondo de Cultura Económica.

Mirra, N., Morrell, E., & Filipiak, D. (2018). From digital consumption to digital invention: Toward a new critical theory and practice of multiliteracies. *Theory Into Practice, 57*(1), 12–19. https://doi.org/10.1080/00405841.2017.1390336

Morrell, E. (2005). Critical English education. *English Education, 37*(4), 312–321.

Morrell, E. (2008). *Critical literacy and urban youth: Pedagogies of access, dissent, and liberation.* Routledge.

Pahl, K. (2014). The aesthetics of everyday literacies: Home writing practices in a British Asian household. *Anthropology & Education Quarterly, 45*(3), 293–311.

Paredes, A. (1958). *With his pistol in his hand: A border ballad and its hero.* University of Texas Press.

Paredes, A. (1976). *A Texas-Mexican cancionero: Folksongs of the lower border.* University of Illinois Press.

Rodriguez-Mojica, C., & Briceño, A. (2018). Sentence stems that support reading comprehension. *The Reading Teacher, 72*(3), 398–402. https://doi.org/10.1002/trtr.1705

Romo, V. (2023, May 5). *The unstoppable appeal of Peso Pluma and the Regional Mexican music scene.* NPR. https://www.npr.org/2023/05/05/1174139133/the-unstoppable-appeal-of-peso-pluma-and-the-regional-mexican-music-scene

Saldívar, J. D. (1990). The limits of cultural studies. *American Literary History, 2*(2), 251–266.

Saldívar, J. D. (1991). Chicano border narratives as cultural critique. In H. Calderon & J. D. Saldívar (Eds.), *Criticism in the borderlands: Studies in Chicano literature, culture, and ideology* (pp. 167–180). Duke University Press.

Saldívar, J. D. (1997). *Border matters: Remapping American cultural studies*. University of California Press.

Simonett, H. (2000). Popular music and the politics of identity: The empowering sound of technobanda. *Popular Music and Society, 24*(2), 1–23. https://doi.org/10.1080/03007760008591765

Tatar, M. (2009). *Enchanted hunters: The power of stories in childhood*. W. W. Norton & Company.

Winn, M. T. (2018). *Justice on both sides. Transforming education through restorative justice*. Harvard Education Press.

Chapter Eight

Queering Critical Literacy and English Education

Mollie V. Blackburn

Critical English education has come, mostly, to include sexual and gender diversity. The beginnings of this are evident in Hoffman's (1993) teaching of *Torch Song Trilogy* in a high school creative writing classroom, Greenbaum's (1994) teaching of a variety of literature with gay and lesbian texts and subtexts in high school English classrooms, Athanases's (1996) report of "Dear Anita: Late Night Thoughts of an Irish Catholic Homosexual" being read and discussed in a tenth-grade literature course, and Reese's (1998) teaching of *Jack*, a young adult novel about a teenage boy whose father comes out as gay, in an eighth grade literature course. This scholarship is *critical* in that it makes visible and interrogates inequitable power dynamics—in these cases, with respect to sexuality and gender, albeit primarily with respect to gay and lesbian sexual identities. Critical, yes, but not queer. Queer is distinctive in that it "attends to multiple, variable, and fluid notions of identity, but with particular attention to sexual and gender identities beyond heterosexual [and cisgender] hegemony" (Blackburn & Schey, 2017, p. 42). Queer is more aligned with the poststructural turn in critical theory than earlier versions of critical theory. The critical is still there but with a more complex understanding of the notion of truth and the role of language in power dynamics (Kamberelis & Dimitriadis, 2005).

The aforementioned projects are grounded in English education in that they focus on reading, writing, speaking, and listening in English language arts classrooms, although these focus heavily on reading. That said, to understand the queer in critical English education, one must broaden one's scope beyond classrooms. Work in classrooms, like that described above, was important in terms of combating homophobia, but it was not as effective at documenting the agency of queer youth. This kind of scholarship could be done—at least at this time, around the turn of the century—most powerfully in out-of-school contexts, like queer youth centers (Blackburn, 2002/2003, 2003, 2005a, 2005b). Here, literacies in out-of-school contexts were studied but not English language arts in classrooms.

I say all of this to explain what I'm talking about when I say critical English education and how I stretch it when I talk about queer literacies in education. Critical English education—the making visible and interrogation of power dynamics through reading, writing, speaking, and listening texts, construed broadly, in classrooms—is at the core of the concepts I explore in this chapter. Layered on top of this is an understanding of sexuality and gender as intersecting with many other identities, all of which may (or may not) be experienced as fluid. At this point, this understanding is commonly shared by scholars in the field of critical English education. Beyond this, there is an awareness that while ELA classrooms are central to the field, they do not define the parameters of the work needed to understand critical English education with respect to sexual and gender diversity, as well as other minoritized, surveilled, and marginalized identities. Sometimes—in the past, the present, and the future—in some places, the work just needs to happen beyond the confines of state institutions, including but not limited to schools.

Next, I turn to the roots of queer literacy scholarship before exploring its past, present, and future.

A Pair of Origin Stories

A story about critical English education might start with how critical theory was inspired by Marxism, fostered in the Frankfurt School, and coined by one of the directors, Horkheimer, in Germany during the 1920s and 1930s (Deranty, 2021). This story could then continue to tell how Freire (1983) brought critical theory to education, even literacy education, both broadly construed. Then, how Giroux (1993), along with McLaren, brought critical theory to schooling—more specifically, in North America—with the concept of critical pedagogy. And McLaren, along with Lankshear, shone a critical light on reading and writing in education with the idea of critical literacies (Lankshear & McLaren, 1993). Lankshear went further to broaden understandings of literacy by focusing on digital media. Throughout, educational scholars who focused on critical literacy turned to critical scholars (Anzaldúa, 1987; Collins, 2009; Crenshaw, 2013) and other provocative thinkers outside of the field (Lorde, 2012; Rich, 1980) to disrupt the whiteness and masculinity of critical theory in literacy education, broadly, and critical English education, more specifically. Other critical English educators forged this path within the field (e.g., Morrell, 2002, 2004, 2005; Morrell & Duncan-Andrade, 2002).

A story about the queering of critical theory in literacy education would echo some of the story about critical English education, but this story might start with how French philosophers like Derrida, Deleuze, and Barthes breathed life into poststructuralism in the 1960s (Merquior, 1987). Among those was Foucault (1990), who attended to sexuality, and Butler (1989), in the United States, who brought gender to the fore. Thus, Foucault and Butler laid the foundation for queer theory (Jagose, 1996). Pinar (1998) led the way in bringing queer theory to education in his 1998 groundbreaking edited volume *Queer Theory in Education.* To contextualize this volume, it was just after it came out that the American Educational Research Association's Lesbian and Gay Special Interest Group deliberated, voted, and became the Queer Studies Special Interest Group. In Pinar's edited book, Luhmann (1998) conceptualized queer pedagogy, echoing Lankshear and McLaren's critical pedagogy. Some scholars in Pinar's volume (Miller, 1998; Sumara & Davis, 1998) made connections among queer theory, education, and literacy. One of these scholars—Britzman (1995)—had previously asserted that queer pedagogy demands that scholars "stop reading straight" (p. 164), that is, stop pretending that readings are ever "innocent, normal, or unmediated"; instead, acknowledge that all readings already "provok[e] uncertainties, misrecognitions, ignorance, and silences" (p. 164). As such, she made a decisive and powerful move to bring queer theory to literacy education. In

2015, Miller proposed a "queer literacies framework," and just a few years later, van Leent and Mills (2018) proposed a "queer critical media literacies framework." Echoing scholars in critical theory again, educational scholars who were focused on queer theory and education (Brockenbrough, 2015) turned to queer scholars of color (Cohen, 2020; Johnson, 2001; Muñoz, 1999), particularly the notion of queer of color critique (Ferguson, 2004), to disrupt the whiteness of queer theory. This scholarship has been since taken up in the field of literacy or English education (e.g., Dozono, 2022).

Queer and Critical Literacy Education

Out of these came queer and critical studies of literacy education. Some of these took place outside of schools. For example, I worked with queer youth, primarily youth of color, to study their engagement with literacies for purposes of social change in an LGBTQ youth center in Philadelphia (e.g., Blackburn, 2002/2003, 2003, 2005a, 2005b). Later, Jim Buckley, Caroline Clark, Jeane Copenhaver-Johnson, and I initiated and facilitated a teacher inquiry group focused on combating homophobia and transphobia in Central Ohio schools (Blackburn, Clark, Kenney, & Smith, 2010; Blackburn, Clark, & Schey, 2018). Almost all of the participating teachers were English teachers and struggled with the tension between their students, particularly those in their schools' Gender and Sexuality Alliances (GSAs), wanting to read queer-inclusive texts and some of their administrators and students' parents not being supportive. In response, Caroline Clark and I began facilitating a book discussion group at the local queer youth center where the teachers in the teacher inquiry group could bring their students to select, read, and discuss queer-themed literature (Blackburn & Clark, 2011; Blackburn, Clark, & Nemeth, 2015). And they did so for three school years, showing how youth, including but not limited to queer youth, could engage with queer-themed literature in ways associated with schools—that is with their classmates and teachers, even if not in schools: making visible a queer version of critical English education in relation to schooling rather than in opposition to it.

This inspired me and others (e.g., Helmer 2016a, 2016b) to study LGBTQ-themed literature courses in relatively queer-friendly schools. Ryan Schey and I, for example, taught an LGBTQ-themed literature course at a charter school for the arts that actively recruited queer and queer-friendly students and staff (Blackburn & Schey, 2018; Schey & Blackburn, 2019). Students, straight and gay, cis and trans, and lots in between, read about, wrote about, talked about, and listened to issues and topics pertinent to queer people. Both the students and the literature were diverse in many ways. They did not all agree with one another about every issue or topic, but they had opportunities to articulate and explain their positions, consider those of others, and sometimes, but not always, rearticulate their positions as a result (Blackburn, 2022). Thus, these students embodied queer critical English education in a school. More of this scholarship is reviewed elsewhere (e.g., Blackburn & Schey, 2017), so at this point, I turn to more contemporary studies in queer literacy education.

Contemporary Studies

Recent scholarship that explores and examines queer critical English education builds on these traditions. For example, in 2016 and 2017, Ryan Schey conducted a literacy ethnography in a racially diverse public high school in the Midwestern region of the United States. In reporting on it, he points back to recent history that showed an increase of "scholarship in literacy education considering LGBTQ-themed texts and LGBTQ people in English language arts classrooms" (2019, p. 38). That said, he is explicit about the constraints schools, as homophobic and transphobic institutions, impose on queer and critical English education. He found that when youth engaged with queer-themed texts and topics that they selected in their classes, they were made more vulnerable. He highlights several examples where "[i]ndividualized visibility resulted in interpersonal isolation," meaning students were "vulnerable to queer marginalization," so they worked to protect themselves by decreasing their visibility (p. 56). Schey recognizes these efforts as "survival tactics" (p. 56). He also found, though, that some students at some moments in time experienced "local, concrete, and vivid" queer affirmation from both teachers and classmates (p. 57). As a result, they became interconnected and interdependent as they engaged in queer and critical work. Ultimately, he argues that it is

> deeply problematic and ethically and professionally irresponsible for literacy educators to rely on forms of queer-affirming literacy sponsorship that result in classroom readers becoming individually spotlighted and isolated such that they need to rely on whiteness or other forms of privilege and capital for protection if they choose to read queer texts. (p. 64)

But this argument is made possible by the moments when students experienced queer-affirming literacy events sponsored by their teachers and supported by their classmates. These moments happened in 2016 and 2017; this argument was made in 2019.

A lot changed in those two to three years, as evidenced by the introduction of Schey's 2022 article in which Schey reports on the same study. He writes:

> As I write this introduction, during 2022, a wave of legislation has unfolded during the past year in states such as Alabama, Florida, Georgia, Iowa, South Dakota, and Tennessee that has sought to illegalize classroom discussions of topics such as queerness, transness, anti-Blackness, and white supremacy and has had the effect of increasing the hostility of school climates. (pp. 428–429)

He notes the aforementioned change. In this context, it is imperative, he argues, to look to school-based literacy events in which queer and trans students are positioned as knowers, or not knowers, and consider the consequences of such positioning. In this article, he asserts that LGBTQ+ curriculum is something but not enough. It does not, in his words, "inevitably or uniformly foster a classroom context that is necessarily safe or affirming" (p. 439). But this time, in this article just a few years later, he notes "political and cultural acts to erase and illegalize representations of queer and trans lives from curricula are a form of epistemic injustice if not epistemic violence" (p. 438). He goes on to say that "the presence of epistemic injustice does not mean that queer and trans youth are defined by the harm or solely exist in a state of victimhood" (p. 438), and shows young people enacting "small resistances . . . in the tight spaces of the classroom" (p. 438). Again, we hear echoes, this time from the turn of the century when queer critical literacy education moved in significant ways from classrooms to youth centers.

A year later, Schey (2023) published another article about the 2016–2017 ethnography. It begins similarly, with an acknowledgment of increased hostility in society and schools, but here he advocates for "attending to youth's experiences and actions, particularly those of LGBTQ+ youth, through a framework of intersectionality" as a way of shifting LGBTQ+ curriculum, even "questioning the limits and silences of any curriculum" (p. 83). More explicitly, he suggests "rather than unilaterally constructing the official, institutional curriculum, educators can co-construct curriculum with youth, including texts they select and even author themselves" (p. 83). In other words, by this time, Schey not only recognizes the dire situation LGBTQ+ students are in, but he also sees their agency, as he did in the previous study, and challenges educators to engage with this agency to work within and against the constraints of the current context.

Of course, there are spaces in schools beyond classrooms where educators and students engage in LGBTQ+-themed content. In 2015–2016, Latrise Johnson (2017) documented her teaching in an after-school writing club at a high school in a college town in the southeast region of the United States. Nearly all the students at the school were African American. In the after-school club, "students read examples of how Black and Black queer writers have used writing to examine and interrogate issues of sexual identity and race. . . . [Johnson had] shared [her] own writing that described aspects of [her] Black queer identity." Further, she provided each student a journal and encouraged them "to write freely" (pp. 18–19). In this context, Johnson found that Black queer students' "journal entries, stories, poems, and prose provided practice not only for being gay, gender nonconforming, and queer, but also for just being" (p. 29). Thus, students "used writing to (re)claim, proclaim, and understand the self" (p. 23).

This contrasted with what she saw in classroom discussions and writing where "queer students and adults [including (her) were] discouraged from sharing their non-normative experiences" (p. 23). Ultimately, she argues that "how well teachers teach English in classrooms that includes Black queer youth will depend largely on how willing they are to know *all* of their students" (p. 30). So, rather than working in the "tight spaces of the classrooms," in Schey's words, Johnson works in an after-school club and provokes robust thinking and feeling through writing. Still, she demands those in "tight spaces" get to "know *all* of their students."

Jon Wargo (2017) studied three queer youth across contexts, including in school, after school, outside of school, and online. Thus, he attended to the "tight spaces" but also looked increasingly beyond them, which is the focus of this article. He studied the tattoo of a cis Latina lesbian; the livestreaming of a biracial, gay, gender queer youth; and the digital photography of a gay transmasculine white youth. He found that outside of school and online, these young people composed multimodal (counter)stories as ways of connecting to communities, "coping and engaging in action" (p. 157), and "counter[ing] heteronormative harm and cultural injustice" (p. 158). He argues that multimodal storytelling represents "extra-curricul[ar] . . . literacy learning" (p. 157) and is therefore a "rich site for inquiry for teachers to examine young people's production, consumption, and dissemination of digital products" (p. 158), particularly when examining the work of LGBTQ+ youth. Teachers were not a part of this literacy learning, or at least not in any direct way, but Wargo could imagine that they might be.

shea martin and Cody Miller (2022), however, explored literacy learning in a not just out-of-school but entirely away-from-school context. They initiated and facilitated three cohorts of a "national online book club dedicated to reading, analyzing, and celebrating LGBTQ+ young adult literature with LGBTQ+ youth" (p. 14) during the early part of the pandemic in 2020. They balanced creating a safe and secure space, being what they call "backstage managers" and following the lead of young people as they led the conversations or, in martin and Miller's words, "took center stage" (p. 17). That said, martin and Miller were "intentional in balancing both the content of the books as well as the order of reading to avoid conflating queerness and transness with trauma" (p. 19). Moreover, they deliberately "prioritize[d] care, affirmation, and holding space for the full presence of the LGBTQ+ youth who showed up" (p. 15). Ultimately, they offer recommendations for secondary English (and social studies) teachers, encouraging them to "incorporate and center narratives of QTPOC characters and people in their curriculum," to consider texts as sites "to interrogate oppressive structures and systems" with students, and to reflect on their own policies and practices that prevent LGBTQ+ youth from living fully in their classrooms (p. 21). Even though their project was removed from schools, they still conclude with a call for teachers to step up.

Trevor Boffone and Sarah Jerasa examine another digital book club centered around queer-inclusive texts. Initiated around the same time as martin and Miller's, this one was not only created *for* teens, but it was also created *by* teens on TikTok, specifically BookTok. The focal club for this article is about *Cemetery Boys* (Thomas, 2020), which is by and about a trans Latinx young man. Based on their analysis of this club, Boffone and Jerasa argue that "TikTok enables queer teens and allies to engage with queer YA literature," something they note is "often excluded from in-school literacies" (p. 10). Additionally, they explicitly name more recent dynamics of "book banning or censorship" (p. 14). Still, they encourage teachers "to consider these out-of-school literacy practices as authentic reading communities" and to "become allies in this work, which, in turn, can transform in-school literacies" (p. 10). They further suggest that teachers "include texts that reflect LGBTQ+, BIPOC, and other nondominant communities," "be visible allies for queer students," and "center their pedagogy in critical literacy" (p. 14). Like martin and Miller, Boffone and Jerasa make their calls for teacher action from far outside the classroom.

Other scholars push the boundaries beyond book clubs and "school-ish texts" (Smith & Wilhelm, 2002, p. 87). Addie Shrodes (2022), for example, studied critical digital literacies in the everyday activities of trans and queer youth. She "employed interview and visual participatory methods to theorize with and alongside young people through storytelling and to understand how young people constructed narratives with and in response to digital artifacts such as images, videos, and posts" (Shrodes, 2023, p. 345). In one of the articles to come out of her larger study, she focuses on how young people, particularly those with disabilities, imagined the future in relation to the digital cultural artifacts with which they engaged (Shrodes, 2023, p. 345). Participants selected, shared, and discussed three digital artifacts, one of which represented, for them, the future. Shrodes found that the narratives of these queer and trans young people "clarify that experiences with disability give rise to valuable practices of meaning-making and imagination needed for liberatory futures" (p. 354). In her work, Shrodes offers a vision of what queer critical literacy education might look like not only from far outside of the classroom but even removed from "school-ish" literacies. This agility, from inside the ELA classroom to far beyond it and even beyond texts young people might experience as "school-ish" while looking all the while back into schools, is imperative as we move critically, queerly, into the future of English education.

Moving Forward with Agility

Legislation that hinders or prevents talking about race and racism in schools, talking about gender in any way that disrupts cisnormativity, and talking about sexuality in any way that challenges the heteronormative—legislation that strives to push critical (English) education right back out of schools—seems to be coming from every direction right now in the United States. Certainly, it is coming more from some directions than others, but it is ubiquitous nonetheless.

In some ways, it feels like we are back where we were twenty-five years ago, enacting queer critical English education in out-of-school contexts as a way of seeing LGBTQ+ youth as agents rather than victims, as a way of imagining queer critical English education in school contexts. But we are not there, not exactly. We have a robust body of scholarship across places and spaces and time that goes beyond calls to interrupt homophobia in schools and acknowledge the existence of gay people beyond schools. Critical English educators understand the broad range of sexual and gender identities now; we understand the nuance and complexity of how those identities intersect with so many others. We talk about the importance of queering cisheteronormativity, not just interrupting homophobia. Some of these educators already have practice incorporating diverse queer-themed texts in their curriculum and supporting students in multimodal composition for self-advocacy; others are poised, ready to do so. And, yes, they are constrained and even threatened by some local and state laws, federal policies, and practices, but they stand on the shoulders of those whose only options were to work within and against such hostility. They are ready to heed the calls of Schey, Johnson, Wargo, martin and Miller, Boffone and Jerasa, and Shrodes, among many others. The times have gotten worse, but the critical English educators have gotten better and better. We are ready for the challenge. We are agile.

References

Anzaldúa, G. (1987). *Borderlands/la frontera: The new mestiza*. Spinsters/Aunt Lute.

Athanases, S. Z. (1996). A gay-themed lesson in an ethnic literature curriculum: Tenth graders' responses to "Dear Anita." *Harvard Educational Review, 66*(2), 231–256.

Blackburn, M. V. (2002/2003). Disrupting the (hetero)normative: Exploring literacy performances and identity work with queer youth. *Journal of Adolescent & Adult Literacy, 46*(4), 312–324.

Blackburn, M. V. (2003). Losing, finding, and making space for activism through literacy performances and identity work. *Penn GSE Perspectives on Urban Education, 2*(1). https://urbanedjournal.gse.upenn.edu/archive/volume-2-issue-1-spring-2003/losing-finding-and-making-space-activism-through-literacy-perfo

Blackburn, M. V. (2005a). Agency in borderland discourses: Examining language use in a community center with Black queer youth. *Teachers College Record, 107*(1), 89–113.

Blackburn, M. V. (2005b). Co-constructing space for literacy and identity work with LGBTQ youth. *Afterschool Matters, 4*, 17–23.

Blackburn, M. V. (2022). *Moving across differences: How students engage LGBTQ+ themes in a high school literature class.* State University of New York Press.

Blackburn, M. V., & Clark, C. T. (2011). Analyzing talk in a long-term literature discussion group: Ways of operating within LGBT-inclusive and queer discourses. *Reading Research Quarterly, 46*(3), 222–248.

Blackburn, M. V., Clark, C. T., Kenney, L. M., & Smith, J. M. (Eds.). (2010). *Acting out! Combating homophobia through teacher activism.* Teachers College Press.

Blackburn, M. V., Clark, C. T., & Nemeth, E. (2015). Examining queer elements and ideologies in LGBT-themed literature: What queer literature can offer young adult readers. *Journal of Literacy Research, 47*(1), 11–48.

Blackburn, M. V., Clark, C. T., & Schey, R., with Penn, J. I., Johnson, C., Williams, J., Sutton, D., Swensen, K., & Vanderhule, L. (2018). *Stepping up! Teachers advocating for sexual and gender diversity in schools.* Routledge.

Blackburn, M. V., & Schey, R. (2017). Adolescent literacies beyond heterosexual hegemony. In K. A. Hinchman & D. A. Appleman (Eds.), *Adolescent literacies: A handbook of practiced-based research* (pp. 38–60). Guilford Press.

Blackburn, M. V., & Schey, R. (2018). Shared vulnerability, collaborative composition, and the interrogation and reification of oppressive values in a high school LGBTQ-themed literature course. *Journal of Literacy Research, 50*(3), 335–358.

Boffone, T., & Jerasa, S. (2021). Toward a (queer) reading community: BookTok, teen readers, and the rise of TikTok literacies. *Talking Points, 33*(1), 10–16.

Britzman, D. P. (1995). Is there a queer pedagogy? Or, stop reading straight. *Educational Theory, 45*(2), 151–165.

Brockenbrough, E. (2015). Queer of color agency in educational contexts: Analytic frameworks from a queer of color critique. *Educational Studies, 51*(1), 28–44.

Butler, J. (1989). *Gender trouble: Feminism and the subversion of identity.* Routledge.

Cohen, C. J. (2020). Punks, bulldaggers, and welfare queens: The radical potential of queer politics? In C. McCann, S.-k. Kim, & E. Ergun (Eds.), *Feminist theory reader* (pp. 311–323). Routledge.

Collins, P. H. (2009). *Another kind of public education: Race, schools, the media, and democratic possibilities*. Beacon Press.

Crenshaw, K. W. (2013). Mapping the margins: Intersectionality, identity politics, and violence against women of color. In M. Fineman & R. Mykitiuk (Eds.), *The public nature of private violence* (pp. 93–118). Routledge.

Deranty, J.-P. (2021). Critical theory and/as political philosophy. In P. Giladi (Ed.), *Hegel and the Frankfurt School: Traditions in dialogue* (pp. 267–296). Routledge.

Dozono, T. (2022). Queer of color literacies as subversive reading practice: How queer students of color subvert power in the classroom. *Equity & Excellence in Education, 56*(1–2), 28–41.

Foucault, M. (1990). *The history of sexuality: An introduction* (Vol. 1). Vintage.

Freire, P. (1983). The importance of the act of reading. *Journal of Education, 165*(1), 5–11.

Giroux, H. (1993). Literacy and the politics of difference. In C. Lankshear & P. L. McLaren (Eds.), *Critical literacy: Politics, praxis, and the postmodern* (pp. 367–378). State University of New York Press.

Greenbaum, V. (1994). Literature out of the closet: Bringing gay and lesbian texts and subtexts out in high school English. *English Journal, 83*(5), 71–74.

Helmer, K. (2016a). Queer literacies: A multidimensional approach to reading LGBTQ-themed literature. In D. Linville & D. L. Carlson (Eds.), *Beyond borders: Queer eros and ethos (ethics) in LGBTQ young adult literature* (pp. 181–198). Peter Lang.

Helmer, K. (2016b). Gay and lesbian literature disrupting the heteronormative space of the high school English classroom. *Sex Education, 16*(1), 35–48.

Hoffman, M. (1994). Teaching *Torch song*: Gay literature in the classroom. *Rethinking Schools, 8*(4), 16–17.

Jagose, A. (1996). *Queer theory: An introduction*. New York University Press.

Johnson, E. P. (2001). "Quare" studies, or (almost) everything I know about queer studies I learned from my grandmother. *Text and Performance Quarterly, 21*(1), 1–25.

Johnson, L. P. (2017). Writing the self: Black queer youth challenge heteronormative ways of being in an after-school writing club. *Research in the Teaching of English*, *52*(1), 13–33.

Kamberelis, G., & Dimitriades, G. (2005). *On qualitative inquiry: Approaches to language and literacy research*. Teachers College Press.

Lankshear, C., & McLaren, P. L. (Eds.). (1993). *Critical literacy: Politics, praxis, and the postmodern*. State University of New York Press.

Lorde, A. (2012). *Sister outsider: Essays and speeches*. Crossing Press.

Luhmann, S. (1998). Queering/querying pedagogy? Or, pedagogy is a pretty queer thing. In W. F. Pinar (Ed.), *Queer theory in education* (pp. 141–155). Lawrence Erlbaum Associates.

martin, s. w., & Miller, H. C. (2022). The category is "pandemic queer." *The Radical Teacher*, (124), 13–23.

Merquior, J. G. (1987). *Foucault*. University of California Press.

Miller, J. (1998). Autobiography as a queer curriculum practice. In W. F. Pinar (Ed.), *Queer theory in education* (pp. 301–308). Lawrence Erlbaum Associates.

miller, sj. (2015). A queer literacy framework promoting (a)gender and (a) sexuality self-determination and justice. *English Journal*, *104*(5), 37–44.

Morrell, E. (2002). Toward a critical pedagogy of popular culture: Literacy development among urban youth. *Journal of Adolescent & Adult Literacy*, *46*(1), 72–77.

Morrell, E. (2004). *Becoming critical researchers: Literacy and empowerment for urban youth* (Vol. 227). Peter Lang.

Morrell, E. (2005). Critical English education. *English Education*, *37*(4), 312–321.

Morrell, E., & Duncan-Andrade, J. M. (2002). Promoting academic literacy with urban youth through engaging hip-hop culture. *English Journal*, *91*(6), 88–92.

Muñoz, J. E. (1999). *Disidentifications: Queers of color and the performance of politics*. University of Minnesota Press.

Pinar, W. F. (Ed.). (1998). *Queer theory in education*. Lawrence Erlbaum Associates.

Reese, J. (1998). Teaching tolerance through literature: Dealing with issues of homosexuality in English class. *International Schools Journal, 17*(2), 35–40.

Rich, A. (1980). Compulsory heterosexuality and lesbian existence. *Signs, 5*(4), 631–660.

Schey, R. (2019). Youths' choices to read optional queer texts in a high school ELA classroom. *English Education, 52*(1), 38–69.

Schey, R. (2022). Queer and trans youth (not) knowing: Experiences of epistemic (in)justice in the context of an LGBTQ+-inclusive secondary curriculum. *English Teaching: Practice & Critique, 21*(4), 428–442.

Schey, R. (2023). Youth's experiences of LGBTQ+-inclusive curriculum in a secondary U.S. classroom at the intersections of sexuality, gender, race, and class. *Equity & Excellence in Education, 56*(1–2), 72–86.

Schey, R., & Blackburn, M. V. (2019). Queer ruptures to normative literacy practices: Toward visualizing, hypothesizing, and empathizing. *Research in the Teaching of English 54*(1), 58–80.

Shrodes, A. (2022). *Learning practices of livability toward elsewhere: Critical digital literacies in the everyday activities of trans and queer youth* (Publication No. 29256961) [Doctoral dissertation, Northwestern University]. ProQuest Dissertations & Theses Global.

Shrodes, A. (2023). "The word 'getting over' is really weird": Storying disability in desired futures. *Curriculum Inquiry, 53*(4), 339–358.

Smith. M. W., & Wilhelm, J. D. (2002). *"Reading don't fix no Chevys": Literacy in the lives of young men.* Heinemann.

Sumara, D., & Davis, B. (1998). Telling tales of surprise. In W. F. Pinar (Ed.), *Queer theory in education* (pp. 164–182). Lawrence Erlbaum Associates.

Thomas, A. (2020). *Cemetery boys.* Swoon Reads.

van Leent, L., & Mills, K. (2018). A queer critical media literacies framework in a digital age. *Journal of Adolescent & Adult Literacy, 61*(4), 401–411.

Wargo, J. M. (2017). Designing more just social futures or remixing the radical present? Queer rhetorics, multimodal (counter)storytelling, and the politics of LGBTQ youth activism. *English Teaching: Practice & Critique, 16*(2), 145–160.

Chapter Nine

Abolitionist Multiliteracies within and beyond English Language Arts Classrooms

Rubén González
Antero Garcia

Over two decades ago, Dr. Ernest Morrell (2005) urged the English education and English language arts (ELA) profession to engage in "critical English education" as a means to be "explicit about the role of language and literacy in conveying meaning and in promoting or disrupting existing power relations" in which students develop various academic skills "that allow them to create their own critical texts that can be used in the struggle for social justice" (p. 313). He described how critical English education engages in a problem-posing process that situates language and literacy within a larger sociopolitical context for youth to develop various capacities for social transformation. In other words, the goal of critical English education is to not solely name the role of language and literacy in creating and/or refuting different forms of oppression but, more importantly, to center youth in their ability to evoke their language and literacy skills toward creating more socially just present and future lifeworlds. This is coupled with sociocultural literacies scholarship emphasizing the cultural and linguistic diversity shaping classroom communities globally (e.g., New London Group, 1996), and these sites are spaces from which our pedagogical commitments must attune toward freedom.

In more recent years, and in response to the antiBlack police violence that served as the impetus for the Black Lives Matter (BLM) movement, English education scholars have built on

Morrell's foundational work by explicitly focusing on the role of race and racism within ELA teaching and learning (Baker-Bell, 2020a; Baker-Bell et al., 2017; Johnson, 2018). We extend this work to better address the root causes of racism, antiBlackness, and other forms of interlocking forms of oppression such as settler colonialism and white supremacy, all of which are ubiquitous within and beyond ELA classrooms (Baker-Bell, 2020b; de los Ríos et al., 2019; Flores, 2024; Martínez & Mejía, 2020; Martínez et al., 2019; Morrell, 2009, 2015). In response, and in drawing on speculative and abolitionist approaches to teaching and learning toward alternative worldbuilding, we describe *abolitionist multiliteracies* as a framework for our work with multiply marginalized youth of Color within and beyond ELA classrooms. Abolitionist multiliteracies are guided by three tenets:

- Center the experiences of multiply marginalized people of Color who experience and resist different forms of carcerality in favor of creating humanizing and liberatory alternatives;
- Foreground individual and collective social dreaming toward movement building against carceral practices, policies, and ideologies in favor of creating humanizing and liberatory alternatives; and
- Support collective, interactive, and practice-based approaches to develop and enact literacy skills toward the abolition of prisons, police, and all forms of carcerality in favor of creating humanizing and liberatory alternatives.

In this chapter, we present abolitionist multiliteracies as both a theoretical and pedagogical approach to ELA teaching and learning. We first explain how our work is informed by speculative (Garcia & Mirra, 2023a) and abolitionist (Love, 2019) pedagogies. We then offer empirical examples from our ongoing scholarship to elucidate how abolitionist multiliteracies are developed and enacted by K–12 multiply marginalized youth of Color. Finally, we call on the profession to seek and to work toward a (re)imagination and (re)configuration of not only English education and ELA through a speculative and abolitionist perspective but to enact such disposition in *how* and *what* we teach via abolitionist multiliteracies.

A Speculative and Abolitionist Approach to English Language Arts

English education and K–12 English language arts classrooms, literally and figuratively, are consumed by whiteness and white supremacy (Badenhorst et al., 2023; Cook, 2022; Sleeter, 2017) and have long been racist and violent spaces and places for multiply marginalized youth of Color (Baker-Bell, 2020b; de los Ríos et al., 2019; Johnson, 2018). This ecosystem results in ELA classrooms serving as "sites of suffering" (Dumas, 2014) that are embedded in carceral logics against multiply marginalized youth of Color (Beneke et al., 2022; Souto-Manning et al., 2022; Yeh et al., 2023). Annamma (2017) describes carceral logics as the ideas and practices that naturalize labeling, surveilling, and criminalizing the bodies, minds, and behaviors of multiply marginalized youth of Color to maintain social control. While such violence as a result of whiteness, white supremacy, and carcerality are not limited to ELA classrooms, the ELA classroom has long been interconnected toward carceral practices, policies, and ideologies against Black, Indigenous, Latinx, and multiply marginalized youth based on race, gender, class, disability, and language (Baker-Bell, 2020b; Beneke et al., 2022; Cabral, 2022; Coles et al., 2021; Martinez, 2017; Rosa, 2019; Souto-Manning et al., 2022; Yeh et al., 2023). We must not only focus on the problems within ELA teaching and learning, but, more importantly, we must be attuned to and work toward possibilities for alternate current and future lifeworlds. Toward this end, below we draw on speculative (Garcia & Mirra, 2023a) and abolitionist (Love, 2019) approaches to K–12 ELA teaching and learning to outline our conceptualization of abolitionist multiliteracies.

Speculative education (Garcia & Mirra, 2023a) builds on the work of Afro, Indigenous, and queer futurism (brown, 2017; Dillon, 2012; Hartman, 2019)—which centers the practice of multiply marginalized people of Color dreaming and working toward alternative present and future lifeworlds. Regarding Afrofuturism, Toliver (2021) defines it as:

> a cultural aesthetic in which Black authors create speculative texts that center Black characters in an effort to reclaim and

> recover the past, counter negative and elevate positive realities that exist in the present, and create new possibilities for the future. (p. xxi)

Similarly, through an Indigenous epistemology, ontology, and axiology of "storywork" (Archibald, 2008), San Pedro and Kinloch (2017) conceptualize "storying" as the process in which people collaboratively converge theory and practice as a means to be "invited into relationships where we dialogically listen and give back to the stories shared and questions that arise with others" (p. 378). This act of communal listening and giving back to others creates a relationship in which "the story and the storyteller both serve to connect the past with the future, one generation with the other, the land with the people, and the people with the story" (Smith, 2021, p. 166). Through engaging in these Afro and Indigenous speculative approaches to present and future world building, abolitionist multiliteracies work toward alternative lifeworlds that are devoid of all forms of carcerality and rooted in humanizing and liberatory alternatives for ourselves and others.

Furthermore, as we are reminded by queer pleasure activist adrienne maree brown (2017), the speculative is not limited to a far-off "when" and/or "what if," nor is it something that is limited to a speculative space and place that is out of our present realm of reality. Instead, as brown declares:

> The future is not an escapist place to occupy. All of it is the inevitable result of what we do today, and the more we take it in our hands . . . the more the future knows we want it, and that we aren't letting go. (p. 164)

Speculative education demands that we recognize and analyze our current material conditions—the "good," the "bad," and everything in between and beyond—while we individually and collectively seek and work toward decentering the carceral state and foregrounding ethical relations as the basis of civic trust; fostering an ethos of collaborative practice as the work of world-building; and engaging in joyful struggle toward just futures (Garcia & Mirra, 2023a, p. 4). Such an approach to ELA teaching and learning does not fixate on the different forms of oppression we seek to abolish; rather, it focuses on the building of alternative present and future lifeworlds we desire to materialize that are free of not only the various forms of oppression but the societal conditions that allow for such oppression to exist.

In their empirical work (re)imagining ELA classrooms via a speculative approach to teaching and learning, Mirra and Garcia (2020; 2022) engaged with youth from six geographical areas across the United States as part of a digital democratic dialogue (3D) project. In this work, youth privileged collaborative approaches toward democratic interrogation and innovation over democratic integration into existing sociopolitical power structures (Mirra & Garcia, 2022). Mirra and Garcia (2022) documented how youth engaged in what they term as a "speculative civic literacy framework" of decentering formal state-sanctioned institutions, engaging in dialogic practice, and striving for justice via exerting civic agency during social uncertainties. The speculative civic literacy approaches developed and enacted by youth included (re)imagining their positioning and agency regarding civics and the present and future lifeworlds they desire to build for themselves and for others (Mirra & Garcia, 2020). Namely, youth engaged in speculative civic literacies rooted in skill development and consciousness raising across geographical and ideological differences with specific attention to how guns and gun violence shaped their sociopolitical realities (Mirra & Garcia, 2022). In this scholarship, speculative education served as an approach to ELA teaching and learning where youth interrogated and extended traditional models of civic education in which youth pushed against integration into existing sociopolitical power structures and toward (re)imagining civic participation and society writ large.

Similar to speculative education, prison and police abolition has long been rooted in a radical Black, Indigenous, and feminist imaginary toward present and future world building (Carson, 2022; Davis et al., 2022; Turner et al., 2022). Abolition is both the vision and the action of dismantling prisons and police but, more importantly, dismantling the societal conditions that create the environment in which carcerality is an accepted way of being and thinking. Abolition works toward creating and sustaining a new "normal" in society free of all forms of carcerality and rooted in community care, harm reduction, and collective liberation, in which we are engaged in the practice where we are "willing to end the conditions that justify marginalization" (Stovall, 2020, p. 4). This world-building endeavor toward an alternative "normal" without carcerality includes historical examples of abolishing US chattel enslavement of Black people (Du Bois, 1935; Painter, 1997), along with contemporary examples of police and police abolition (Davis, 2003; Kaba, 2021). More recently, educational scholars have engaged in abolitionist work within K–12 schooling contexts, namely with a focus on the school-prison nexus and the experiences of multiply marginalized youth of Color (Meiners, 2007; Meiners & Winn, 2010). While this scholarship is important, there remains a need to empirically explore abolition related to ELA teaching and learning.

Regarding ELA teaching and learning, the foundational work of Dr. Bettina Love (2019) has brought abolition into the general K–12 schooling lexicon. Love provides an expansive framework of what they term "abolitionist teaching," which they define as an individual and collective practice of:

> imagination, creativity, refusal, (re)membering, visionary thinking, healing, rebellious spirit, boldness, determination, and subversiveness of abolitionists to eradicate injustice inside and outside of schools. (2019, p. 2)

While scholars have taken up the call to engage in abolitionist work within K–12 school contexts (Cabral, 2023; Coles et al., 2021a; Love, 2019; Souto-Manning et al., 2022; Stovall, 2018), much of this work remains conceptual. In this larger context, there is nascent conceptual scholarship at the intersection of abolition and ELA. Coles and colleagues (2021b) theorize about "abolitionist perspectives on critical literacy" in which they outline the "abolitionist literacies working against" the ideologies of antiBlackness and white supremacy that have become ubiquitous to schooling within the United States (p. 365). In doing so, they urge the profession to engage in educational scholarship and practice that "demands direct participation in social movement and being in the streets, shoulder-to-shoulder with those struggling towards an abolitionist vision of self-determination and collective power" (p. 368). In the realm of early literacy classrooms, Beneke and colleagues (2023) theorize about the carceral logics that are deeply embedded in these spaces and explore how to counter various widely accepted practices that often pathologize and criminalize multiply marginalized youth. Other early education scholars (Yeh et al., 2023)—via reflecting on their experiences as education scholars, motherscholars, and community workers—conceptualize the power of employing an abolitionist ethos to attend to the survivance of young children and communities of Color as part of the work toward creating and sustaining more humanizing schooling experiences.

In conceptual scholarship with pedagogical implications, Souto-Manning and colleagues (2022) describe how abolition in ELA classrooms can serve as the impetus for a "healing pedagogy of communicative belonging" against racialized notions of language and literacy. In addition, and with a specific focus on early childhood literacy instruction, Bryan et al. (2022) provide "prison abolition literacies" as an approach to "bring awareness to the injustices of the carceral state and encourage young children to become prison abolitionists" (p. 383), and Garcia and de Roock (2021) argue for an "abolitionist lens" and "civic dimensions" to critical digital literacies. Regarding the limited empirical scholarship related to abolition and ELA to date, Turner (2022) reveals how youth of Color create and sustain an "abolitionist classroom community" via collective practices of care. Related to curriculum and instruction, González (2024) elucidates how preservice teachers of Color employ "pedagogies of abolitionist praxis" in elementary and high school ELA classrooms, along with scholarship (González & Jones, 2025) on how elementary students of Color develop and enact an abolitionist praxis after learning about the concepts of freedom dreaming and the abolition of prisons and police.

Overall, while the scholarship at the intersection of abolition and ELA is promising, there is a need for more empirical work exploring how abolition is enacted within and beyond various ELA classrooms, with particular attention to how youth develop and enact abolition via their use of language and literacy.

Multiliteracies as Abolitionist Social Futures

The speculative and abolitionist framing of the possibilities of critical English education build on what have been, to this point, implicit assumptions on the critical and sociocultural nature of literacy (e.g., Freire & Macedo, 1987; Gutiérrez, 2008; Morrell, 2015). Importantly, literacy research in the 1990s and beyond have called for explicitly naming the multiple kinds of litera*cies* at play. Three decades ago, the New London Group (1996) built on this understanding to name multiliteracies as a way to describe both "the multiplicity of communications channels and media, and the increasing saliency of cultural and linguistic diversity" (p. 61). This salvo within the literacy research community shaped how scholars engaged in digital literacies scholarship, critical work in an era of rapid globalization, and the impact of multilingual and transnational youth in schooling contexts for three decades.

Reflecting on the impact of the New London Group's literacy contributions two decades after initial publication, NLG member Allan Luke noted:

> What's surprised me is the degree to which many versions of multiliteracies are taught as neutral tools, sans discussion of all of the key ethical and political issues of surveillance and control, truth and lies, bullying and exploitation, profit and ownership. (Garcia, Luke, & Seglem, 2018, p. 76)

As a reminder of how critical scholarship can get subsumed in normative practices that shave off their ontological pushes toward justice, Luke's reflection highlights how multiliteracies have shaped multiple pathways toward "social futures." As such, Luke reaffirms that the very foundation of multiliteracies has been a response to "a persistent unequal distribution of capital, wealth, and power" (p. 74). By focusing on the root causes of injustice fomented in classrooms, abolitionist multiliteracies renew the New London Group's vision of multiliteracies that respond to the harms shaping classrooms globally.

Taken as a whole, we draw on speculative and abolitionist approaches to understanding contemporary multiliteracies.

We conceptualize abolitionist multiliteracies in our work with multiply marginalized youth of Color within and beyond ELA classrooms. The collective teaching and learning and the enactment of an abolitionist praxis is a "beautiful experiment" of current and future worldbuilding (Hartman, 2019) in which we engage in "centering possibility" in our work by focusing on "who [or what] we're 'fighting for,' and to a far lesser extent, who or what we're 'fighting against.'" (Warren, 2021, p. 5). Below, we reveal examples from our ongoing work related to how youth develop and enact abolitionist multiliteracies within and beyond ELA classrooms.

Abolitionist Multiliteracies and English Language Arts

It is not enough to simply identify, analyze, and critique different forms of carcerality in our work with multiply marginalized youth of Color within and beyond ELA classrooms. There must be action toward alternative world building away from carcerality and toward collective liberation. To recognize that the world is situated in normalized carceral policies, practices, and ideologies that are deeply imbued in antiBlackness, settler-colonialism, and white supremacy should not be the goal of our teaching and learning. The goal of our work should be to have students recognize, analyze, critique, *and* take action against different forms of carcerality within and beyond the classroom, school, and larger community settings. Toward this end, there is a need to push the field of English education and ELA to consider *what* and *how* we teach through an abolitionist ethos and the implications for youth to develop and enact abolitionist multiliteracies within and beyond ELA classrooms via their language and literacy skills and practices. While we have supported youth to engage in this work during our time as ELA teachers, our current research as teacher educators elucidates the explicit teaching and learning of abolitionist multiliteracies in ELA elementary and high school settings.

In my (Rubén) ongoing work with the same group of novice K–12 teachers of Color across their preservice and inservice teaching experiences, I have explored the teaching and learning of prison and police abolition through abolitionist multiliteracies within and beyond ELA classrooms. This has included how two women preservice teachers of Color centered Black, Indigenous, and feminist imaginaries and action-research approaches to their ELA instruction in the teaching of prison and police abolition in elementary and high school classrooms (González, 2024), along with how elementary students of Color develop and enact an abolitionist praxis as part of a Freedom Dreaming literacy unit exploring prison and police abolition (González & Jones, 2025). Below, I elucidate how two first-year teachers of Color enacted abolitionist multiliteracies in their work within and beyond ELA classrooms during the 2023–2024 academic year.

"We can't get rid of prisons or police right now, but we can try."

Lorena,[1] a Latina first-year fourth-grade teacher in Southern California, enacted abolitionist multiliteracies in the teaching of prison and police abolition via a social movements unit she created as part of her ELA instruction. Through the use of children's literature, informational texts, and short videos, her curriculum and instruction included, although it was not limited to, teaching about Black, Indigenous, and Latinx abolitionist social movements in the United States. Lorena, after teaching this unit, designed the summative assessment to be small-group action research projects in which students identified an issue of carcerality on campus or in their larger community, researched the root causes through various forms of data collection, and presented findings and abolitionist recommendations to teachers and administrators, parents and guardians, and community members. She explained,

> I want students to take their learning seriously. It's not enough to just know about abolition; you have to do something with that information. Yeah, these issues are still going on, prisons and police are still a problem, but people are working against it, and that includes [the students]. They need to know they're part of these movements, too.

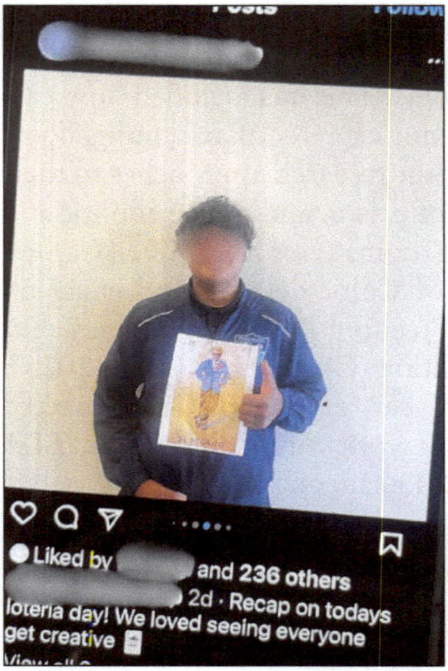

FIGURE 1.

Students worked on selecting topics for their action-research projects and, sparked by an antiBlack post on the school's Instagram page (see Figure 1), two groups of students combined to explore the intersection of carcerality and antiBlackness on campus.

Veronica, an outgoing Latina girl, explained her reasoning to her peers for wanting to select this topic, stating, "That post was racist against Black people, and nobody at school did anything until we told Ms. Lorena. I think we should look for other examples of racism against Black students." Mario, an often reserved Latino boy, agreed, drawing on what he learned in the social movement unit and commenting, "We can do a protest, something like the Black Panthers."

The two groups of students ultimately elected to create posters to depict the experiences of their Black peers on campus, which students used as artifacts during their protests on campus. When asked about what informed their creation of these posters, a Black-Mexican girl named Brittany revealed about her Black peers: "They told us they felt everyone assumed negative things of them in school, and they felt picked on, just like Black people are picked on with cops outside of school." She concluded with, "We learned a lot from them and we used their words to do something. We made these posters with 'to protect and serve' because that's what cops say they do, but the picture is what they actually do—hurt people." Leveraging the words of their peers to inform their actions, these posters were employed by students in their protests they conducted before school, during lunch, and after school, in which they chanted against carcerality and antiBlack violence on their campus and in their broader community. This social

FIGURE 2.

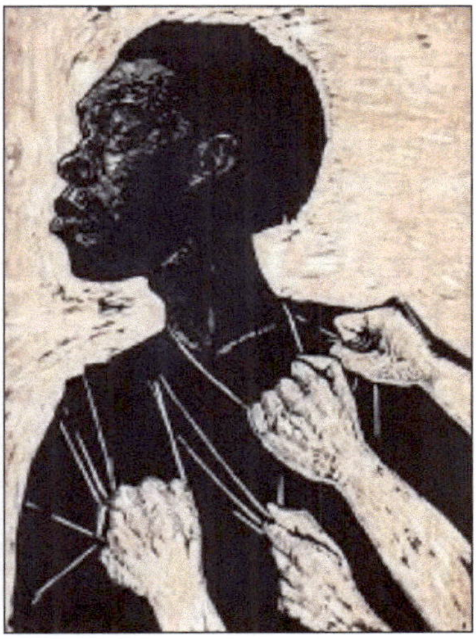

FIGURE 3.

movement building drew the attention of their peers, teachers and administrators, and parents and guardians. As a result and with support of Ms. Lorena, students presented their findings of carcerality and antiBlackness at school and their abolitionist recommendations to the school's administrative team and grade-level team leaders.

For the students, their work toward addressing carcerality and antiBlackness on campus sparked their motivation to continue to engage in abolitionist movement building. In a focus-group interview at the end of the academic year, Chris, who self-identified as a Latino boy, revealed:

> Learning about the Black Panthers, Brown Berets, and all the others who were against prisons and police motivated me to do something. If they used their words to do something, we can, too. We can't get rid of prisons or police right now, but we can try.

Yoseline, a Latina girl, agreed and commented:

> We can't be okay with other students being picked on and getting in trouble and getting referrals and suspensions for no reason. It's not okay, and that's kind of what happens with

> police too—they pick on some people, and then they get arrested and put in jail. We can help people know that it's not right, and there is another way.

Lorena's abolitionist multiliteracies approach to teaching about prison and police abolition and carcerality writ large exemplifies how an abolitionist multiliteracies approach can serve as the catalyst for students to develop and enact various literacy skills and practices toward activism and social transformation. In learning about Black, Indigenous, and Latinx abolitionist activism, students leveraged their understanding of social movement building to identify and counter antiBlack carcerality on campus through offering humanizing and liberatory alternatives beyond their present realities. Students engaged in this work via collective and practice-based literacy practices through the use of multimodal literacies such as identifying and researching notions of antiBlack carcerality, creating posters to use during their protests, employing calls against carcerality and antiBlackness during their protests, and presenting their research findings and abolitionist recommendations to key educational actors. In doing so, students' various literacy skills and practices were not confined to their reading, writing, speaking, and listening as part of Lorena's unit but were leveraged and enacted both within and beyond their ELA classroom.

"You can be 'locked up' in a way, even without police or prisons."

Azul, a queer and non-binary Latinx first-year tenth-grade English teacher in Northern California, enacted abolitionist multiliteracies in their teaching of literature across the fall term. This included, but was not limited to, their teaching of *Song of the Hummingbird* (Limón, 1996) and *Homegoing* (Gyasi, 2016) by integrating an anti-carceral and abolitionist perspective, which included supplementing informational texts about prison and police abolition (i.e., documentaries, newspaper articles, and art) to teach about the abolition of different forms of carcerality in favor of humanizing and liberatory alternatives within and beyond the novels students read. Azul, after teaching both texts during the fall term, had their students create multimodal "zines" to demonstrate their understanding of the novels they read, prison and police abolition, and the abolition of different forms of carcerality within their school site and broader community. Azul explained:

> The books have themes of carcerality, like chattel slavery and prisons, settler colonialism, and these big institutions, and then how these things play out in the interactions between characters. It's all there. Zines are a creative way for students to combine what they learned in the books with the documentaries and articles I included in the unit and then to share their learning with others.

The zines were created in class and presented at the school's "Winter Student Academic Exhibition Night," during which students shared one aspect of their learning to peers, teachers, administrators, parents and guardians, and community members in an after-school setting. Azul was intentional in having students present their zines in this context rather than completing a traditional essay at the end of the term, which was the common practice for their grade-level colleagues, as Azul wanted students to "extend what they learned outside the classroom and inform others about it."

The exhibition night was well attended, with Azul's students proudly describing and explaining their digital and analog zines to various interested parties. As students presented, they demonstrated a nuanced understanding of carcerality and abolitionism, using the novels they had read in class to situate different forms of carcerality within and beyond the institutions and systems of prisons and police. Ricky, a Latino boy, described his zine to a group of his peers:

> I wanted to show how slavery is still going on. In *Homegoing*, it was a certain type of slavery against people brought from Africa, but now slavery against their descendants and other Black people looks like prisons. It's a little different now, but it's pretty much the same—it's still slavery.

Marisol, a Latina classmate who stood a few feet away from Ricky, was asked by a school administrator about her thought process in creating her zine. Marisol explained:

> I wanted to show how the life of Huitzitzli [in *Song of the Hummingbird*] is connected to me and the life of other Latina girls. How she was controlled and policed because of her gender and race, and how you can be "locked up" in a way, even without police or prisons.

For Azul's students, the creating and presenting of their zines was the culmination of learning about the abolition of prisons, police, and carcerality writ large that was incredibly influential to their way of thinking and being as people of Color. In a focus-group interview at the end of the academic year, students discussed how reading the novels in class with an abolitionist perspective provided them with a new analytical lens. Alma, who identified as Chicana, commented:

> I hadn't thought about how prisons and police are related to everyday toxic masculinity. It's all about control of certain people and really women of Color. I think that really resonates with us, especially the girls in class. I hadn't really thought about how I'm policed for being a Latina until this class.

FIGURE 4.

FIGURE 5.

Violet, a Latina who recently moved from Southern California, built on this idea, revealing:

> Yeah, in *Hummingbird* it was people being policed with settler colonialism and *Homegoing*, it was policed with racism against Black people. And I just realized that the characters doing this were all men. It connects to toxic masculinity and shows how policing is not just prisons or police, but then we do those things, too.

Similar to Lorena, Azul's curriculum and instruction, grounded in abolitionist multiliteracies, provided a space for students to develop and enact various literacy skills and practices toward abolitionist movement building. Azul was strategic in using curriculum and schoolwide events they were expected to follow and centering the teaching and learning of prison and police abolition, and carcerality writ large, in a mode that helped students engage in a more critical approach to ELA. This, in turn, provided students with various opportunities to enact their multiliteracies skills and practices to demonstrate their understanding of abolishing different forms of carcerality in favor of humanizing and liberatory alternatives within their lives and the lives of others. As students read various novels from an abolitionist perspective, they were able to leverage their literary analysis toward exploring their own experiences with carcerality, but, more importantly, students engaged in action toward informing other educational actors about the need for abolitionist activism.

Abolition and Multiliteracies as the Bedrock of ELA Classrooms

As the example in the fourth-grade classroom reminds us, sophisticated literacy engagement around abolition must not wait until students are years into their adolescence. Rather, students' interest in their own freedoms, their own cultural identities, and in learning contexts that match their present world are not only present in every ELA classroom but are a necessary pathway toward critical English education pedagogy. From participatory approaches to utilizing student interests for data collection and critical inquiry (e.g., Garcia, 2017) to collective storytelling that imagines untold futures (Toliver, 2021), it is young people's ability to build on their own ingenuity, storytelling, and abolitionist desires that can drive where and how ELA learning transpires. This does not mean, though, that such work happens divorced from the guidance of powerful pedagogy.

Just as the New London Group emphasized the role of *design* for "social futures" (Penuel & O'Connor, 2018), abolitionist multiliteracies must work toward youth-envisioned, carceral-free, and liberatory futures through settings structured for their existing repertoires of literacy practice. For example, leaning on the technological-facing aspects of multiliteracies, what kinds of tools abet student explorations of their world and its policies? Such tools might be the existing hardware and software that students already rely upon in their day-to-day social practice and teacher supports will have to shape classroom space for unpacking and experimenting with such tools. Likewise, exploring the linguistic and cultural resonance of multiliteracies, we must ask ourselves: From what kinds of texts and in what kinds of linguistic registers can students both consume and produce texts that freedom dream in ways that students expressed earlier in this chapter?

Ultimately, abolitionist multiliteracies are shaped by the tools, cultural interests, and linguistic expertise of the students who are using them. Such is the mantle that English teachers must take up in our classrooms every day.

An Abolitionist Turn to English Language Arts

In *Freedom Dreams: The Black Radical Imagination*, Dr. Robin D. G. Kelley (2002) posits, "Without new visions, we don't know what to build, only what to knock down" (p. xii). We argue abolitionist multiliteracies challenge scholars and teachers to (re)imagine and (re)configure the role of English language arts (ELA) as a space beyond language and literacy development and toward a space for youth to engage in seeking and working toward creating alternative lifeworlds free of carcerality and rooted in liberation for all. This is a fundamental shift in how ELA teaching and learning is to be approached, as the field must be attuned to the carceral policies, practices, and ideologies—rooted in antiBlack, settler colonialism, and white supremacy—that undergird all forms of oppression but more importantly, must engage in an action-oriented approach that seeks and works toward humanizing and liberatory alternatives rooted in collected liberation. This will not be accomplished through isolated changes in curriculum and/or occasional literacy practices that thinly address the experiences of multiply marginalized people of Color as they pertain to their oppression and resistance against carcerality in favor of creating liberatory present and future realities. In working toward enacting abolitionist multiliteracies, the focus should not be on whether English education scholars and ELA teachers should engage in the teaching of prison and police abolition. Instead, the focus should be on how we collectively do so within and beyond the classroom as we seek and work toward a society free of all forms of carcerality in favor of humanizing and liberatory alternatives.

Note

1. All names are pseudonyms, and all ethnoracial and gender categories were self-selected by participants.

References

Annamma, S. A. (2017). *The pedagogy of pathologization: Dis/abled girls of color in the school-prison nexus*. Routledge.

Archibald, J.-A. (2008). *Indigenous storywork: Educating the heart, mind, body, and spirit.* UBC Press.

Badenhorst, P., Tanner, S. J., & Grinage, J. (Eds.). (2023). *Reckoning with the Whiteness of English education: Transformative pedagogies in English language arts and beyond.* Teachers College Press.

Baker-Bell, A. (2020a). Dismantling anti-Black linguistic racism in English language arts classrooms: Toward an anti-racist Black language pedagogy. *Theory Into Practice*, *59*(1), 8–21.

Baker-Bell, A. (2020b). *Linguistic justice: Black language, literacy, identity, and pedagogy*. Routledge.

Baker-Bell, A., Butler, T., & Johnson, L. (2017). The pain and the wounds: A call for critical race English education in the wake of racial violence. *English Education*, *49*(2), 116–129.

Beneke, M. R., Machado, E., & Taitingfong, J. (2022). Dismantling carceral logics in the urban early literacy classroom: Towards liberatory literacy pedagogies with/for multiply-marginalized young children. *Urban Education*, *59*(6), 1871–1904.

brown, a. m. (2017). *Emergent strategy: Shaping change, changing worlds*. AK Press.

Bryan, N., McMillian, R., & LaMar, K. (2022). Prison abolition literacies as pro-Black pedagogy in early childhood education. *Journal of Early Childhood Literacy, 22*(3), 383–407.

Cabral, B. (2023). Linguistic confinement: Rethinking the racialized interplay between educational language learning and carcerality. *Race Ethnicity and Education*, *26*(3), 277–297.

Carson, G. L. (2022). Tribal sovereignty, decolonization, and abolition: Why tribes should reconsider punishment. *UCLA Law Review*, *69*(1076), 1078–1128.

Coles, J. A., de Roock, R. S., Malone, H.-L. S., & Musser, A. D. (2021). Critical literacy and abolition. In J. Z. Pandya, R. A. Mora, J. H. Alford, N. A. Golden, & R. S. de Roock (Eds.), *The handbook of critical literacies* (pp. 363–372). Routledge.

Coles, J. A., Ohito, E. O., Green, K. L., & Lyiscott, J. (2021). Fugitivity and abolition in educational research and practice: An offering. *Equity & Excellence in Education*, *54*(2), 103–111.

Cook, M. P. (2022). ELA teachers and Whiteness: Hesitancy as barrier to teacher agency development. *English Education*, *54*(4), 273–293.

Davis, A. Y. (2003). *Are prisons obsolete?* Seven Stories Press.

Davis, A. Y., Dent, G., Meiners, E. R., & Richie, B. E. (2022). *Abolition. Feminism. Now*. Haymarket Books.

de los Ríos, C. V., Martínez, D. C., Musser, A. D., Canady, A., Camangian, P., & Quijada, P. D. (2019). Upending colonial practices: Toward repairing harm in English education. *Theory Into Practice*, *58*(4), 359–367.

Dillon, G. (Ed.). (2012). *Walking the clouds: An anthology of Indigenous science fiction.* University of Arizona Press.

Du Bois, W. E. B. (1935). *Black reconstruction in America, 1860–1880.* Harcourt, Brace & Company.

Dumas, M. J. (2014). "Losing an arm": Schooling as a site of black suffering. *Race Ethnicity and Education, 17*(1), 1–29.

Flores, N. (2024). *Becoming the system: A raciolinguistic genealogy of bilingual education in the post-Civil Rights era.* Oxford University Press.

Freire, P., & Macedo, D. (1987). *Literacy: Reading the word and the world.* Bergin & Garvey.

Garcia, A. (2017). *Good reception: Teens, teachers, and mobile media in a Los Angeles high school.* The MIT Press.

Garcia, A., Luke, A., & Seglem, R. (2018). Looking at the next 20 years of multiliteracies: A discussion with Allan Luke. *Theory Into Practice, 57*(1), 72–78.

Garcia, A., & Mirra, N. (Eds.). (2023a). *Speculative pedagogies: Designing equitable educational futures.* Teachers College Press.

Garcia, A., & Mirra, N. (2023b). Other suns: Designing for racial equity through speculative education. *Journal of the Learning Sciences, 32*(1), 1–20.

Garcia, A., & de Roock, R. S. (2021). Civic dimensions of critical digital literacies: Towards an abolitionist lens. *Pedagogies: An International Journal, 16*(2), 187–201.

González, R. A. (2024). "I've always had the abolitionist spirit in me": Preservice teachers of color and pedagogies of abolitionist praxis. *English Education, 56*(3), 143–169.

González, R. A., & Jones, B. L. (2025). From dreaming of freedom to freedom dreaming: Developing students' abolitionist praxis through interdisciplinary literacy instruction. *The Reading Teacher, 78*(5), 267–278.

Gutiérrez, K. D. (2008). Developing a sociocritical literacy in the Third Space. *Reading Research Quarterly, 43*(2), 148–164.

Gyasi, Y. (2016). *Homegoing.* Vintage.

Hartman, S. (2019). *Wayward lives, beautiful experiments: Intimate histories of riotous black girls, troublesome women, and queer radicals*. W. W. Norton & Company.

Johnson, L. L. (2018). Where do we go from here? Toward a critical race English education. *Research in the Teaching of English*, *53*(2), 102–124.

Kaba, M. (2021). *We do this 'til we free us: Abolitionist organizing and transforming justice*. Haymarket Books.

Limón, G. (1996). *Song of the hummingbird*. Arte Público Press.

Love, B. L. (2019). *We want to do more than survive: Abolitionist teaching and the pursuit of educational freedom*. Beacon Press.

Martínez, D. C., Rojo, J., & González, R. A. (2019). Speaking Spanish in white public spaces: Implications for literacy classrooms. *Journal of Adolescent & Adult Literacy*, *62*(4), 451–454.

Martínez, R. A., & Mejía, A. F. (2020). Looking closely and listening carefully: A sociocultural approach to understanding the complexity of Latina/o/x students' everyday language. *Theory Into Practice*, *59*(1), 53–63.

Meiners, E. R. (2007). *Right to be hostile: Schools, prisons, and the making of public enemies*. Routledge.

Meiners, E. R., & Winn, M. T. (2010). Resisting the school to prison pipeline: The practice to build abolition democracies. *Race Ethnicity and Education*, *13*(3), 271–276.

Mirra, N., & Garcia, A. (2020). "I hesitate but I do have hope": Youth speculative civic literacies for troubled times. *Harvard Educational Review*, *90*(2), 295–321.

Mirra, N., & Garcia, A. (2022). Guns, schools, and democracy: Adolescents imagining social futures through speculative civic literacies. *American Educational Research Journal*, *59*(2), 345–380.

Morrell, E. (2005). Critical English education. *English Education*, *37*(4), 312–321.

Morrell, E. (2009). Critical research and the future of literacy education. *Journal of Adolescent & Adult Literacy*, *53*(2), 96–104.

Morrell, E. (2015). *Critical literacy and urban youth: Pedagogies of access, dissent, and liberation*. Routledge.

New London Group. (1996). A pedagogy of multiliteracies: Designing social futures. *Harvard Educational Review, 66*(1), 60–92. https://doi.org/10.17763/haer.66.1.17370n67v22j160u

Painter, N. I. (1997). *Sojourner Truth: A life, a symbol.* W. W. Norton & Company.

Penuel, W. R., & O'Connor, K. (2018). From designing to organizing new social futures: Multiliteracies pedagogies for today. *Theory Into Practice, 57*(1), 64–71. https://doi.org/10.1080/00405841.2017.1411715

San Pedro, T., & Kinloch, V. (2017). Toward projects in humanization: Research on co-creating and sustaining dialogic relationships. *American Educational Research Journal, 54*(1), 373S–394S.

Sleeter, C. E. (2017). Critical race theory and the Whiteness of teacher education. *Urban Education, 52*(2), 155–169.

Smith, L. T. (2021). *Decolonizing methodologies: Research and Indigenous peoples.* Zed Books.

Souto-Manning, M., Martínez, D. C., & Musser, A. D. (2022). ELA as English language abolition: Toward a pedagogy of communicative belonging. *Reading Research Quarterly, 57*(4), 1089–1106.

Stovall, D. (2018). Are we ready for "school" abolition? Thoughts and practices of radical imaginary in education. *Taboo: The Journal of Culture and Education, 17*(1), 51–61.

Toliver, S. R. (2021). *Recovering Black storytelling in qualitative research: Endarkened storywork.* Routledge.

Turner, K. (2022). The making of abolitionist classroom community: A call for critical collective practices in the English classroom. In A. Brown (Ed.), *Racial literacies informed by the sociopolitical and sociocultural contexts for youth* (pp. 35–42). National Council of Teachers of English.

Turner, K., Wallace, D., Miles-Langaigne, D., & Deras, E. (2023). Toward Black abolition theory within radical abolition studies: Upending practices, structures, and epistemes of domination. *Journal for Multicultural Education, 18*(3), 275–288.

Yeh, C., Agarwal-Rangnath, R., & Albarran Moses, A. (2023). Abolition and ethnic studies in early care and education. *Contemporary Issues in Early Childhood, 24*(2), 208–225.

Chapter Ten

On the Speculative Undercurrent of Critical English Education

Stephanie Toliver

> *As I am advocating for a radical transformation of the discipline and the practice of training English teachers, I am also imagining a time when English educators participate collectively in movements for educational and social justice. . . . I imagine collectives of English educators who take to the streets, who lobby and advocate strongly, who protest, who seek to use the discipline to transform the world.*
>
> —Ernest Morrell

Critical English education (CEE) has always been about deconstruction and disruption, a means to counter the hegemony of white patriarchal dominance that encompasses the field of English education. It has been a means to disturb current and historical power relations and to challenge deficit framings by acknowledging that young people's literacies are not confined to the reading, writing, and speaking tasks that occur in the school building. It has been a framework for educators looking to challenge the status quo and position themselves as activists and intellectuals through a rethinking of textual consumption, textual production, and literacy pedagogy (Morrell, 2005). In centralizing the complicated relationship between language, literacy, culture, and power, CEE has made room for literacy stakeholders to not only acknowledge and challenge "what is" in English education (e.g., the oppression, the violence, the hegemony, the white supremacy) but to also consider "what if" and envision "what might be," to imagine and create a more anti-oppressive stance for the future of literacy pedagogy.

This speculative thread was woven through Morrell's (2005) initial essay. As examples, he argued for the imagining of pedagogical practices that increase students' access to various texts and ability to deconstruct those texts. He dreamed of a literacy education that makes room for young people to position themselves as change agents rather than passive learners of literacy content. He envisaged a world where English educators embraced their power and sought to use the English language arts for the purpose of dismantling oppression in and outside of the classroom. More than dream, he showcased how his work moved from imagination to creation, providing explicit detail that suggests this dream could become a reality if literacy stakeholders worked together to make it so. In this way, CEE described a dream for a better English educational future where young people could "create their own critical texts that can be used in the struggle for social justice" (Morrell, 2005, p. 313), where youth could construct texts that suggested new futures beyond oppression. It depicted a space where literacy scholars and educators could imagine and create more equitable literacy futures, could envision ways to honor new digital and analog means of communication, could dream of education spaces where multiple literacies are validated, not discounted. It presented a call for literacy stakeholders to "put in motion the critical, democratic principles necessary for nurturing an equitable society" (Gordon, 2017, p. 2). And yet, even with this speculative undercurrent that embraced the imaginative and creative, CEE's association with the speculative is underexplored.

Thus, in this chapter, I consider how CEE is (and has always been) connected to the creative, the imaginative, the speculative. To do so, I first briefly trace how the act of speculation is critical to the foundation of CEE. Then, I detail the importance of connecting this undercurrent to Afrofuturism as a means of creating equitable literacy spaces in which Black students can thrive. Lastly, following Morell's (2005) conceptual template, I consider my own work and the work of other literacy scholars who have used the speculative to expand upon the possibilities and promises of CEE over the past several years. I conclude by calling for educators to consider how imagination and creativity are essential to the future of pro-Black English language arts learning spaces.

Speculation as Foundation for Critical English Education

Speculation and imagination are key for social justice because they are foundational to personal and social transformation (Goessling et al., 2020). Imagination enables us to construct empathy between the self and others, and it is what gives us permission to "give credence to alternative realities. It allows us to break with the taken for granted, to set aside familiar distinctions and definitions" (Greene, 1995, p. 3). It enables us to grasp at other worlds and create new ones that are drastically different from the world we inhabit. Imagination provides us with the ability to see past the despicable conditions of everyday life and envision otherwise the possibilities that might push the world past the violence of current injustices (Kelly, 2002). It offers us a means to make clear the distinctions between "what is" in the world around us and "what could be" if we look toward other vantage points. Essentially, as shown by activists throughout time, imagination is one of our greatest tools (Love, 2019) because, once new potential futures are imagined, we can work toward the creation of those alternate pathways. We can look at things "as if they were otherwise" (Greene, 1995, p. 112), and we can refuse and challenge the status quo embedded in the structures that dominate this world (Stetsenko, 2018).

While the view toward otherwise is essential, Khasnabish and Haiven (2014) remind us that collective action is the goal of a critical, radical imagination:

> Imagination is not just about understanding how power works, or dreaming up blueprints for a new society, though these are important (especially if we do them together). Instead, it's about transforming our social lives and relationships, transforming who and what we imagine are valuable, and transforming ourselves. We do this by building alternative social structures

> and institutions in our own lives. These can be concrete and material, like housing cooperatives, community gardens and organized social movements. But they can also be more abstract and intimate: building new relationships with friends and family, building new reading and discussion groups. The radical imagination exists in collective practice only. (para. 12)

In other words, visualizing, creating, and predicting are important, but it is equally important to move those dreams toward actions, whether concrete or abstract. Imagination is essential to the construction of a socially just future, as it makes space for people to think beyond the contemporary moment and envision new worlds and alternative futures. But the goal is for people to create more than just mental images of possible otherworlds; instead, they can engage in action—to resist, challenge, critique, reject, demand, transcend, and rebel against—injustice. It is this journey, from imagination to creation to action, that underlies CEE.

Take, for instance, Johnson's (2017) work on critical race English education that illustrates how we might use our imaginations to radically change English classrooms. In describing his dream for pro-Black literacy spaces undergirded by a CEE framework, he stated the following:

> To (re)***imagine*** ELA classrooms, educators have to work to ***create*** the world that we hope to see. . . . I ***envision*** classrooms where the stories of Black people are told through liberatory literacy practices such as movement, media, art, song, dance, and poetry. I ***envision*** classrooms where educators love the multiple ways people from different racial and ethnic backgrounds express their pain and work toward liberation. I ***imagine*** classrooms where Black children are taught to love every ounce of their Blackness and that, as Africa's children, they are born from generations of kings and queens, scientists, writers, and mathematicians, from resilience and determination. I ***imagine*** classrooms where educators believe in the possibility of Black children and youth—classrooms where Black students know their Black skin, education, health, spirit, voice, life, and humanity do matter. Lastly, I ***imagine*** classrooms where the teachers and students all have riots in their souls (Baszile, 2006) and are not afraid to join the revolution in a time of racial chaos by making a commitment to racial justice—a commitment to their cause, our cause, and the cause of human freedom. (p. 121, emphasis added)

Johnson recognized CEE's call to engage in multimodality (movement, media, art, song, dance, poetry) alongside its demand for educators to commit to the cultivation and maintenance of socially just classrooms by embracing activism and advocacy (have riots in their souls; join the revolution, commit to the cause of human freedom). More importantly, though, he brought forth the speculative aspects of CEE, as his words suggest the great importance of imagination and creation to the development of equitable classrooms, to the radical transformation of literacy education, and to the creation of more just futures for Black youth.

But Johnson is not the only one, as numerous researchers throughout time have emphasized the speculative as part of CEE, even if the connection was not directly stated. As examples, Morell and Duncan-Andrade (2002) imagined an English classroom in which hip-hop was used to promote critical literacy and consciousness. To move from abstract to concrete, they developed a unit that incorporated the musical genre into a "traditional" English class, thereby disrupting what and who are deemed important enough to be studied in schools. Godley and Minnici (2008) believed in classrooms that refused to privilege certain linguistic dialects while stigmatizing others. Studying the use of African American vernacular English in three tenth-grade classrooms, they constructed a pedagogical method that questioned language ideologies and acknowledged students' literacy assets within and outside of the classroom. Aukerman (2012) envisioned a classroom in which teachers and texts could be viewed as fallible, as capable of being critiqued. She posited that cultivating this classroom would require a dialogic engagement between teacher, student, and text to ensure that students understood the value of multiple perspectives and interpretations. Coleman (2021) dreamed of English language arts classrooms that could dismantle the colonial, white supremacist, queerphobic frames that dominate the field. He proposed that upending these ideologies demanded English teachers and teacher educators engage in affective self-reflection to "dismantle the literacy normativities that perpetuate harmful ways of reading, writing, and imagining in ELA classrooms" (p. 257). Each of these scholars saw literacy intertwined with power relations, and they each imagined and created classrooms where these power relations were challenged and/or dismantled. They moved from imagination to action because that is what CEE requires.

Largely, discussions on CEE can be described as wide-reaching efforts to dismantle oppression in the literacy field. Toward this aim, literacy researchers have explored how young people experience CEE (Gordon, 2017), how they critique and create text (Marsh et al., 2021; Sarigianides, 2019; Spector, 2010), how they might use other literacy forms to develop academic literacies (Brown & Rodesiler, 2016; Camangian, 2008), and how they use their literacy practices to challenge power (Thakurta, 2023). Scholars have also investigated how English educators might reconceptualize their ELA classrooms toward a more culturally relevant and social justice-informed pedagogical praxis (Dyches & Sams, 2018; Knight, 2011; Lopez, 2011; Skerrett, 2010), and teacher educators have used CEE to examine their own approaches to the teaching of literacy pedagogy in English methods courses (Berchini, 2014; Gatti et al., 2018; Olan & Richmond, 2017). Across many pedagogical, conceptual, and empirical articles, scholars have shown that CEE is about the business of analyzing and deconstructing dominant institutions while also creating space to do things differently in ELA.

Still, scholars employing CEE perspectives could do more to centralize the critique and dismantling of anti-Black violence that permeates the field of English education. As Johnson (2022) argued, "The anatomy of modern classrooms serves as a space of anti-Black racism and non-being for Black people" (p. 2), and "state-sanctioned curriculum exercises violence and has historical and contemporary roots in the reproduction of anti-Black racism through perpetuating a curriculum that is rooted in white supremacist patriarchal control" (p. 3). That is, ELA classrooms are often violent spaces for Black children, where they experience assault via pedagogy, text selection, and cultural erasure. If the goal of CEE is to promote "change in focus of literacy pedagogy, textual consumption, and textual production," (Morell, 2005, p. 319), then it is imperative that we focalize Blackness as an essential project of a speculative CEE.

The Black Speculative and Critical English Education

Currently, Black children are positioned as monstrous Other, forced to sit in learning spaces in which they are consistently exposed to racial violence (Baker-Bell et al., 2017; Love, 2016; Thomas, 2019). Currently, the stories of Black youth are criminalized, outlawed in English classrooms, and removed from library shelves (Opoku-Agyeman, 2023; Parker, 2023). Currently, Black people are often forced to beg others to see the value in our unique and nuanced literacy practices, with various people (including educators) viewing Black literacies through deficit lenses rather than seeing the assets Black people bring to the learning environment (Johnson et al., 2017; Mauldin & Johnson, 2021). CEE acknowledges these realities while arguing for pedagogies that challenge and dismantle them. But a radical transformation in English education needs imagination and requires the envisioning of alternative, anti-oppressive futures. Additionally, a "radical transformation of the discipline and the practice of training English teachers" (Morell, 2005, p. 319) requires a focus on disrupting anti-Black realities and imagining and enacting futures in which all Black students can thrive.

So, when considering the future of Black youth in CEE spaces, a generic speculative focus will not do. Instead, imagination steeped in Blackness is needed. For this reason, it is imperative that educators take Afrofuturism into consideration.

Afrofuturism and Critical English Education

Afrofuturism is a fluid term, one that defies definition and boundary. It is an aesthetic, a theory of knowledge, a Black-conscious movement, and a set of tools that connects race to space and technology to art in order to assist Black people in analyzing contemporary and historical issues and disrupting oppressive interpretations of Black people's pasts and futures (Morris, 2012, 2016). It exists as a program for "recovering the histories of counter-futures created in a century hostile to Afrodiasporic projection and as a space within which the critical work of manufacturing tools capable of intervention within the current political dispensation may be undertaken" (Eshun, 2003, p. 301). It is a global and popular aesthetic movement that utilizes various genres, media, and forms of artistry to tell Black speculative fiction stories, retrieve and recount lost Black histories, and examine the impact of recovered histories on ideas about a more equitable Black future (Yaszek, 2005, 2006, 2013). Although a concrete definition is elusive due to the broad nature of the term, to employ Afrofuturist ideals is to engage in various processes of deconstruction, recovery, and production that makes space for Black people to reclaim and recover the past, counter negative and uplift positive realities that exist in the present, and present new possibilities for the future (Toliver, 2022).

Broadly, the process of deconstruction, retrieval, and creation necessary to engage in Afrofuturism aligns the aesthetic with CEE. For instance, CEE is clear in how it works to deconstruct dominant texts and make space for young people to create their own critical texts that can be used as they push for a more socially just world. Afrofuturism allows for the same examination of text because in order to recover lost histories and/or counter negative and uplift positive realities, educators must understand how dominant texts have always attempted to erase the stories and histories of Black peoples. We must know how to critique "traditional" texts of erasure so that we may arrive at different truths. We must know that Black authors have always engaged in the creation of liberatory texts, and we must give these texts the same (if not more) time and attention we give to white-centric texts.

Additionally, with its focus on the past, present, and future, Afrofuturism connects to CEE in the ways it enables literacy stakeholders to engage in a historical and contemporary "investigation of language and literacy in cultures and communities" (Morrell, 2005, p. 316). Community and culture are not static things; instead, they are living, breathing, fluid. It is impossible to understand the intricacy of students' cultural or communal background if literacy stakeholders are imprisoned by thoughts of the past or bound to what they see in the present. To truly explore young people's language and literacy practices is to examine the whole of their histories while also deeply considering the possibilities of their present moments. But it cannot stop there, for the goal is to use these examinations to imagine and create potential futures. We cannot examine the past and present to remain static. Instead, we must engage in this exploration in order to consider how the past and the present might contribute to potential futures.

Lastly, countering negative and uplifting positive realities aligns with CEE in how scholars can "explicitly address issues of violence, race, whiteness, white supremacy, and anti-black racism within school and out-of-school spaces" and emphasize "how language and literacy can be used as tools to uplift the lives of people who are often on the margins in society" (Johnson, 2018, p. 108). Afrofuturism asks that we focus on the retrieval of Black histories and stories erased from dominant texts and shunned in anti-Black classrooms. By adopting a critical approach to English education, literacy stakeholders can make room to engage in in-depth examinations of Black culture that extend beyond one moment in time, so they can acknowledge and appreciate Black youth's historical and contemporary language and literacy practices.

Of course, while CEE and Afrofuturism are greatly aligned, there is still room to grow. So much of the literacy research landscape is focused on the past and the present, but Afrofuturism does not stop at the examination of history or the contemporary moment, as futurity is an essential component of the aesthetic. Afrofuturism requires the act of creation of speculative texts, the deliberate telling of stories featuring Black people in far-out futures and other worlds, an intentional imagining of new ways of existing in community with one another. It asks that we don't only think of what used to be or critique what is currently happening; instead, it demands that we create the impossible, that we dream in community to compose more anti-oppressive futures. Moreover, Afrofuturism requires that we see Black people as not only participants in the future but as content creators and world makers. It compels us to look to the dreams of Black youth in order to envision and compose more equitable futures in which all people are free. Futurity, imagination, and the speculative, however, are aspects that are not yet prominent in CEE, and Afrofuturism is even less so.

But a lack of prominence doesn't negate existence, as there are literacy researchers who have utilized Afrofuturistic ideals to explore Black youth's pasts, presents, and futures. For instance, Griffin and Turner (2021) created space for elementary and middle school Black girls to use multimodal creations to critique the contemporary world and imagine Black worlds in which Black people might live freely from the white gaze. They invite literacy educators to make space for Black livingness. Similarly, Coles (2023) facilitated a summer writing course that provided space for Black high school youth to create and share artifacts where they challenged anti-Blackness through Afrofuturist counterstories. In doing this work, he noted that developing the ability "to story against the non-human/superhuman anti-Black narratives that work to frame the treatment of Black youth, educators must be transformed by the Afro-futurist counterstories of Black youth" (p. 460). Additionally, Kaler-Jones (2022) cocreated a healing space in which she and eight Black girls engaged in artistic explorations of storytelling, history, and social justice. Through her work with the girls, Kaler-Jones gave the following advice:

> We must support space for Black girls to explore and determine the fullness of their freedom dreams—from examining history, to refuting stereotypes, to creating their identities, to thinking about future aspirations, to dreaming a new world into existence, to developing demands to enact those futures. We also must not solely listen, but act in service of those demands. (p. 15)

These scholars, among others, have engaged in speculative CEE, showcasing how literacy educators might use their research and teaching to explore how Black youth understand their realities and to engage Black youth in the creation of new futures (Player et al., 2023; Turner, 2023; Watson & Knight-Manuel, 2020). They have also suggested ways we might examine teacher education more closely, to pinpoint how these programs engage in anti-Blackness and to consider how we can challenge white supremacy in these spaces (Carey, 2020; Coles & Stanley, 2021). They challenge literacy educators to make space for imagination, art, creativity, and livingness to uplift Black youth in a white supremacist society.

In my own work, I have drawn heavily from CEE and Afrofuturism to explore Black girls' speculative thinking and to better understand their dreams for more anti-oppressive futures. As examples, I created a speculative fiction writing group for middle school girls in which we used science fiction, fantasy, and horror writing to discuss their experience with social injustice and to imagine worlds in which they have the power, support, and resources to promote social change (Toliver, 2020, 2021b, 2022). I have also analyzed Black speculative fiction to consider the speculative futures and other worlds Black people compose for themselves and others. For instance, I've examined young adult science fiction and fantasy narratives to consider how Black authors illuminate the complex ways in which overlapping systems of oppression affect Black youth and how they challenge those systems through storytelling (Toliver, 2021a, 2023). Lastly, I have considered how CEE might benefit from the inclusion of the speculative and what is at stake if Black futures are omitted from teacher preparation programs (Toliver & Hadley, 2021). Specifically, I've made space in my teacher preparation classrooms for preservice teachers to use art and imagination to develop and forward their racial literacy practices. Like scholars before and after me, I utilize the imaginative, the speculative, and the creative as a mechanism through which Black youth can use their literacy practices to challenge the current world and imagine new ones.

Ultimately, across my studies and the studies of other scholars who consider the speculative and Black youth in the context of CEE, one thing is clear: A critical approach to English education must include the speculative and the creative. We cannot just be aware of future possibilities; we must also find ways to create them.

So, Where Might We Go from Here?

Over the years, critical English educators have attempted to imagine a more equitable literacy education, one that aligns with the call Morrell (2005) presented years ago. Still, there is much to do if we are ever to completely realize the fullness of our collective dreams. To truly reach the promises and possibilities of CEE (teachers as activists, young people as textual producers, the centering of Black liberatory thought, rebellion against dominant texts), literacy stakeholders must consider the past and present but also think about how to bring imagination and creation into English education. We must engage in more direct analyses of Afrofuturist texts to consider how Black authors are composing their own futures, how they are engaging in the redefinition, reclamation, and expansion of Black people's identities within and beyond the parameters of dominance. We must open space for Black youth to write about their pasts and presents, but we must also ask them to dream of boundless, untethered futures. We must make space and encourage young Black people to create literary portals to new worlds, to engage in new ways of thinking and doing, to compose new stories for themselves and others. We must assist teachers in letting go of realistic constraints so they can not only dream of Black liberation but can be an integral part of the movement toward freedom. If a radical transformation is what we seek in CEE, then we must make room for our dreams to become realities, but we must center those dreams more prominently before creation will manifest.

Conclusion

The speculative undercurrent in CEE has always been there, etched into the idea from the very beginning. But so many of us have been moored by oppression, fixed to the realistic because the future seems too farfetched. So many of us have been stuck in the stage of dreaming, hoping that one day our fantasies will somehow become reality if we close our eyes and wish with all our might. But if we truly seek to transform the world for our students, especially those who are most minoritized in a white supremacist system, we must find ways to create, to transform our dreams into actions.

References

Aukerman, M. (2012). "Why do you say yes to Pedro, but no to me?" Toward a critical literacy of dialogic engagement. *Theory Into Practice, 51*(1), 42–48.

Baker-Bell, A., Butler, T., & Johnson, L. (2017). The pain and the wounds: A call for critical race English education in the wake of racial violence. *English Education, 49*(2), 116–129.

Berchini, C. (2014). Learning to teach and critical pedagogy: Struggling with a "do as I say, not as I do" pedagogy. *English Education, 46*(3), 247–267.

Brown, A., & Rodesiler, L. (2016). *Developing contemporary literacies through sports: A guide for the English classroom.* National Council for Teachers of English.

Camangian, P. (2008). Untempered tongues: Teaching performance poetry for social justice. *English Teaching: Practice & Critique, 7*(2), 35–55.

Carey, R. (2020). Making Black boys and young men matter: Radical relationships, future oriented imaginaries and other evolving insights for educational research and practice. *International Journal of Qualitative Studies in Education, 33*(7), 729–744.

Coleman, J. J. (2021). Affective reader response: Using ordinary affects to repair literacy normativities in ELA and English education. *English Education, 53*(4), 254–276.

Coles, J. A. (2023). Storying against non-human/superhuman narratives: Black youth Afro-futurist counterstories in qualitative research. *International Journal of Qualitative Studies in Education, 36*(3), 446–464.

Coles, J. A., & Stanley, D. (2021). Black liberation in teacher education: (Re)envisioning educator preparation to defend Black life and possibility. *Northwest Journal of Teacher Education, 16*(2), Article 6.

Dyches, J., & Sams, B. L. (2018). Reconciling competing missions of English education: A story of pedagogical realism. *Changing English: Studies in Culture and Education, 25*(4), 370–383.

Eshun, K. (2003). Further considerations on Afrofuturism. *CR: The New Centennial Review*, *3*(2), 287–302.

Gatti, L., Masterson, J., Brooke, R., Shah, R., & Thomas, S. (2018). English education as democratic armor: Responding programmatically to our political work. *English Teaching: Practice & Critique, 17*(2), 116–131.

Godley, A., & Minnici, A. (2008). Critical language pedagogy in an urban high school English class. *Urban Education, 43*(3), 319–346.

Goessling, K. P., Wright, D., Wager, A. C., & Dewhurst, M. (2020). A critical mixtape for the movement: Reflecting on creative and critical youth practices in research. *International Journal of Qualitative Studies in Education, 33*(1), 1–7.

Gordon, C. T. (2017). Critical literacy and the arts: Using one-act plays to promote social justice. *Ubiquity: The Journal of Literature, Literacy, and the Arts, 4*(2), 75–89.

Greene, M. (1995). *Releasing the imagination: Essays on education, the arts, and social change*. Jossey-Bass.

Griffin, A. A., & Turner, J. (2021). Toward a pedagogy of Black livingness: Black students' creative multimodal renderings of resistance to anti-Blackness. *English Teaching: Practice & Critique, 20*(4), 440–453.

Johnson, L. L. (2018). Where do we go from here? Toward a critical race English education. *Research in the Teaching of English, 53*(2), 102–124.

Johnson, L. L. (2022). *Critical race English education: New visions, new possibilities.* Routledge.

Johnson, L. L., Jackson, J., Stovall, D. O., & Taliaferro Baszile, D. (2017). "Loving Blackness to death": (Re)imagining ELA classrooms in a time of racial chaos. *English Journal, 106*(4), 60–66.

Kaler-Jones, C. (2022). "I rewrote their story and you can, too": Black girls' artistic freedom dreams to create new worlds. *Frontiers in Education, 7*, 1–17.

Kelley, R. D. G. (2002). *Freedom dreams: The Black radical imagination.* Beacon Press.

Khasnabish, A, & Haiven, M. (2014, August 9). *Lessons from social movements: Six notes on the radical imagination.* Truthout. https://truthout.org/articles/lessons-from-social-movements-six-notes-on-the-radical-imagination/

Knight, S. D. (2011). Using narrative to examine positionality: Powerful pedagogy in English education. *English Teaching: Practice and Critique, 10*(2), 49–64.

Lopez, A. E. (2011). Culturally relevant pedagogy and critical literacy in diverse English classrooms: A case study of a secondary English teacher's activism and agency. *English Teaching: Practice & Critique, 10*(4), 75–93.

Love, B. (2016). Anti-Black state violence, classroom edition: The spirit murdering of Black children. *Journal of Curriculum and Pedagogy, 13*(1), 22–25.

Love, B. (2019). *We want to do more than survive: Abolitionist teaching and the pursuit of educational freedom.* Beacon Press.

Marsh, V. L., Lammers, J. C., & Conroy, E. (2021). Students as change makers: Five steps to advocacy research. *English Journal, 111*(2), 56–63.

Mauldin, C., & Johnson, L. L. (2021). Black lives mattering in and out of schools: Anti-Black racism, racial violence, and a hope for Black imagination in educational research. In C. E. Matias (Ed.), *The handbook of critical theoretical research methods in education* (pp. 272–283). Routledge.

Morrell, E. (2005). Critical English education. *English Education, 37*(4), 312–321.

Morrell, E., & Duncan-Andrade, J. M. R. (2002). Promoting academic literacy with urban youth through engaging hip-hop culture. *English Journal, 91*(6), 88–92.

Morris, S. (2012). Black girls are from the future: Afrofuturist feminism in Octavia E. Butler's *Fledgling. WSQ: Women's Studies Quarterly, 40*(3–4), 146–166.

Morris, S. (2016). More than human: Black feminisms of the future in Jewelle Gomez's *The Gilda stories. The Black Scholar, 46*(2), 33–45.

Olan, E. L., & Richmond, K. (2017). Storying our journey: Conversations about the literary canon and course development in secondary English education. *The Wisconsin English Journal, 49*(1–2), 238–266.

Opoku-Agyeman, A. G. (2023, June 2). The heavy cost of banning books about Black children. *TIME.*

Parker, K. N. (2023). "I think you should read it anyway": Black readers and book bans. *Voices from the Middle, 30*(4), 15–18.

Player, G., Animashaun, O., & Thornton, T. (2023). "Getting lost in stars and glitter": Black girls' multimodal literacies as portals to new suns. *International Journal of Qualitative Studies in Education, 36*(3), 411–429.

Sarigianides, S. T. (2019). Performative youth: The literacy possibilities of de-essentializing adolescence. *English Education, 51*(4), 376–403.

Skerrett, A. (2010). Teaching critical literacy for social justice. *Action in Teacher Education, 31*(4), 54–65.

Spector, K. (2010). Classroom provocateurs and ethical classroom practice. *Changing English: Studies in Culture and Education, 17*(4), 363–373.

Stetsenko, A. (2018). Creativity as dissent and resistance: Transformative approach premised on social justice agenda. In I. Lebuda & V. Glaveanu (Eds.), *The Palgrave handbook of social creativity research* (pp. 431–446). Palgrave Macmillan.

Thakurta, A. (2023). Solidarity-as-project: Charting democratic co-inquiries in an Asian American girl and woman-centric English education community. *English Education, 55*(4), 257–278.

Thomas, E. E. (2019). *The dark fantastic: Race and the imagination from Harry Potter to the Hunger Games.* New York University Press.

Toliver, S. R. (2020). Can I get a witness?: Speculative fiction as testimony and counterstory. *Journal of Literacy Research, 52*(4), 507–529.

Toliver, S. R. (2021a). Afrocarnival: Celebrating Black bodies and critiquing oppressive bodies in afrofuturist literature. *Children's Literature in Education, 52*(1), 132–148.

Toliver, S. R. (2021b). Freedom dreaming in a broken world: The Black radical imagination in Black girls' science fiction stories. *Research in the Teaching of English, 56*(1), 85–106.

Toliver, S. R. (2022). *Recovering Black storytelling in qualitative research: Endarkened storywork*. Routledge.

Toliver, S. R. (2023). "Weird is normal": A womanist discourse analysis of Black girl nerd's community building. *Equity & Excellence in Education, 56*(1–2), 206–220.

Toliver, S. R., & Hadley, H. (2021). Rhetorically speaking: On white preservice teachers' failure to imagine an anti-racist *English education. English Teaching: Practice and Critique, 20*(4), 485–500.

Turner, J. (2023). Celebrate with me: A Black adolescent girl's speculative multimodal design of intersectional college and career futures. *English Teaching: Practice & Critique, 22*(3), 271–284.

Watson, V., & Knight-Manuel, M. G. (2020). Humanizing the Black immigrant body: Envisioning diaspora literacies of youth and young adults from West African countries. *Teachers College Record, 122*(13), 1–28.

Yaszek, L. (2005). An Afrofuturist reading of Ralph Ellison's *Invisible man. Rethinking History*, *9*(2–3), 297–313.

Yaszek, L. (2006). Afrofuturism, science fiction, and the history of the future. *Socialism and Democracy*, *20*(3), 41–60.

Yaszek, L. (2013). *Race in science fiction: The case of Afrofuturism.* A Virtual Introduction to Science Fiction. http://virtual-sf.com/wp-content/uploads/2013/08/Yaszek.pdf

Chapter Eleven

What Black English Reveals about Black Power

Jamila Lyiscott

If my work is to confront a reality unlike that received reality of the West, it must centralize and animate information discredited by the West—discredited not because it is not true or useful or even of some racial value, but because it is information held by discredited people, information dismissed as "lore" or "gossip" or "magic" or "sentiment."

—Toni Morrison

In the lives of Black people across the world, language is memory and witness. It wields the pain and possibilities of political pasts. It hides what we refuse to forget and performs what we want you to remember. Culture lives in the rhythm of our tongues. Our genius takes refuge here. It is an untamable site of refusal. It remains a site of political, historical, cultural, and ideological struggle. In May of 2022, I stood on 8288 Khumalo Street in Soweto, South Africa, a space of memory and witness where the Hector Pieterson Museum was erected to memorialize the hundreds of school-aged children who lost their lives in the 1976 Soweto Student Uprising that took place just two short blocks away. A gruesome black-and-white image of twelve-year-old Hector Pieterson, lifeless next to his grieving sister, filled me with pain and possibility. As I stood there, I recalled that I was twelve years old—the age of Hector—when my father gave me what he refused to forget: a VHS copy of the 1992 movie *Sarafina* that dramatized this peaceful protest. The film performed what he wanted me to remember.

Mobilized by the South African Students Movement, on June 16, 1976, the day had arrived for thousands of politically conscious students in Soweto to peacefully protest the compulsory government mandate that forced their instruction and assessments to all be conducted in the language of Afrikaans—the West Germanic language of white South Africans. It was my first lesson in the interwoven depths of racial and linguistic hatred. The students refused the deceit of a curriculum that painted African histories, languages, and cultures as unworthy of the classroom. They refused the ways that the 1953 Bantu Education Act cemented racism in the veins of their education system. I must have watched the film a thousand times. Eyes widened, first by scenes of a coming-of-age protagonist, Sarafina, moving through love, learning, and life. Then by the impending doom of a radical teacher, Mary Masembuko, who dared to teach her African students about the true history of Africa against the sanctioned curriculum that was explicitly designed with the imperative that "natives (blacks) must be taught from an early age that equality with Europeans (whites) is not for them" (Rethinking Schools, n.d.). The white armed guards standing outside of her classroom door to ensure she stuck to the script bristled my spirit. I drank the story into my young consciousness as I watched the school-aged children organize their peaceful protest.

What happened next in the film's coverage of true history stunned my young mind. The children, who looked like me, who were filled with such curiosity and ambition that they demanded the kind of education that they deserved, chanted peacefully and were met by heavily armed soldiers and officers equipped with military tanks and assault rifles. Across ten days of ongoing protests, the official death toll was over 174 people, with over 1,200 wounded and over 1,200 arrested. Today, on 8288 Khumalo Street, the heritage site that stands in honor of these children is an untamable site of refusal. Following these uprisings, in July of 1976, Black schools were given the option to choose their language of instruction and "ninety-six percent of Black schools chose English, not one of their African languages" (Phaswana, 2003, p. 120) for fear that their education in their tribal African languages would be weaponized by the Apartheid government to divide Black South Africans. That students lost their lives to reject the looming colonial language of Afrikaans and felt that their safest passage was through yet another colonial language that is English illuminates the pervasive violence of colonial and racist logic that shapes the reality of Black people across the African Diaspora and the enduring need for critical perspectives of English education.

In 2019, NAEP reported that only 15 percent of Black eighth graders in the United States were reading at or above grade level.[1] Mirroring the logic that framed apartheid South Africa's refusal to value the language, history, and culture of Black students in favor of an Afrikaan-centered (white) curriculum, Black students' strained relationship to English education in the United States must be understood against the backdrop of educational logics that continue to discredit and weaponize their own languages and cultures in favor of Eurocentrism. Too often, efforts to address disparities in English education frame Black students as illiterate (Alim, 2011) and their English as "broken." With Bourdieuian finesse, theorists, school leaders, and educators alike view the English classroom as an avenue to equip Black students with the canonical knowledge and language of middle class America (Yosso, 2005) in order to prepare them for "success" in the "real world" with the loud message that their own linguistic repertoires are unworthy of regard.

However, over four decades of research has established the validity, rigor, and distinctness of Black English as well as the imperial, colonial, and racist factors that continue to discredit it (Baker-Bell, 2020; Boutte et al., 2021; TEDx, 2018; Makoni et al., 2003; Smitherman, 1977). For example, in "Revisiting the Promise of Students' Right to Their Own Language," Kinloch (2005) lifts up the words of June Jordan, arguing that "our Black English is a political fact suffering from political persecution and political malice" (p. 84). That Black English is a political fact is unquestionable, but more than the political correctness and is-ness of Black English is the essential power of its function in Black life. Kinloch insists, "the subordination and relegation of Black English to otherness" is a result of the attempted extinction of "a communicative tongue that has historically represented the lived experiences of African American people" (p. 84). While for critical English educators today the argument that Black English has its own distinct value when viewed beyond the white gaze is not new (Boutte et al., 2021; Lyiscott, 2025; Smitherman, 2000; Young, 2007), little has been done to turn toward and utilize the *power* of Black English as an animate and agentic site for addressing the alarming disparities disproportionately affecting Black students. Thus, this chapter moves beyond arguing for the validity of Black English and argues that what should now be seen as the common-sense power of Black English must be leveraged by critical English educators as a source of both social inquiry *and* direct social transformation in teaching and learning.

Rooted in critical theory, critical English perspectives question hegemonic perspectives of English and its associated ideologies (Morrell, 2005). I argue that because critical and social perspectives of language have long argued for the ways that English is imbued with history, culture, politics, and power (TEDx, 2018), Black English, when viewed through a critical lens, gives us a window into Black history, Black culture, Black politics, and Black power that can be leveraged for tangible social change.

Black Power Is Black Language

In 1968, linguistic scholar Dr. Geneva Smitherman proclaimed at a Black Power rally, "Black power is Black language!" (Smitherman, 1972). The statement gestured toward emerging research by Smitherman and her contemporaries, who began tracing the etymological, phonological, and heritage roots of Black English all the way back to West Africa and how these survived the Middle Passage despite enslavers' best efforts to annihilate the languages of enslaved Africans (Baker-Bell, 2013). Smitherman's proclamation had built on the wildly popularized phrase "Black Power," made (in)famous by Stokely Carmichael and other Civil Rights leaders in the previous two years. On June 16, 1966, in Greenwood, Mississippi, Trinidadian-born activist Kwame Toure (aka Stokely Carmichael) shook up the Civil Rights Movement with a speech that called for "Black Power." "We been saying freedom for six years, and we ain't got nothin'. What we got to start saying now is Black Power! We want Black Power!" (Ligon, 2016), he said to the crowd as he introduced the phrase to the world. As the chairman of the Student Nonviolent Coordinating Committee (SNCC), Carmichael, along with SNCC activists, decided that "Freedom now!" the phrase that branded their movement up until June 16, was too hollow and did not move Black people toward galvanizing their true power in the name of visible structural change. Black Power was also meant to capture Carmichael's frustration with Martin Luther King Jr.'s nonviolent agenda. In the face of unrelenting racialized violence against Black communities, the phrase called for militant separatism, posing some ideological divides within the Civil Rights Movement.

The media frantically denounced "Black Power" as violent and hateful toward white America. Mainstream outlets and federal authorities alike worked to make the use of the phrase punishable and poured their rage into refuting the audacity of Black Power as a concept rather than dismantle the racist conditions that Civil Rights leaders had been illuminating for the previous decade. When given the opportunity to define and reclaim the spirit of Black Power, Carmichael quickly noted that it was telling that white America insisted on controlling the language of the Civil Rights Movement as they sought to reduce the concept of Black Power to violence. In subsequent works, he clarified that Black Power was a call for Black people (a) to unite, (b) to recognize their heritage, (c) to build their communities while defining their own goals, and (d) to advocate for Black political and economic power within their own communities (Carmichael, 1967). Smitherman's assertion that "Black power is Black language" must be understood within this context.

Echoing the sentiments of SNCC, in the face of the physical, mental, spiritual, linguistic, and discursive anti-Black violences throughout the Civil Rights Movement, Smitherman's claim that "Black power is Black language" was a call to recognize the unified tapestry of Black English and its heritage roots while wielding its power to facilitate self-definition in the lives of Black people. Far from the lie espoused by right-wing America that diversifying curriculum for an increasingly diverse student body is anti-American, research has shown unequivocally that when Black students see Black English texts valued in classrooms, it taps into powerful background schema, increases engagement, strengthens self-efficacy, and better prepares them to connect with other cultures and knowledges in school (Baker-Bell, 2012; Boutte et al., 2021; Haddix, 2012; Kinloch, 2005; TEDx, 2018). At the heart of staggering disparities in reading and writing is a staggering disregard for the language practices that Black students bring organically into the classroom. To date, the goal of English classrooms has been content and canon instruction, the mechanics and science of reading and writing, and preparing students for high-stakes testing. Educators and students can work together to shift the culture of English education to better serve Black students for whom, based on current literacy rates, the traditional English classroom is not working. However, the answers to enduring questions about healing racial disparities in school will not be found in the privileged center but in the discredited margins.

For these reasons, I ask, "What (when valued) does Black English reveal about Black Power?" to raise questions about how centering Black epistemological, linguistic, and cultural practices might provoke direct social action cocreated by the students and teachers who are typically constrained by the limited mechanisms of schooling. To begin answering this question, I first discuss how Black English has been discredited and devalued by anti-Black linguistic racism in the United States, encouraging critical English educators to turn toward it as the first step to valuing and wielding its power to disrupt normative schooling. I then discuss how valuing Black English through critical perspectives of English provides us with a lens to actually witness its agentic power that has long been obscured by white supremacy. Finally, I offer a path to support critical educators with moving beyond validating Black English and toward leveraging its power.

Black English as Discredited Knowledge

A long history of global anti-Black violence has made it so that Black people are regularly required to abandon the tongues that have nurtured them and to shed the cultural milieu that they call home in order to climb ladders of success. In keeping with this history, within the US, complex Black Language practices are most often (mis)read as lazy or bad English in the mainstream imagination. Benign everyday cultural practices in Black communities are relegated to delinquency. African American English, for example, shares features such as copula absence (i.e., the absence of the verb "to be," as in, "she goin' to the store" rather than "she is going to the store") with many West African languages. This shared linguistic history is an emblem of remembrance discredited by school knowledge as "informal," erroneous, and even punishable. Thus, traditional educational experiences in the lives of Black people are marked by a redemptive narrative meant to heal this laziness, to atone for the perceived ratchet uncivilized nature of our cultures, and to lure us into the unrelenting invitation to perform whiteness.

The transformative capacity of Black English to point us toward the nuances of Black power for the field of English education first requires critical English educators who are willing to turn toward what Toni Morrison calls "discredited knowledges" (Morrison, 1984). For Morrison, discredited knowledges are organic ways of knowing and being in the lives of Black people that are illegible to the white gaze. It is knowledge that is dismissed, ignored, even scoffed at, but when turned toward reveals insights "unlike the received reality of the West." She writes,

> If my work is to confront a reality unlike that received reality of the West, it must centralize and animate information discredited by the West—discredited not because it is not true or useful or even of some racial value, but because it is information held by discredited people, information dismissed as "lore" or "gossip" or "magic" or "sentiment." (1984, p. 388)

When we turn to discredited knowledges in education, we make visible the power of alternate truths, alternate histories, and alternate onto-epistemologies forged in the margins of our society. We give ourselves permission to bring these to the fore in our classrooms, our communities, and in our research in place of the fragmentation that is typically required of Black students, who are asked to disregard their repertoires with the message that their Englishes have no cultural or intellectual value in schools.

Black English has been discredited by what April Baker-Bell (2019) calls *anti-Black linguistic racism*. According to Baker-Bell, "Anti-Black linguistic racism refers to the linguistic violence, persecution, dehumanization, and marginalization that Black Language (BL) speakers endure when using their language in schools and in everyday life" (p. 9). Anti-Black linguistic racism is a form of discrimination that relies on white supremacist logics to obscure the power of Black English. This form of discrimination has several features. First, it relies on standard language ideology, which is a belief in a fixed hierarchy that positions "standard" white mainstream English as superior to other language practices. This feature of anti-Black linguistic racism discredits Black English by obscuring the power of Black English, which functions as a leading influential force in popular culture and society writ large for mass appeal. For example, marketing strategies rely heavily on Black English because it has demonstrated its power to influence global popular culture, yet it remains discredited in school as an ineffective form of communication. The next feature of anti-Black linguistic racism is that it is historically situated within a history of anti-Black violence that has worked to discredit Black people and the languages and cultures that emerge from Black communities. This feature of anti-Black linguistic racism obscures the power of Black English by seeking to limit its historical validity (i.e., there is a long history of devaluing it) and subsequently, its capacity to formally shape social futures. For example, we can hardly imagine a future that respectfully and meaningfully integrates Black English into all facets of society. Another feature of anti-Black linguistic racism relies on the idea that language is homogenous, fixed, and one-size-fits-all. This seeks to discredit Black English by ignoring the reality that all languages are socially constructed and always evolving. Although Black English is just as rule-governed and complex as any other language that has been constructed throughout history, the illusion prevails that European Romance languages are "real" languages and that they exist in a fixed standardizable state.

Baker-Bell (2019) discusses the myriad ways that these features of anti-Black linguistic racism show up in the classroom. These include,

> teachers' silencing, correcting, and policing students when they communicate in [Black Language] . . . the belief that there is something inherently wrong with [Black Language] therefore, it should be eradicated. It is denying Black students the right to use their native language as a linguistic resource during their language and literacy learning. It is requiring that Black students reject their language and culture to acquire White Mainstream English (WME), and it is also insisting that Black students code-switch to avoid discrimination. (p. 9)

Yet even in the face of linguistic racism, Black students are not abandoning the language practices that so meaningfully shape their identities (TEDx, 2018). Instead, their language practices persist in keeping with a history that has required Black people to engage in fugitive consciousness and practices to survive (Givens, 2021). To credit these ways of knowing, then, would provide a powerful window into student schema. The fact is that, despite social consequence, students often labeled as "disengaged" are fully engaged with their languages of nurture in spaces beyond the classroom. To credit these ways of knowing is just an initial step toward understanding and wielding their power.

Witnessing the Agentic Power of Black English

To witness the discredited power of Black English that has survived the enduring threat of anti-Black linguistic racism, I draw on *fugitive literacies* as a critical lens to acknowledge its complex history, one that has been fraught with survival, refuge, preservation, and hope. Elsewhere, I define fugitive literacies as

> rooted in the bodily, linguistic, cultural, and spiritual acts of flight that were carried out by the enslaved. . . . Fugitive literacies are literacy practices that endure in the lives of Black and Brown people in ways that ignore, reject, and refuse the sanctioning of white hegemony. (2025)

We can use such critical perspectives of English to witness and leverage the power available to us in Black English when that power is not obscured by white supremacist logics. If indeed this power, according to Smitherman as inspired by SNCC, is evidenced in (a) the unified tapestry of Black English, (b) its heritage roots, (c) its capacity to facilitate self-definition, and (d) its situatedness in Black culture, then these should be viewable once placed in a fugitive light—one that breaks free from the status quo and finds refuge; one that persists in the precarity of that refuge while still surrounded by social structures that render Black English disposable; one that, much like the fugitive Black bodies of the enslaved, views Black English with the kind of value, love, and care that believes in its power to be self-determined and free.

During the slave trade, captured West Africans speaking the same language were separated and shipped to different parts of the world to ensure they could not communicate and rebel. Similar to practices in states such as North and South Carolina—where the creolized Gullah Geechee language of the enslaved was made punishable—during colonial and imperial reigns in Africa, South America, and the Caribbean, speaking in a mother tongue in school resulted in corporal punishment or shaming strategies to reinforce the dominance of colonial Western Romance languages. From 1740 to 1834, anti-literacy laws were in place in the US, outlawing reading and writing for free and enslaved Black people. Mirroring the criminality of those who fled from slavery (i.e., the Fugitive Slave Acts of 1850 and 1872 made escape from slavery a criminal act and mandated that those who escaped from slavery, even into "free" states, be returned as property), the ramifications for engaging in fugitive acts of literacy were punishable and even deadly. Despite this, learning how to read and write persisted covertly in the lives of Black people in the US throughout the eighteenth and nineteenth centuries. A long history of these covert acts of learning during slavery and in the Jim Crow South serves as the blueprint for present-day fugitive literacies—acts of rhetorical and linguistic refusal within the shared discourse practices of Black communities.

Critical English educators who turn toward the discredited ways of knowing available within Black English must then contend with its fugitive and agentic nature. Where those who absconded from slavery sought to preserve their bodies and minds, fugitive literacies work to preserve heritage knowledge, memory, and culture through language. Where those who charted their way to freedom through the cover of night sought to locate themselves beyond the physical confines of their master's reach, fugitive literacies function as a form of racial positioning that locates its speakers as grounded in self-definition uninhibited by the circumscription of the status quo. And where those who dreamed of liberty sought to imagine futures where, no longer reduced to chattel, they were free to create worlds marked by the fullness of their heritage and humanity, fugitive literacies perpetually create new, dynamic, hybrid forms of expression that capture our collective imaginations. This is the power of Black English.

Wielding the Power of Black English

When educators turn toward discredited ways of knowing and make meaning of the agentic fugitive nature of Black English (i.e., as opposed to relegating it to the margins in their classrooms), then its capacity for engaging and transforming the educational experiences of all students is made visible in new ways. However, too often, English educators working to value Black English in their classrooms send the subtle message that it is only appropriate for certain settings. For example, Black English will be readily included in a poetic unit but excluded from intellectual endeavors that are labeled as more rigorous in the classroom. To combat this limiting view of Black English and its utility for learning, we must unpack the ways that this logic mirrors the logic of segregation. When Stokely Carmichael called for Black Power and Dr. Geneva Smitherman echoed the sentiment of the Black Power Movement in her fight for linguistic and racial justice, they did so against the backdrop of a segregationist society that rendered the bodies of Black people as only appropriate for certain settings. Black power, then, was not just a call to acknowledge the value of Black people while still keeping them on the margins of a "whites only" society, but it was a call for the US to integrate and contend with the power of Black life that it had long disparaged.

For English educators who wish to move beyond merely valuing Black English and into the realm of nurturing its power to transform the English classroom and the educational lives of students, several pedagogical possibilities exist. One example of such a shift is available within hip-hop pedagogy. While proponents of hip-hop pedagogy have situated the value of Black English and culture as common sense for the classroom, too often its use is limited to reifying normative school practices that harm Black students. In *Beats, Rhymes, and Classroom Life* (2009), Hill argues for the pedagogical possibilities available within hip-hop given its global influence but warns against merely valuing hip-hop without leveraging its power. Centered on his experiences teaching a hip-hop-centered English class at an alternative high school, he asserts that students' identities are renegotiated when hip-hop culture is bridged with their learning in the English classroom. He writes,

> Instead of carefully unpacking the complex relationships that are forged between youth and hip-hop culture, current classroom research has focused primarily, if not exclusively, on narrow conceptions of educational success such as attendance and standardized test scores. (p. 2)

If we are to truly take up Smitherman's call to engage with the unified tapestry of Black English and tap into its power to facilitate self-definition in the lives of Black people, then rather than use hip-hop texts in the English classroom for narrow avenues toward student success, English educators should consider how the Black English practices within hip-hop texts offer windows into the social politics and situated worlds of artists and engage students in critical analysis, self-reflection, and argumentation around relevant issues.

When we usher Black English out of the shadows of white supremacist colonial logics that discredit its value, we also have the opportunity to illuminate its power of mass appeal globally and, by extension, its power to appeal to the deep engagement of students who are otherwise disengaged in the classroom. The saturation of Black English throughout popular culture, advertising, and marketing is evidence of its social currency as a mode of influence and engagement. In an increasingly globalized society where popular culture has massive influence and impact, this facet of Black power available within Black English cannot be ignored. In 2012, Alim and Smitherman wrote a book exploring

Black Language and race in the US through an analysis of Barack Obama's position as president of the United States. Dubbing President Obama "orator-in-chief," the book examines the racial politics of language and centers on the power of some of his "Blackest" rhetorical and linguistic exchanges while in office. For example, during an exchange in Chicago's Ben's Chili Bowl, Obama engaged in *styleshifting* with his response to the cashier, "Nah, we straight" (Alim & Smitherman, 2012, p. 5). Alim and Smitherman unpack the social and political currency connected to Obama's ability to access the language practices of Black communities as well as the West African linguistic features (such as copula absence) that show up in those three little Black English words. This speaks to the power of Black English to not only create paths of access and influence but also to tap into a West African heritage that persists even in our contemporary uses of Black Language.

Critical English educators have moved beyond silencing Black English and perpetuating the message that it is broken or inferior in their classrooms. Yet the mere presence of Black English in the "less-rigorous" places in our curriculum as we adhere to increasingly marginalizing standards undermines the goal of truly valuing the power of Black English. To truly disrupt the ethos of the English classroom, English educators must move beyond valuing Black English at the surface level and turn toward it as a powerful discredited knowledge with the capacity to transform the educational lives of students. When released from the grips of anti-Black linguistic racism through critical perspectives, Black English reveals the power of Black interior worlds, Black English reveals the power of Black influence, and Black English reveals the power of Black heritage knowledge to shape teaching and learning.

Note

1. Based on the 2019 National Assessment of Educational Progress (NAEP) Reading Assessment.

References

Alim, H. S. (2011). Global ill-literacies: Hip hop cultures, youth identities, and the politics of literacy. *Review of Research in Education, 35*(1), 120–146.

Alim, H. S., & Smitherman, G. (2012). *Articulate while Black: Barack Obama, language, and race in the U.S.* Oxford University Press.

Baker-Bell, A. (2013). "I never really knew the history behind African American language": Critical language pedagogy in an advanced placement English language arts class. *Equity & Excellence in Education, 46*(3), 355–370.

Baker-Bell, A. (2019). Dismantling anti-Black linguistic racism in English language arts classrooms: Toward an anti-racist Black language pedagogy. *Theory Into Practice, 59*(1), 8–21.

Baker-Bell, A. (2020). *Linguistic justice: Black language, literacy, identity, and pedagogy.* Routledge.

Bigelow, W. (1987–1988). Education in South Africa: Challenging "gutter education." *Rethinking Schools, 2*(2), 8–9. https://rethinkingschools.org/articles/education-in-south-africa-challenging-gutter-education/

Boutte, G. S., King, J. E., Johnson, G. L., & King, L. J. (Eds.). (2021). *We be lovin' Black children: Learning to be literate about the African diaspora.* Myers Education Press.

Carmichael, S., & Hamilton, C. V. (1967). *Black power: The politics of liberation in America.* Random House.

Givens, J. R. (2021). *Fugitive pedagogy: Carter G. Woodson and the art of Black teaching.* Harvard University Press.

Haddix, M. M. (2012). Talkin' in the company of my sistas: The counterlanguages and deliberate silences of Black female students in teacher education. *Linguistics and Education, 23*(2), 169–181.

Hill, M. L. (2009). *Beats, rhymes, and classroom life: Hip-hop pedagogy and the politics of identity.* Teachers College Press.

Kinloch, V. F. (2005). Revisiting the promise of "students' right to their own language": Pedagogical strategies. *College Composition & Communication, 57*(1), 83–113.

Ligon, T. (2016, June 7). *"Turn this town out": Stokely Carmichael, black power, and the march against fear.* Rediscovering Black History.

https://rediscovering-black-history.blogs.archives.gov/2016/06/07/turn-this-town-out-stokely-carmichael-black-power-and-the-march-against-fear/

Lyiscott, J. (2025). Decolonial and fugitive literacies. In *The encyclopedia of applied linguistics*. Wiley. https://doi.org/10.1002/9781405198431.wbeal20263

Makoni, S., Smitherman, G., Ball, A., & Spears, A. (Eds.). (2003). *Black linguistics: Language, society, and politics in Africa and the Americas.* Routledge.

Morrell, E. (2005). Critical English education. *English Education, 37*(4), 312–321.

Morrison, T. (1984). Memory, creation, and writing. *Thought: Fordham University Quarterly, 59*(4), 385–390.

Phaswana, N. E. (2003). *Contradiction or affirmation? The South African language policy and the South African national government.* In S. Makoni, G. Smitherman, A. F. Ball, & A. K. Spears (Eds.), *Black linguistics* (pp. 117-131). Routledge.

Smitherman, G. (1972). "Black power is black language." In G. M. Simmons, H. D. Hutchinson, & H. E. Simmons (Eds.), *Black culture: Reading and writing black* (pp. 85–91). Holt, Rinehart and Winston.

Smitherman, G. (1977). *Talkin and testifyin: The language of black America.* Wayne State University Press.

Smitherman, G. (2000). *Talkin that talk: Language, culture, and education in African America.* Routledge.

TEDx. (2018, May 23). *Why English class is silencing students of color | Jamila Lyiscott* [Video]. YouTube. https://www.youtube.com/watch?v=u4dc1axRwE4

Yosso , T. J. (2005). Whose culture has capital? A critical race theory discussion of community cultural wealth. *Race Ethnicity and Education, 8*(1), 69–91.

Young, V. A. (2007). *Your average nigga: Performing race, literacy, and masculinity.* Wayne State University Press.

CHAPTER TWELVE

Five E's of Rehumanizing Critical Literacy Pedagogy

LAURENCE TAN

Context: The Past 25 Years as an Urban Educator

I am in my twenty-fifth year of credentialed teaching and have been primarily in upper grade (third through fifth) elementary the entire time. Within those years, I have served urban communities of Watts, South Central Los Angeles, and East Oakland, which boasts a predominantly Black and Latinx demographic in marginalized communities. The school districts I have taught in mandate literacy curricula that they purchase, and they create a pacing plan that is enforced. In this chapter, I uplift student voices and experiences from the most recent years since the pandemic while also drawing from teaching experiences, pedagogies, and practices throughout my twenty-five years of teaching and learning.

Overstating the Problem

The state of literacy education in urban centers where I have taught has not changed throughout my twenty-five-plus years of student and credentialed teaching. Over this time, schools and school districts have purchased and changed curriculum, sometimes as often as every five years. And within that span, the same issues and challenges have been prevalent across schools and districts when considering the "success" of BIPOC (Black, Indigenous, People of Color) communities by standardized measures. Paulo Freire and Donaldo Macedo (1987) would refer to this as the illiteracy of literacy, where literacy is not based on the experiences of the learner but instead where students should be agents of their own education, not just recipients of dominant knowledge.

In 2020, COVID-19 altered the face of education. Educators scrambled to create and adjust to teaching exclusively online. Creative tactics, such as incorporating innovative technologies and strategies, had forced us to figure out how to reengage students in meaningful ways. Gloria Ladson-Billings (2021) mentioned how this was the opportunity to reexamine and redesign how education could and should be; instead, schools and districts couldn't wait to go "back to business as usual" as soon as possible. Because of many factors, including the previously stated, our students have been playing "catch-up" ever since "learning loss" became the topic of conversation. Ladson-Billings (2021) notes that

> Although many educators and policymakers insist that we have to "get back to normal," I want to suggest that "going back" is the wrong thing for children and youth who were unsuccessful and oppressed in our schools before the pandemic. Normal is where the problems reside. (p. 68)

The following academic year (2020–2021) presented a seismic struggle and challenge for my colleagues, the communities I served, comrades, and me. Not only were we all going through the pandemic, which rocked us in almost every facet of life, but the world was exposed to our historic treatment of Black folks in the highly publicized George Floyd murder. Out of these significant moments, we had an opportunity to fully reimagine, recreate, and transform how our nation would move forward toward healing from these incidents, but instead, we rushed and hurried back to "normal."

This was wholeheartedly felt in the field of education. As soon as students were able to come back to school in person, testing, and programs centered around it, resumed. Funds were allocated to support "learning loss," which allowed for reading tutors and other positions to further make sure we got back to "grade level." However, the funding for extra support was limited and has run its course. COVID-19 monies for extra staffing and supplies have halted, causing some positions to be closed, and no budget remains for things like paper towels and tissues in classrooms. The onus was placed on the teachers and their families to fill these gaps. This narrative of the haves and have-nots in schools has long been told, only now it has a slightly different spin on it with COVID-19.

In the aftermath of George Floyd's murder, initiatives emerged to address the centuries of mistreatment of Black folks, with variations depending on the cities implementing them. To the credit of the school district I teach in, Oakland Unified School District (OUSD) was one of only two school districts in California to create a Black Reparations Initiative. In this initiative, task forces were created to abolish oppressive structures in the district that highly impacted Black students and families, creating conditions that promoted Black students and families thriving in and out of schools. One of the overall goals of the district initiative is to abolish oppressive structures.

OUSD's Reparations for Black Students—Resolution No. 2021-0037 states:

> WHEREAS, OUSD seeks to take immediate action to stop and repair the harm to Black children and families caused by decades of structural racism and also by the differential impact of COVID-19 on Black communities by creating a targeted plan to monitor and invest federal, state, county and local funds for Black Students and for Thriving Community Schools in Black communities.

This is a necessary and worthwhile task that OUSD is undertaking by meeting with stakeholders to develop measures for Black students and families regarding reparations and thriving matters. However, structural racism also includes how we have approached education and how we continue to do so within a "business as usual" model. April Baker-Bell (2020) suggests an antiracist Black language pedagogy as an approach that English language arts teachers can implement in an effort to dismantle anti-Black linguistic racism and white cultural and linguistic hegemony in their classrooms. Yet that isn't the case. If ongoing educational models and approaches continue to yield the same results, demonstrating that predominantly BIPOC students—particularly Black students and families—are "failing" or have "failed," then why do we keep using the same methods and approaches? The one thing that seems to have changed over time is the increasing rate of teacher burnout and pushout.

Over the years, I have experienced various shifts in scripted literacy curriculum to be more culturally relevant. As more and more curriculum companies and school districts have tried to forefront BIPOC learners and their representation, what teachers and students are receiving is a "wolf in sheep's clothing" approach. Purchased curriculum cursorily incorporates BIPOC representation and selections but continues to use the same structures, tasks, and lessons as before. Instead, utilizing antiracist Black language pedagogy provides a framework for teachers that recognizes and includes our varied language learners (Black English, African American English, Chicanx English, etc.) in our English language arts, which can dismantle white cultural and linguistic hegemony (Baker-Bell, 2020).

Along this line of thinking, the curriculum has started to incorporate core narratives featuring BIPOC characters, such as Esperanza Rising and Jackie Robinson. These narratives engage with themes that many culturally responsive educators are likely to endorse, including human rights, women's suffrage, and education across global contexts. However, the teaching approaches, structural frameworks, tasks, and pacing remain largely consistent with practices that have been in place for at least twenty-five years.

When I entered the teaching profession, "culturally relevant" was the key buzzword. My school district in Southern California invested significantly to ensure our libraries were filled with diverse faces and authors that reflected our student population. They hoped this would enhance test scores, but like many promising initiatives—such as "growth mindset" and social-emotional learning—they ultimately fell short in terms of genuine intention and effective implementation. The notion that my students would improve their literacy scores or develop a love for reading simply because we had a copy of Will Smith's book, *Just the Two of Us*, did little to foster engagement, care, or investment in reading or our reading programs.

A New Coat of Paint Doesn't Make the Engine Run Any Better

Over twenty-five years ago, culturally relevant pedagogy became the prevailing trend in education. Districts embraced programs and resources with the belief that materials featuring faces that reflected those of their students would lead to improved test scores. This notion was similarly carried forward with the introduction of culturally responsive pedagogy. Amid these shifts, though, many failed to grasp the deeper significance of these approaches. It was often those innovative educators, willing to explore and engage deeply with the true essence of both pedagogies, who recognized that the impact extended far beyond simply having relatable faces, artifacts, and creators.

Currently, the stakes are even higher for our BIPOC communities, yet districts continue to use the same tactics, resulting in all-too-familiar outcomes.

The "all-in-one" approach to a literacy program shortchanges instruction to monopolize the school day. Most purchased curriculum programs will have daily lesson plans that span ninety minutes to three hours on paper and in a vacuum. Yet in practice, much of the planning actually takes more than that to fully implement each designed component. To compensate for the monopoly of instructional minutes, companies will deftly include units that embed science and social studies units to allow educators to check those subjects off. Educators can shy away from designated time to wrap their heads around and teach those subjects because it is covered in their literacy program. If the teacher chooses this route (which many do), this approach shortchanges the experiences of students to engage in deeper and more meaningful curriculum in the areas of science and social studies. Even more, it shoots down the "out-of-the-box" opportunities for lessons and learning on technology, ethnic studies, social-emotional learning, mindfulness, and wellness.

Currently, our district has adopted another scripted curriculum that is very culturally responsive to urban populations. Many of the themes and even book selections are great; I've used some of the books in my own personal practice over my years of teaching. However, many of the tasks, lessons, and activities are very much the same as other scripted literacy programs. It just doesn't engage youth or make learning helpful to students—these remain tasks to be completed simply to receive grades (see Figure 1 below).

Now, I am not saying that there isn't value in this or any other bought program. When I helped to design and open a school, I made the mistake in thinking that every educator needed to create their own literacy curriculum that took into account state standards and the needs of their students, choosing their own key texts to center their curriculum on. It was something I was constantly doing for many years of teaching. So initially, when we opened up the school, everyone struggled. Not everyone had experience and had developed a "bag of resources." I even realized that I had always based my curriculum on a mandated one.

Starting with an adopted curriculum is *not* the problem. Rather, the problem is that schools and districts adhere to the rigidity of the program, layer seemingly unrealistic pacing plans, and do not allow for flexibility (even with solid "standards-based" decisions, alterations, and supplements).

I highlight one example—a unit on the rainforest for fifth graders. The topic itself is engaging and has the potential to be responsive, to infuse social justice and ethnic studies elements, to be cross-curricular with science, and to include supplemental

GRADES K-5 LANGUAGE ARTS
Module Topics

	Module 1	Module 2	Module 3	Module 4
Kindergarten	Toys and Play	Weather Wonders	Trees are Alive	Enjoying and Appreciating Trees
Grade 1	Tools and Work	The Sun, Moon, and Stars	Birds' Amazing Bodies	Caring for Birds
Grade 2	Schools and Community	Fossils Tell of Earth's Changes	The Secret World of Pollination	Providing for Pollinators
Grade 3	Overcoming Learning Challenges Near and Far	Adaptations and the Wide World of Frogs	Exploring Literary Classics	Water Around the World
Grade 4	Poetry, Poets and Becoming Writers	Animal Defense Mechanisms	The American Revolution	Responding to Inequality: Ratifying the 19th Amendment
Grade 5	Stories of Human Rights	Biodiversity in the Rainforest	Athlete Leaders of Social Change	The Impact of Natural Disasters

FIGURE 1.

resources both old and current. Many great core curricular texts could have been used to hit the program goals to cover particular standards. Yet the book chosen for the unit has been the most disengaging, non-culturally responsive selection based on years of student and teacher input. The book does have its merits as a resource for rainforest biodiversity research, but it isn't good enough to sustain fifth graders for a whole unit. Moreover, the narrative writing task asks students to create a first-person narrative from the perspective of the main character's sons as they venture into the canopy of a rainforest.

Students already struggle with engaging in writing tasks in general. Asking them to relate to characters they could not care less about in a story that they are not connected to is an instant "game over."

In my experience, one of the keys to successful and engaging writing is to center it on each student's experiences and interests. Aligning student experience and interest with my purpose to critically serve their needs allowed us to create a third space together, "where teacher and student scripts intersect, . . . creating the potential for authentic interactions and a shift in the social organization of learning and what counts as knowledge" (Gutiérrez, 2008, p. 152). I have done cross-curricular units like Create Your Own Pokémon or Develop Your Own Comic Book or Graphic Novel. Asking students to create autoethnographies or even their own novels through the NaNoWriMo (National Novel Writing Month) Project led me to see their genuine and active participation rate greatly increase. Whether students were tapping into their youth culture by creating, designing, and writing their own Pokémon or comic origin stories, creating their own novel based on whatever genre they were interested in, or focusing on a powerful moment that greatly impacted them and connecting it to what was happening around them at the time, the students were centered in the projects, activities, and tasks. Personal connections were drawn from and validated. Aligning student experience and interest with my purpose to critically serve their needs allowed us to create a third space together, where "teacher and students scripts intersect, creating the potential for authentic interactions and a shift in the social organization of learning and what counts as knowledge" (Gutiérrez, 2008, p. 152).

In 2009, I wrote a piece about my pedagogy and practice in the *Handbook of Social Justice in Education* titled "The 5 E's of Emancipatory Pedagogy." The embodiment of my pedagogy centered around Engage, Educate, Experience, Empower, and Enact. These components were evidenced in my planning, construction, and delivery of every aspect of my teaching. Heavier emphasis was placed on the Engage, Educate, and Experience portions, but all aspects were touched upon in any given lesson or unit. Eleven years later, the Five E's still hold strong, and I will focus on how this pedagogy specifically applies to critical literacy.

Five E's of Emancipatory Literacy

Engage

This component is the most weighted. This requires a genuine investment in what students are into, consuming, and ultimately, learning from. Based on the knowledge that students already have, an educator can turn youth culture into powerful literacy and learning moments. You can utilize these moments to cover foundational standards-based activities and develop critical literacy skills for the youth to "read the world and the word," as Paulo Freire said (1987). Students are already making sense of the things around them, so why not help to facilitate the correlations, connections, and skill-building?

The following is a sample of students' voices, based on a reading and reading reflection done with a recent class (2023–2024):

> *Key*
> **EL Ed** is our district adopted reading program.
>
> **SIPPS** is an intervention reading program that supports students in acquiring fluency.
>
> **iReady** is a reading and math supplemental computer program that is adaptive to a diagnostic score.
>
> **Diagnostic** testing is frequent throughout the trimesters and year.

DT, fifth grader

I don't like our school reading program because they gave us the most boring book in the world, The Most Beautiful Roof in the World. *I'm not in SIPPS. I'm in the highest reading group in our school, and I hate iReady for some reason. My least favorite thing about reading being taught in school is the diagnostic.*

FSJ, fifth grader

My personal thought on reading is I don't like it because of big words, and sometimes my head starts hurting.

KW, fifth grader

My thoughts and feelings about reading is . . . most of the time, it's boring.

My genuine thoughts and feelings about reading taught in school are that they make us read the most boring books ever.

My least favorite part about how reading is taught is that we have to do iReady.

AA, fifth grader

My thoughts and feelings about reading in general are that I don't really like reading because I think it's boring and just generally not fun.

My genuine thoughts and feelings about how reading is being taught in school is that I like some of the books we read in reading groups, but most books I don't like.

My least favorite part about how reading is being taught in school is doing the test because they're really stressful.

PB, fifth grader

In my opinion, reading is fun when you choose to read, but when the teacher or your mom tells you to read, it doesn't feel fun because you're forced to.

I don't like reading programs on computers like iReady. It is kiddish and not to the point. It has tons of extra steps that are not reasonable. I would like it if it were simple. I like SIPPS because we are all on the same level, so we can read and grow together.

There are tons of things that make me excited to read. For me, I have a hard time finding books that I enjoy, so when I find one that makes me excited to read it over and over again and maybe even other books from that writer.

TW, fifth grader

I do not like iReady and stuff like that makes you do a test because I do not like researching things unless it is looking into something I want to, like looking into police harassment against black people instead of looking into some boring old white lady.

My least favorite part about when reading is taught is when there is a diagnostic or when we have to read a super long book that is boring.

FS, fifth grader

I like reading and all but I hate!!!!!!!! when people tell me to read, also when it's information and word books.

I think when reading is put on EL Ed, and SIPPS, etc. It's boring no matter what.

I don't have any favorite things about reading in school or how it's taught.

GF, fifth grader

My genuine thoughts and feelings about reading being taught here is that it's kinda interesting and I kind of like it except when it's a boring or racist book.

JKE, fifth grader

My thoughts and feelings about reading can be good and bad. Good because I could be reading a very interesting book. Bad because I could be reading something boring.

My least favorite part of how reading is taught is that some people don't feel interested in reading the book, but they force them to read the book, even though they're not interested.

Something I would suggest to make learning better is to make sure students are reading the book they want to read.

Things that make me interested to read are reading graphic novels because I can actually see pictures, and sports books because I love sports.

AI, fifth grader

My thoughts about reading are bad, and when I read, I feel like my blood is boiling because I don't feel like reading.

My least favorite part about how reading is taught in school is when they want to make us read hard stuff.

I would suggest making teaching and learning reading better by making us read some fun stuff like song lyrics.

The things that make me excited about reading are nothing because reading is not my thing, it makes me really nervous, and when I pronounce something wrong I feel embarrassed, but it's okay.

TDA, fifth grader

My genuine thoughts and feelings about reading in school are that it's good, but there are some points of improvement in the curriculum, like if we could choose what we read and we could share ideas about the book.

My least favorite part about reading is that we can't choose the books.

I don't have anything to suggest about the reading and learning except that we should vote on the book we read.

There needs to be accountability across multiple decision-makers. Policy-makers, leaders, schools, educators, and adopted curricula need to reevaluate what are considered meaningful texts and worthwhile selections. Critical pedagogues would count multimedia and what's around (advertisements, posters, neighborhood landscape) as text. Comic books and graphic novels currently are highly engaging physical texts that often are overlooked and not included, yet can offer the same literacy and critical literacy opportunities in a more youth-consumable package. Even though it is not in scripted curriculum, students gravitate toward this medium more by choice. You can cover the same sort of standards-based skills but in ways that truly excite and validate students' choices.

Often, schools and educators demonize and dissuade popular trends that youth gravitate toward. Negative judgments are made regarding popular youth culture. If students are too into it, schools tend to ban it or take it away the moment things get "out of hand," and yet we force-feed students what they should be consuming and reading. Even with the best of intentions—because it's culturally relevant, responsive, a classic, our favorite, it's part of our curriculum, or we feel it's what's best for our students—education stifles youth engagement, agency, and overall buy-in. Instead of shutting down youth from what they like, you can highly engage them and equip them with academic and critical skills to make better-informed decisions for themselves. In doing so, moreover, you can harness and transfer those developing skills to traditional text and print.

Engagement falls into the levels of trust and respect we develop with students. The more we can earn, the more willing they are to trust us and what we may bring to the table. One of the best ways to do this would be to invest heavily in what the students are into in genuine ways. Why is Monster High or Pokémon back in popularity with our youth? When did "skibbidi toilet" and Gen Z slang dominate the active conversation among youth? How did the term "sus"—short for "suspect," which became popular during the pandemic with the *Among Us* video game—get merged with "baka," which is a popular Japanese word for "idiot" used frequently in Japanese anime (also a genre of media consumption heightened during the pandemic), to form a popular youth phrase "sussy baka"? "Sussy baka" not only became a popular phrase with youth but was heavily coded to become a homophobic slur, all because it had gone viral on TikTok. In investing time and energy to learn both from youth and for youth, you can see how deeply complex it can get. How can we use what we learn about youth culture to genuinely create opportunities and meaningful learning experiences that can build youth's literacies and skills?

Through authentic engagement moments, students and student wellness are genuinely validated. Trust and respect are further developed on a deeper level, and students are more apt to be in a position to learn from the educator.

Educate

This component refers to a balance between developing crucial foundational literacy skills with multifaceted critical literacy skills. Learning and teaching literacy doesn't always have to come from a standardized system, curriculum, expert, or physical text. Harnessing the ability to "read the world" and incorporate lived experiences in social and cultural situations creates entry points into academics that allow students to develop tangible skills.

Experience

We need to recognize that our students come in with a variety of lived experiences that they have learned from, just as much as educators do. Yet as soon as students start an academic literacy block, we rush to fill every minute teaching and cramming skills for them to master with varying degrees of success. Schools create opportunities for intervention because students are far below grade level in reading, taking over more of the school day. Therefore, a student's school experience can be filled with disengaging traditional literacy learning moments. But by tapping into a more robust and whole student-centered literacy learning experience, educators can continue to build their genuine base knowledge of their students and can bring in, invite, and create spaces and moments for students to experience literacy through different lenses and ways of doing.

This is a two-way street in growing experience. We, as educators, need to build our capacity to receive from our students, strengthen and add to our experience with each other, and truly invest in students' interests in and out of school. We must do right by them by incorporating what we experience and learn from this process directly back into our practice, curriculum, and class. If we can do this effectively enough, our students will be more open to new experiences we present to them.

Empower

Instead of replacing youth culture, we are validating and showing ways to help students make sense of what they are already highly engaged in and consuming, which is reading and comprehending words and the world. Recognizing their expertise and building critical skills and tools to solidify it gives students agency.

I do a comic and graphic novel unit or lesson series. We take the comics and graphic novels that students are already reading and critically analyze them. Students easily identify standards-based elements like story plot, theme, figurative language, author's and artist's purpose, and more. They also develop their critical thinking and problem-solving literacy skills by analyzing how characters are represented, aspects of leadership and heroism, issues of race and gender, how body types are portrayed, and more. Once we engage, educate, and validate the students, they gain experience and skills that transfer over to other forms of literature. More importantly, students have authentically bought in and are ready for more. We tackle other comics like political cartoons from Dr. Seuss and his commentary on the Japanese during World War II juxtaposed with George Takei's graphic novel *They Called Us Enemy*. Or we stay community responsive and tackle excerpts from Tony Medina's graphic novel *I Am Alphonso Jones,* which addresses police and gun violence. From there, students go through a variety of lessons that transform them from mere consumers of this form of literature and media to critical producers (Duncan-Andrade & Morrell, 2008). They take the skills they have acquired and create their own comic book or graphic novel that centers aspects of themselves directly or indirectly. The literacy learning that students engage in becomes meaningful in real-time ways as they are empowered to create.

Enact

Once students have developed critical literacy skills throughout the 5 E's process, they also develop civic responsibility and efficacy. Students develop their agency along with their skills, and this allows them to create transformative actions that are imbued with greater purpose because the students have spearheaded these actions themselves.

How often are students made to use their skills to apply to meaningful real-life tasks? The overarching message in schools is that students should learn to read so they can do well on tests, get good grades, and try to go to college. Many students and their families buy into that narrative, and it can become a motivating factor to put forth energy and effort. However, it's not always the case. So, how do we make literacy practice and usefulness tangible within the realities that many students face?

The following examples answer this question by showing students drawing on their personal connections to world events and using their agency to create change and awareness.

Current global situations should not be swept under the rug. They are a *key* opportunity for developing critical literacy and agency skills. Just as the tragedy of George Floyd and others called for mass movements, it was a call to action in the classroom, as well. For our students, it was the spark for highly engaging activities that provoked them to study history, make critical connections, and engage in high-level literacy. Today, the same can be said for what is happening in regards to Palestine. Students are asking questions, are interested in learning the truth, and want to do their part to affect action and change.

Our entire fifth-grade class conducted a similar project as Rethinking Columbus's *The People vs. Columbus et al.* Our students completed *The People vs. Israel*, which had them reading, writing, and unpacking all sides of the situation in order to create their claims and defenses. The activity met fifth-grade content standards, but the students were motivated to perform at a higher level because the they wanted to, and because they had a say in what they were doing.

When It's Not Broken . . . Tweak It

Paulo Freire was able to teach literacy centered around what people experienced and were heavily involved in on a regular daily basis. He validated what people came in with and he met folks at their level. People make attempts to replicate that practice but tend to miss the mark with today's youth because there is a cultural disconnect from the students. I found myself in that situation in my second year of teaching when trying to create a literacy lesson using hip-hop that I listened to instead of going straight to the hip-hop music my students were listening to. That day, I learned to always genuinely invest time and energy in participating, learning, questioning, and having dialogue with my students about the things that they engage in. That meant consuming the same things that they did regardless of my thoughts and critiques.

Authentically Meaningful Learning Opportunities

The concept of "the classics" no longer applies in this day and age, because in this TikTok generation, trends rapidly change and so do the students' influences. You can be pretty "up on game" or aware of what is trending one week but then quickly be out of date the following weeks all at the speed of a viral TikTok. And while you may never understand what's going on, students are heavily consuming trends and making them part of their everyday. An educator does not have to always master every nuance of trending youth culture; however, it is crucial for that educator to open themselves up for moments to participate in dialogue, teachable moments, and moments to be taught or "put on game." More powerfully, an educator can take being "put on game" and create meaningful learning and teaching moments, activities, lessons, and units that invite their students to authentically participate.

Authentically engaging today's youth in critical literacies becomes an educator's deep investment in those they serve. Complete immersion into trends, language, and cultural phenomena requires intensive attention. And while using hip-hop to support learning is still responsive, educators need to go beyond that to include TikTok, AI, anime, and more.

Regardless of the many critical literacy opportunities that youth culture provides us with, the one thing that has mattered in all my twenty-five years of teaching has been the notion that *if it is meaningful to students, they will buy in, engage, and be up to the challenge.*

Infusing Critical Literacy Opportunities with Youth Culture

The reality educators face is that they will be given curriculum to use with some level of fidelity. Progress and pacing checks are normalized to make sure educators are held accountable to the district's investment. With that said, there are many opportunities within the curriculum and standards to create genuine critical literacy moments for students with some effort from the teacher.

Ernest Morrell and Jeff Duncan-Andrade would pair Shakespeare with 2Pac. Fortunately for me, throughout the twenty-five years of my teaching career, Drake has been in and out of what's trending and popular. In most years, we selectively analyze the lyrics to his discography to tackle foundational, standards-based literacy skills: figurative language, imagery, metaphors and similes, themes, motifs, and author's purpose. We start with his and Trey Songz's song "Successful" to analyze their definition of success and what might have influenced it, which allows students to define or redefine their own idea of success, and ultimately come to a community definition based on varying critical considerations. We then look at other Drake songs throughout his career and continue to analyze themes and motifs as we do an extensive "author's study" over time. Throughout the course of this unit or lesson series, we tackle vocabulary and concepts like misogyny, hegemony, social reproduction, indoctrination, and more.

This type of critical literacy unit, lesson sequence, or lesson plan works if you have the flexibility to teach what you want; however, that is not the case for the majority of teaching conditions. To teach like lives depend on it, Camangian (2015) suggests that teachers "focus more on developing transformative practices rather than the pressures of high-stakes testing . . . [and to] ground . . . their teaching in the articulated needs of their students . . . and treat [their] students' worlds as assets worthy of social analysis and intellectual introspection" (p. 449). With curriculum expected to be followed and carried out as written, lessons like the aforementioned Drake ones must be strategically and creatively woven into the pockets and spaces in a "supplementary" way.

Take for instance my current teaching situation. Just after winter break, we start our third module centered around the theme "Athlete Leaders for Social Change." The main core literature assigned is *Promises to Keep,* which is a biographical account of Jackie Robinson from the perspective of his daughter. The text covers several critical considerations—namely, cultural relevance and responsiveness and opportunities for critical literacy skills—and can be highly engaging for my students.

The curriculum has natural entry points that allow me to supplement and slot in my lessons with Drake due to the tasks and activities it presents. Tasks include finding evidence from the text to show Jackie Robinson's factors and motivation for success. So, before doing the "book task," I recreated the worksheet from the curriculum and had students do the same task but by analyzing Drake and Trey Songz's "Successful" instead. Students were highly engaged and bought into the activity. After doing so, they were able to better engage and independently do the same task with Jackie Robinson and interact with the *Promises to Keep* book. We then took it a step further and filled out a "double bubble map" graphic organizer to compare and contrast Jackie's motivation and ideals about success with that of Drake and Trey Songz. Ultimately, this led to a critical writeup and overall opinion piece about what success was for the people we analyzed and what it was for us as a classroom community.

There are ample opportunities to be able to do similar work within a given curriculum. The standards are broad enough to be able to "supplement" curriculum that is grounded not only in genuine grade-level academics but, more importantly, in authentic youth culturally relevant and responsive critical literacy moments that engage students in meaningful academic experiences.

Using Drake in my English language arts curriculum has always been a highlight for my classes and has easily been among the most remembered class lessons throughout the years. Even when Drake falls out of popularity, he has always been trending enough for students to feel connected to him. There was one moment when my student approached Jeff Duncan-Andrade and a group of adults touring our school and definitively proclaimed that Drake was hegemonic and walked away. That same year, the summer after my students had graduated, a mother texted me and said, "What did you do to my child?" Naturally, not knowing the context, I responded, "It's not my fault." She went on to tell me that her daughter was coming home from a program, listening to music on her Beats headphones, and did not respond to her mother's questions of "How was your day?" and "What's going on?" Instead, that student brushed off her mom and told her she had to quickly find some paper and pen because she needed to write down the messages and analyze the song that she was listening to, which she "blamed" me for teaching her. Genuine meaningful skills can be developed because of the critical considerations an educator makes in choosing what and how they incorporate youth culture into the classroom.

The bottom line is that (a) it can be done, (b) students will be heavily engaged because the lesson speaks genuinely to them, and (c) they will thank you for it to the point that they will continue to trust and respect you enough to see what else you have in store for them.

YPAR: The Culminating Critical Literacy Project

I have worked with many students ranging from fourth grade to college, having them conduct youth participatory action research (YPAR) projects in which they identify issues in their communities that they want to research and work on. They ground themselves in theories, conduct extensive research, collect data (interviews, surveys, and more), synthesize findings, create media, suggest solutions, and present their research. Most of these YPAR projects were multigenerational, mixing high schoolers with middle and elementary students, and allowed for some authentic critical community apprenticeship models to develop.

In the early months of 2024, I decided to conduct a YPAR project with a group of fifth graders that culminated with them presenting as a selected presidential session at the American Education Research Association's annual meeting. Unlike all the YPAR projects beforehand, there were no veteran high schoolers or even experienced middle schoolers to help scaffold and support my group of students. What kept these fifth graders motivated was the idea that the work and challenges asked of them were meaningful and worthwhile to them, their families, their school, and their community.

In my reading group, which was composed of eighteen fifth graders of various reading levels, we used that period to introduce YPAR and then jump into our YPAR project: looking into the equity of Oakland Schools and critically analyzing OUSD's Thriving Black Students and Families Taskforce as part of the

Reparations for Black Students Resolution that stemmed from the George Floyd resolution.

One of the main texts the fifth graders had to tackle, and genuinely struggled with, was Jeff Duncan-Andrade's book *Equality or Equity*. The book served as their main literature review, along with documents from the school district about the Black Reparations Initiative.

The entire group worked together on the first chapter: being introduced to rigorous text, making sense, and learning how to make connections to their realities. They were able to prioritize their interests into three main categories: relationships, relevance, and responsibility. Students were broken into those three groups and focused on the chapters in the book that aligned with their interest; they identified recurring themes and looked for instances that confirmed, countered, or complexified those themes. They conducted expert interviews with Dr. Pedro Noguera, Dr. Gloria Ladson-Billings, Dr. Augustine Romero, Dr. Tyrone Howard, Dr. Tiffani Marie, and Dr. Ann Milne. They also conducted numerous stakeholder interviews with school staff, district employees, families, and even students.

Students devoted themselves to seeing this project through to the very end. They were willing to work extra hours after school, and they even Zoomed into sessions for a few hours a day during their week-long spring break. The project was made more meaningful knowing that a handful were traveling to Philadelphia to present at a national conference, but students also did so knowing they would not be able to travel with us. Students felt the weight of the task asked of them, had their moments, and were even given opportunities to step down from the project. However, despite their struggles and challenges personally and as a group, every student stayed on to finish the project. We had students who were several levels below grade level in reading who flourished when challenged to tackle complex text far beyond their level. When all was said and done, it boiled down to genuine and authentic engagement, meaningful purpose, and complete buy-in.

Within this YPAR project, there were many opportunities for the students to develop their critical and standard literacy skills, their transformative and personal skills, and to use these skills in authentically meaningful and applicable ways. This project was not for a grade, not for an assessment, and not a means to appease the teacher. This project was for them, their school, their family, and their community. And that made the most difference.

The following are a sampling of student reflection responses on the YPAR experience, process, and comparisons to their regular literacy education.

AA, fifth grader

To do college-level work was hard because it felt very stressful, but with adults helping me made me feel more better. It motivated me because I knew this was important work that I was doing and that a lot of people were believing in me.

What made doing this project BETTER than doing normal reading lessons from the book is that it was actually meaningful not like Sara has four cookies she wants to equally distribute them, something like that. This is why I think it's more important.

I think it was important because we are young, and we were doing important work about reparations, and we were a part of the first ethnic studies meeting, I think that's what it's called.

BK, fifth grader

It felt tough to do college-level texts, and that is why it motivated me to do all the work. I did it even though it was super hard, and it motivated me to stay in the group because I couldn't just quit on them, and also I just wanted to help and do the work.

What made this project better was that I was learning college-level work, and also I liked how it challenged me to do the work.

My favorite part of the process was working together as a team.

DT, fifth grader

I chose to stay involved because I wanted to show people that we need reparations in schools and that equity in school is important for POC (people of color).

To be doing college-level work I felt very proud of myself because in the beginning I felt like there was no way I could do this, but when I started, I just got this boost of confidence that told me it was possible and that I could do it.

In my experience, doing this project was better than just reading the regular books.

EG, fifth grader

Why I stay involved with the YPAR Project is that I want to change the way schools push away the students' needs and wants. I was sad that I had to give up my spring break to do work, but if I had to give up my spring break to do work if it helps to better the education of students, then it's fine.

What made it better from doing a normal reading is that we are doing something to help or change the educational system where what we did was just follow what they wanted us to do, but we told them what we wanted to do, and that what made it better.

I do think the work that we did was important because if we didn't do this project, then who would, and the student voice needs to be heard.

JEK, fifth grader

I chose to stay involved with the project because I knew that this was part of a bigger project than many of the others. I also put in that extra work because we were going to influence a lot more teachers or professors than we usually do.

What made doing this project BETTER than doing normal reading lessons was being able to experience learning things that I thought that I would never know (ex. Three Cs of confirming, countering, and complexifying instances), and normal lessons you don't receive the chance. Those lessons just give you information that the school wants you to learn.

The work I did is important because we fifth graders did this work, not PhD professors or teachers—we as kids did this work, and that shows kids can do what we did (hard-level work), not just adults.

NVO, fifth grader

I chose to stay involved with the project because even though I was overwhelmed, stressed, and nervous, I still did it, and I'm really proud that I stayed with the project because it was a good experience, and it made me realize that I am making a change, and

I am doing something that matters to the community and schools. At first, I thought maybe I don't want to do this because it seems like a lot of work, but then somehow I changed my mind, and I stayed, and I was determined to do my best with this project.

I thought that doing college-level texts and reading would be hard, but it wasn't that bad overall. It was actually pretty fun to read college-level texts and reading because I got to get a taste of college a little. It was a good experience.

What made doing this project better than doing normal reading lessons was that we just didn't do normal stuff like in class. We were making a change, we weren't just reading a book. We were reading a college-level book AND making a difference to these school districts.

I think the work I did was important because it will really help school districts by changing the way they teach and making a better community. It will give schools a good impact and a better system.

PB, fifth grader

My overall experience was stressful and challenging BUT it was fun AND important to learn about these things at such a young age!

I chose to stay involved EVEN if it meant giving up my spring break, getting behind in math lessons, AND doing extra work because I was dedicated to fixing these problems that occur in OUSD schools.

Moving Forward: Implications for Educators

We as educators must continue to invest in the students we serve. That means we need to genuinely continue to understand the ever-changing youth culture that our students heavily engage in and understand how loosely fluid it is. In this TikTok generation, where even media producers understand that average attention spans are three minutes nowadays, Japanese cartoon shows are pivoting to a TikTok-like model with three-minute episodes to match youths' attention spans.

On top of that, district pacing plans are incredibly tight, which makes it difficult to always complete novels according to their pacing guides. Many educators, including myself, fall behind and end up moving on to the next module or unit at the expense of never completing literature. Heavy emphasis on cloze reading and "evidence from text"-based skills further encourage truncated passages and excerpts, which are tied to test-taking skills. The messages we are sending to our students about what literacy—much less critical literacy—looks like in the classroom is that it's a very "fast food" model of literacy "dining and digestion." As Freire and Macedo (1987) remind us, literacy is a political act based on the students' material reality and lived experiences. Reading the world and the word is not something you can truncate to an excerpt for literary analysis. Students will continue to miss out on the deeper level skills and meanings that lie outside the short passage.

The YPAR project proved that students can engage with a complex text from start to finish if it holds meaning for them. Throughout the process and in the reflections, the common themes of "making a difference as a kid," "enjoying the challenge with support," and "meaningful work" resonated with the students. Students who were considered "low-reading group," and who had found reading groups disengaging, were not only highly engaged in the reading task and project overall but elevated their abilities to read and, more importantly, read critically when challenged to do so. Research shows that this has tended to be the case, so why not make this more of a common practice throughout schools and districts?

Flexibility: Trusting the Intellectualism of the Students and Educators

Purchased curricula can serve as intentionally thought-out foundations to use as springboards. It is great to have concrete suggestions and considerations, but a curriculum cannot be rigid in its structures, pacing, and planning in a "one-size-fits-all" model that discounts the complexities of each unique situation involving class composition, dynamics, and educators' pedagogies and experience, as well as varying levels and styles. It is great to have programs to draw from with the flexibility to make strategic and intentional adjustments necessary for the situation.

I worked in LAUSD (Los Angeles Unified School District) for fifteen years and was required to use their purchased curriculum at the time. I was also fortunate enough to be allowed to "supplement" the curriculum without any penalties, as long as I could show growth in student achievement and academics via test scores. In that opportunity, I was always creating, designing, and modifying units and lessons that would continue to meet intended standards and learning objectives—but in my own way.

In August of 2015, Roses in Concrete Community School launched, which I helped create with a few folks and Jeff Duncan-Andrade. When asked to design, create, and implement our literacy program, I felt that each teacher should create their own to meet the needs of their particular classes. My initial rationale was that it was hugely successful for me back in LA, so it should not have been a problem moving forward. I was completely wrong, and it was rectified mid-year and throughout the second year. While veteran teachers like myself had enough experience to develop a "bag of tricks" and draw from what had worked for us in the past, our early career staff struggled to create things from scratch or pivot on the fly. Having a foundation to draw from was necessary and essential for teachers with any level of experience; however, the ability to be flexible, and to enhance, supplement, and truly be responsive is crucial.

Student agency in being able to choose what they read and digest is important as well. Instead of forcing students to read a particular selection of books, why not allow them to consume and work on literacy and critical literacy skills that they genuinely engage in? Literacy programs should develop blueprints and structures that encourage students to work on key skills with any text. Anchor texts that model strategies can be from a selection of texts designed to be more responsive to the specific class an educator has, and can support class choice and overall buy-in.

In our constantly changing time, trends move faster than technology becomes outdated. Even theories, pedagogies, and practices that have stood the test of time need to be refreshed and updated to match the ever-changing landscape of youth and youth culture. Educators are asked to be flexible in their roles dealing with their students on a daily basis. It is necessary to have our literacy programs and our education system overall be flexible and allow for flexibility. In doing so, we start to rehumanize literacy with students and for students to authentically engage in all forms of text critically and in meaningful ways. Our marginalized BIPOC students can then begin to receive reparations from their education in transformative ways as they become included and invested in their literacy learning.

References

Baker-Bell, A. (2020). Dismantling anti-Black linguistic racism in English language arts classrooms: Toward an anti-racist Black language pedagogy. *Theory Into Practice, 59*(1), 8–21.

Bigelow, B., Miner, B., & Peterson, B. (Eds.). (1991). *Rethinking Columbus: Teaching about the 500th anniversary of Columbus's arrival in America.* Rethinking Schools in collaboration with the Network of Educators on Central America.

Camangian, P. R. (2013). Seeing through lies: Teaching ideological literacy as a corrective lens. *Equality & Excellence in Education, 46*(1), 119–134.

Camangian, P. R. (2015). Teach like lives depend on it: Agitate, arouse, and inspire. *Urban Education, 50*(4), 424–453.

Drake, & Trey Songz. (2009). Successful [Song]. On *So far gone.* Young Money/Cash Money Records.

Duncan-Andrade, J. M. R. (2022). *Equality or equity: Toward a model of community-responsive education.* Harvard Education Press.

Duncan-Andrade, J., & Morrell, E. (2008). *The art of critical pedagogy.* Peter Lang.

Freire, P., & Macedo, D. (1987). *Literacy: Reading the word and the world.* Routledge.

Gutiérrez, K. (2008). Developing a sociocritical literacy in the Third Space. *Reading Research Quarterly, 43*(2), 148–164.

Ladson-Billings, G. (2021). I'm here for the hard re-set: Post pandemic pedagogy to preserve our culture. *Equity & Excellence in Education, 54*(1), 68–78.

Robinson, S. (2004). *Promises to keep: How Jackie Robinson changed America*. Scholastic.

Tan, L. (2009). The 5 e's of emancipatory pedagogy: The rehumanizing approach to teaching and learning with inner-city youth. In W. Ayers, T. Quinn, & D. Stovall (Eds.), *Handbook of social justice in education* (pp. 485–496). Routledge.

CHAPTER THIRTEEN

A Utopian Vision for Critical English Education

KRIS D. GUTIÉRREZ

On this occasion to think about critical English studies more expansively, I hope to push on current understandings and enactments of critical English education (CEE) and return to some foundational ideas first proffered by Ernest Morrell in 2005 and those advanced in my own work on sociocritical literacies (Gutiérrez, 2005, 2008, 2018) over the past decades. Morrell and I share a few theoretical commitments that are foundational to our studies and praxis, viewing language and literacy as fundamentally socioculturally organized practices (Scribner & Coles, 1999; Street, 1995, 1984)—practices mediated by social and political forces, both locally and historically. Thus, language and literacy have broader possibilities and aims beyond formal schooling.

My work as a critical learning scientist has focused both on consequential forms of literacy learning and learning more generally, as well as on the design of robust learning environments that can serve as developmental ecologies for both literacy and forms of expansive agency as historical actors (Gutiérrez, 2008, 2016, 2025; Gutiérrez et al., 2019). In this work, both youth and educators (as well as researchers) are learners who can become designers of their own social futures as they leverage their repertoires of practice in the processes of becoming (Gutiérrez & Vossoughi, 2010; Gutiérrez & Rogoff, 2003). This expansive theory of learning imagines a transformative literacy in a world as it could be (Gutiérrez, 2008). Importantly, social theories, including Freirean (1970), Chicana feminist (Anzaldúa, 1987; Castillo, 1994), and Black feminist theories (Crenshaw, 1991; Collins, 2009; Wynter, 2003) create a matrix of critical analytical frames that are baked into our analyses of the teaching and learning of literacies for historically minoritized youth and communities. Thus, critical theories are synergistic with if not foundational to critical approaches to cultural historical theories of learning and development.

This understanding of literacy has been both situated in and emergent from the longstanding partnerships with schools, educators, youth, and communities in what I have termed social design-based experiments (SDBE). This utopian methodological approach is concerned with “human flourishing in [the context] of possible futures” (Levitas, 2013, p. xi) and its *proleptic* or future orientation is concerned with who people can become rather than a static version of who they are (Gutiérrez, 2018). Within this view, we would expect to find ingenuity, the playful imagination, and complexity in people’s practices if we observed them across a range of events and contexts. And if we are keenly observant participants, we would capture a more expansive picture of people’s practices and their possibilities (Gutiérrez, 2023; Gutiérrez, et al., 2019).

The conceptual metaphor of Learning as Movement (LAM) serves as an important dimension of capturing people’s full humanity described above and is central to the utopian orientation in my social design-based work[1] (Gutiérrez, 2020, 2025). A Learning as Movement frame argues that understanding people’s full potential or making claims about their potential necessarily involves observing people’s practices across a minimum of several settings/practices across the ecologies in which they participate. What is most relevant here to English educators is that this methodological principle is key to expansive designs for teacher educators who recognize the fundamental role everyday knowledge has in processes of deeper learning. The image of everyday and school-based knowledge growing into one another might be useful here in understanding that learning involves the reorganization of everyday and school-based knowledge, thus rupturing the binary views often held and employed in teaching and learning. LAM’s framework is essential to designing systems that promote consequential learning and a pedagogical imagination and support critical social thought for both teachers and students.

It is not surprising, then, that I come to critical English education with deep appreciation of teachers and students; however, I am persistently troubled by how teachers are apprenticed and socialized into the profession, how we conceive of their work, their learning, and their possibility. I argue instead for the transformative object of a more expansive teacher preparation with utopian ideals. Importantly, utopian here is not about predetermined or fixed endpoints but rather "moving horizons of possibility" (Gutiérrez et al., 2020, p. 331). In other words, utopian visions are always situated locally and historically to iterate on future imaginings.

Critical English Education: A Utopian Conception

A first-order question in the development of a critical English education with utopian ideals might be: What commitments inform and guide the design of a resilient critical English ecology and practice? Here I proffer several commitments that have guided the iterative codesign of social design-based experiments—commitments grounded in critical cultural historical approaches to learning and human development and critical social theories (Gutiérrez, 2008, 2016). These commitments were generated and iterated in partnered work with teachers, schools, and communities and have served as resources in the social imagination of fifteen-year-long social design-based activities: the UCLA Migrant Student Leadership Institute (MSLI) and the UCLA/Moffett Elementary School/Lennox School District *Las Redes* Technology-Mediated After-School Program—collaboratives for which human thriving, ecological resilience, and long-term sustainability were intentional designs. The design principles for social design-based experiments at work here are shown in Figure 1.

These design principles serve as conceptual, methodological, and ethical guardrails in the conduct of socially conscious and rigorous consequential research and could serve as heuristic, a resource for critical English education designs. This utopian methodology, grounded in cultural historical theories of learning and human development, has articulated design commitments around ecological resilience, sustainability, and diversity, bringing

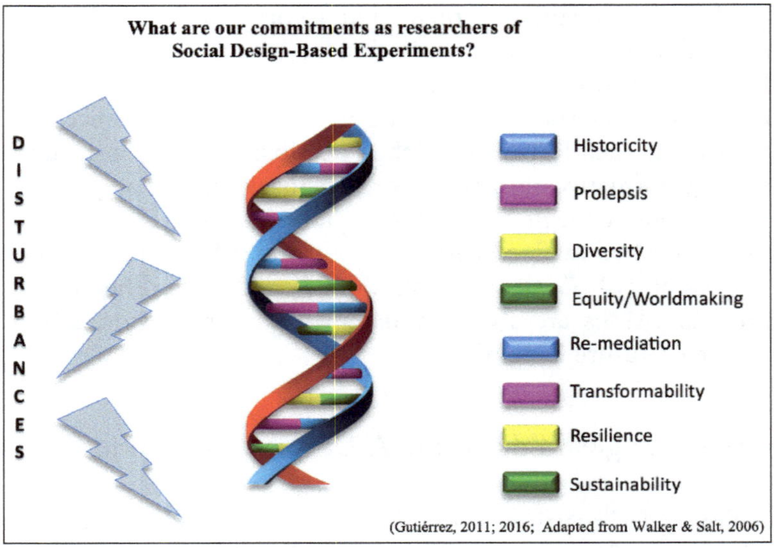

FIGURE 1.

together interpretive and multi-sited ethnographic approaches and sociocritical approaches to literacy and other tools that focus on how youth learn within and across multiple contexts (Gutiérrez, 2025). For this essay, I highlight historicity, prolepsis, transformability, and worldmaking as particularly generative for critical English education, as well as note the jointly agreed-upon commitments that communicate the explicit aims of our work with youth and their instructors:

- to make possible a sustainable and dignified life for all humans in the present and in the future as an overarching commitment
- to address challenges of leveraging cultural diversity and reducing social inequality
- to enact proleptic pedagogies and codesign new futures in mutual relations of exchange with partners
- to seek deep understandings of
    - the resources and constraints of the ecologies that constitute people's everyday lives

- the full range of people's practices understood across at least several activity systems (LAM)
- people's repertoires of practice, including the genesis of those practices
- the regularity and variance in the practices of cultural communities (Gutiérrez, 2016; Gutiérrez & Jurow, 2016)

Critical English education as a utopian project must also develop its commitments around a different form of criticality—one that recognizes that designing for consequential learning involves movement across disciplinary and conceptual borders and across physical and geographic spaces. Thus, criticality would be indexed in the very conceptions and practices of an expansive and future-oriented learning, teaching, and praxis, as discussed above. This boundary crossing necessarily pushes against a kind of monodisciplinarity that ignores or suppresses the inherent interdisciplinarity that critical English demands, as too often English education has been encapsulated within conventional disciplinary boundaries. Here I argue for a vision of an integrated interdisciplinarity that I have sought to use in my design work at different scales and call for a kind of interdisciplinarity that sits at the edges of disciplines, inviting, if not demanding, intellectual and disciplinary boundary crossing (Gutiérrez, 2025). Teacher preparation and teacher learning, for example, would necessarily look different and would involve not only reimagining the curriculum and its underlying epistemologies, but also would bring together individuals traditionally not often in conversation with one another.

A critical approach to English education should be *historicizing* and should rely on reading historical texts and drawing on social theories to understand both subject matter and pedagogical content and, importantly, to connect the past to the present to imagine possible lives (Gutiérrez, et al., 2017). This involves attention to the history of ideas and the social context that helped give rise to those ideas, as well as situating those ideas and practices in particular cultural communities and in particular historical moments. At the level of individual students, this historicizing approach would motivate us to seek rich understandings of youths' history of involvement with literacy broadly speaking rather than focusing on what youth "do not know." In terms of designing supports for youth, for example, accounting for their histories of involvement with literacy, math, etc., would provide richer and more useful information about the knowledge and experience that constitute learners' repertoires of practice—information that would help ensure a rich learning ecology, collaborative pedagogical engagement, and meaningful learning (Gutiérrez & Rogoff, 2003).

Such practices also move educators away from deficit perspectives of students' toolkits and toward more generative practices (Gutiérrez et al., 2009). For example, a routine practice with high school youth from migrant farmworker backgrounds who engaged complex topics and texts in MSLI—practices far beyond what was normally expected of them in their high school classrooms—could be described as follows: The students and their instructional team would gather in a large lecture room and would be introduced to the weekly topic, such as the social and educational consequences of linguistic hegemony and the possibilities of translingual language practices. Instructional conversations about how language policies and practices have been understood ideologically and sociopolitically across time, especially vis-à-vis cultural communities, would ensue. These rich conversations would be followed by reading a range of texts that further historicized and provided social analysis that situated language practices and language ideologies in broader and local sociohistorical contexts.

Students would read Gloria Anzaldúa's "How to Tame a Wild Tongue" (*Borderlands/la frontera,* 1987), with its critical analysis of language use and its link to identity formation, alongside Ana Castillo's "Countryless Woman: The Early Feminista" (*Massacre of the Dreamers,* 1994), Eduardo Galeano's *Open Veins of Latin America: Five Centuries of the Pillage of a Continent* (1997), and C. Wright Mills's *The Sociological Imagination* (1959), bringing together the analytical connections among the historical, the sociopolitical, and the economic, including how language, race and gender are indexed historically and spatially. These ideas and texts would be resituated in the students' present contexts and would provide students with ongoing opportunities to do close readings of texts and engage in discussion, with abundant opportunities to make sense of and write about their own understandings of texts and their relation to broader social issues and individual and collective lives. There would be comprehension circles of small groups of intergenerational learners to deepen understandings, to reflect, to identify tensions and contradictions, and to raise questions still unanswered.

These practices helped to support the development of sociocritical literacies that served as a central tool in the development of new understandings of who youth were and who they could become. Sociocritical literacies both privilege and are contingent upon learners' sociohistorical lives, proximally and distally, and where everyday and institutional literacies are historicized, reimagined, and leveraged toward critical social thought (Gutiérrez, 2008, p. 149; Vossoughi, 2014). A critical CEE also would challenge educational and literacy practices and linguistic ideologies rooted in coloniality and power reproduction that define youths' learning and identities within dominant norms; we might imagine instead studies of language, like those described above, where language is understood as both a resource as well as the object of sanction, regulation, and colonization (Becker & Gutiérrez, 2021). Again, this description should make clear that the texts read and the curriculum were mediating artifacts employed toward some larger and more consequential endpoint. Here, literacy became a powerful resource in the production of new selves and communities.

Within education, dominant ideologies frame certain learners as illegitimate and deviant with particular implications for literacy learning. English educators equipped with an interdisciplinary framework and expansive sensibilities about learning and pedagogy are uniquely positioned to re-signify what it means to be a literate body and to design learning ecologies in which youth move freely across linguistic borders. In line with decolonial perspectives, a utopian view of critical English education also troubles taken-for-granted assumptions about the learning and teaching of literacy for youth from otherized backgrounds and opens up pathways toward visions of alternate epistemic futures.

Historicizing and critical analysis of content and practices also help make visible the consequences of privileging teaching over learning rather than seeing how learning/teaching could be understood as symbiotic, as mutually constitutive and informing. Further, the over-privileging of the English curriculum, i.e., the content of the curriculum, makes the curriculum and the reading and writing of texts the primary object of learning, instead of using the curriculum as a tool for meaning making, for critical social thought. From a critical cultural historical perspective, the curriculum is a tool that mediates or supports learning. Importantly, reframing the curriculum as a mediating tool opens up the possibility of attending to the larger social context of development as a dialogic, plurilinguistic, historicizing, and heteroglossic space.

From my perspective, this is an example of how criticality becomes a meaningful part of learning. I remain concerned about how criticality in English education and literacy studies more broadly is conceptualized and enacted in practice, including how inequity gets made in everyday activity. Notions of equity and social justice have become inert or so amorphous in many institutions and in their policies and their practices that there are few concrete manifestations of transformative change in micro interactions or in the organization of social life in learning contexts.

In my work, equity is best understood as worldmaking in which new worlds are created, designed for; that is "Equity by Design" (Gutiérrez, 2015). Worldmaking is not only an agentic act; it is future oriented but necessarily leverages learners' existing repertoires of practice (Gutiérrez & Rogoff, 2003). Worldmaking, as Goodman noted in 1978, "always starts from worlds already on hand; the making is a remaking" (p. 6). This conception of worldmaking resonates strongly with cultural historical theoretical approaches for which everyday practices (those "already on hand") are fundamental to learning. Worldmaking is also generative as it demands historical and social analysis "evok[ing] sociopolitical transformation and the impossibility of escaping power, history and culture" (Kondo, 2018, p. 29).

I have wrestled with these issues throughout my time as a teacher, an academic, and a researcher—one with critical sensibilities that question how my work can remain relevant and contribute to the social good; thus, I continually iterate my commitments calibrated against mutually agreed upon equity indices that serve as a kind of miner's canary (Gutiérrez, 2008) that signals the health and wellbeing of the learning ecology and its people. Equity indices should address local constraints and historical inequities toward possible social futures. For example, in work with high school students from migrant farmworker backgrounds, high-level equity indices that are empirically observable would have included ongoing analysis of (1) students' opportunities to employ translanguaging practices important to learning and sense-making, etc.; (2) students' access to expansive learning opportunities and meaningful content, including reading difficult texts; (3) availability of a range of supports and forms of assistance tied to consequential learning, including collaborative "collaborate activity"; and (4) students' opportunities to use their full linguistic toolkits in the service of learning, participation, and meaning-making, for example. These equity indices help set up the conditions for worldmaking; they are not the endpoint of newly imagined futures. Of consequence, we started from an understanding that while the group shared histories of inequity and exploitation, there was significant variation in their experience with schooling and in their linguistic repertoires, as well as their range of familial status vis-à-vis US citizenship, country of origin, and immigration stories.

Early Start: An Empirical Vignette

I provide an empirical vignette from a social design-based university/school collaborative experiment in a K–5 setting. I use it because it embodies the same utopian approach, proleptic design principles, pedagogical imagination, and transformative and radical possibilities at work in a critical English education project. These principles transcend gameplay and after-school contexts and can become generative in formal and informal critical English activity.

While at UCLA, Center X teacher education leadership granted me permission to design and implement a social design-based experiment in collaboration with new teacher education students and then-elementary school principal Joanne Isken.[2]

This effort provided a transformative opportunity to work with prospective teachers and public school leadership and teachers in ways that were both utopian in their approach and grounded in robust theories of learning, human development and culture, critical approaches to language and literacy, and pedagogy. The program involved working with an entirely new cohort of prospective bilingual teachers who agreed to enroll early in a course a month before the official university program began. The program of study entailed participation in a daily extended morning and afternoon course on learning, literacy/language/translingualism, culture, and human development co-taught by Principal Isken, UCLA teaching assistants, and me. The cohort teachers simultaneously participated in *Las Redes* (Networks), a 5th Dimension technology-mediated after-school program, in which they collaborated in intergenerational groups of peers, K–5 youth, and UCLA graduate and undergraduate students around gaming activity.[3] The playful imagination was a defining characteristic at this site in which youth and adults could take on a variety of roles and identities and leverage a range of experiences through gameplay. For example, youth, with the assistance of others, corresponded daily with a magical cyber Wizard (intentionally referred to as *El Maga* instead of *La Maga*, the wizard, to unmark gender) to detail their participation for the day; they also participated in board games, computer games, and digital storytelling—all jointly accomplished activities requiring distributed expertise and full participation from all. The joint activity generated in-the-moment feedback, co-problem solving, and assessment for all participants. The participation structures were necessarily fluid, and the role of expert could be assumed by anyone, as well as many, within and across all activity. Here the principle goal was learning through playful imagination, not teaching, and thus the prospective teachers were known as amiga/os who were being introduced to the importance of focusing on learning along with more dynamic and symmetrical participation structures and relational equity (DiGiacomo & Gutiérrez, 2015, 2017). Learning also was regularly supported with various forms of assistance and tools in the context of joint work.

Of significance, the design of this playful environment indexed the very concepts and practices elaborated in the theories and readings with which the prospective teachers engaged in their daily class. For example, the design's emphasis on the playful imagination was supported by reading and analysis of a number of articles on the cognitive and social consequences of play, principally Vygotsky's (1978) conceptions of play and the playful imagination, along with El'konin's (1971) notion of play as a leading activity and its elaboration in the work of Cole and Engeström (2007) and Griffin and Cole (1984). In this work, play is examined empirically and theorized to create opportunities for youth to engage in consequential forms of learning, as play sets the conditions that support youths' development of psychological tools such as language. In other words, the aims and conceptual, analytical, and pedagogical ideas addressed in the course were mirrored in the after-school setting, providing opportunities for the teachers to bring knowledge and experience in a recursive manner from one setting to the other. These were also occasions to test out ideas in situ and to use observation and other evidence to develop small "t" theories of their own as designers of learning/teaching. Importantly, the design of the course/practicum addressed one of the ongoing contradictions in teacher preparation in which course content, practices, and theories examined in the university course are too often in tension with the practices, theories, curricula, and ways of organizing learning and teaching in the actual school setting. At the same time, the university coursework often provides little to no opportunity to situate, examine, test out, redesign or reimagine ideas, practices, and content in situ. This partnered collaboration allowed novice teachers to develop a critical praxis—an emergent repertoire of knowledge, experiences, new practices, tools, and examined assumptions across settings before they had ever entered their formal classroom assignments.

This is key, as understanding the classroom is often a black box in which, without mediation, we can only make sense based on our own previous experiences or folk theories. Why would we put prospective teachers in learning contexts without first providing contexts for learning that were carefully designed to support expansive views of teaching and learning, including their design and organization, or without providing teachers the conceptual, pedagogical and methodological tools to generate new social imaginations about what teaching and learning could be?

In this ecology, there were a number of mediating tools and practices that supported robust teacher learning. First, our research over time found that the cognitive ethnographies (Hutchins, 2003) that teachers wrote after each day in the after-school setting supported the development of a practice in which the teachers learned to (1) document the learning observed (both the youths' as well the adults' learning) in activity and how learning and participation were supported, how and when it broke down, repaired, etc.; (2) document forms of mediation (material and ideational tools) that supported learning; (3) document moment-to-moment accounts of the collaborative activity, both synchronically and diachronically—that is, as interaction unfolded as well as what occurred simultaneously; (4) reflect on what was learned that day across participants, drawing on previous cognitive ethnographies and their feedback, class and peer discussions, and readings to sense-make—to use evidence and theory to conjecture about what worked and why or how to design learning differently; and (5) note tensions with what was being learned or experienced as well as to generate new questions (Gutiérrez & Vossoughi, 2010). These cognitive ethnographies (CEs) became the context for dialogue between course instructors and teachers, engaging the prospective teachers' questions, theorizations, and assumptions. The CEs also became the context in which issues of race, gender, culture could be wrestled with in ways that connected with concrete experiences at *Las Redes*. Specifically, engaging the new teachers with critical cultural historical and learning sciences conceptions of learning and human development, with expansive notions of culture, set up the conditions to challenge and examine deficit views of historically minoritized students and their communities in a supportive, designed context in which theory and practice were in sync and critical and generative feedback was built into all activity, both in the classroom and at the site. Issues of educational and social inequity, race, gender, class, and language, and their intersections were prominently considered in the theoretical approaches examined, research engaged, coursework, and in joint participation in intergenerational ensembles.

Without doubt, across the years, the cognitive ethnographies proved to be the tool that synthesized and integrated what teachers had learned but also became the context for transforming understandings into productive practice and pedagogical imaginaries (Domínguez, 2019). As we (Gutiérrez & Vossoughi, 2010) have previously written, cognitive ethnographies

> focus attention on interactions between the material, cognitive, and social world, that is, distributing attention across cognition, social interaction, and mediating artifacts—what Hutchins called the local cognitive ecology. Through fine-grained ethnographic detailing of the learning at work in situated activity, knowledge of cognitive processes is grounded, and understandings of student learning become more expansive. (p. 105)

Such opportunities to reflect, sense-make, and examine assumptions about learning, pedagogy, youths' practices, and teachers' own held ideologies should be routine practices for teachers, as they were here. What was also different here is that teachers had their own data elaborated in their comprehensive cognitive theories from which to draw; teachers were building important local theories examined *in situ* and with new analytic frames.

Finally, the Early Start SDBE employed the important principle of observing youths' (teachers and people more generally) learning across a minimum of two activity settings to begin to develop fuller accounts of learners' repertoires of practice and the knowledge and experience therein (Gutiérrez, 2023; Vossoughi & Gutiérrez, 2014). Toward this end, the participating teachers were asked to follow the youth with whom they had collaborated at *Las Redes* into their regular school classrooms—a process that involved the youths' classroom teachers. The operant guiding questions for the teachers' cognitive ethnographies of classroom learning included: What do you observe about X's participation and learning in the classroom that is similar or different from X's learning and participation at *Las Redes*? How would you explain observed similarities and differences across the settings (e.g., participation structures, mediating tools, language practices, etc.)? The contrastive analysis was designed to help the teachers focus on robust and equitable forms of learning and how the social organization of learning could enable and constrain learning and participation, observations that could help explain why some contexts of development matter more and are more generative for learners than others.

The Early Start social design-based experiment provides an existence proof of a concrete utopian in which new teachers were respected for the intellectuals, designers, pedagogues, and learners they are and could become. They were afforded what my dear friend and colleague Mike Rose called a *respectful curriculum*, one worthy of their potential and possibility. Early Start was a complex ecology that valued learning and movement across settings and activities, in which tensions and unexamined assumptions became the object of study and analysis, and in which transformational change was a design commitment. Here prospective teachers—empowered with robust and historicized understandings of learning, culture, literacy, and human activity—were active co-participants in intergenerational learning activities in which they could situate and make sense of these conceptions in practice.

A critical English education is not one thing; it is an expansive landscape of multiple ecologies, organized around a matrix of interdisciplinary thinking and knowing in which sociocritical literacies and their critical social thought are tools for academic and social transformation. Within a utopian framework, such interdisciplinarity would be proleptic, would decenter dominant epistemologies, and would bring a diversity of approaches, particularly those imagining what disciplinary perspectives are necessary to develop the sociocritical literacies required to study complex problems and reimagine new forms of worldmaking. Several years ago, Jean Lave (2009) argued for a reconceptualization of taken-for-granted "natural categories" such as "bodies of knowledge, learners, and understandings of cultural transmission" (p. 203). Troubling commonplaces is an important aspect of this transformative reconceptualization.

I end, then, with a rethinking of critical English education toward a utopian and expansive form of criticality that centers historicity, prolepsis, interdisciplinarity that pushes against the edges of disciplines, and cultural and linguistic complexity; centers complexity in human learning and a pedagogical imagination; and resists just "doing the curriculum" of an English education. I take a moment to address the curriculum as a taken-for-granted tool and practice. Importantly, a utopian critical English could never be reduced to the English course subject matter. Within this utopian frame, the critical English education curriculum for youth and their teachers and its pedagogical moves would include recursive attention to the following iterative processes for designing and enacting a consequential and transformative literacy learning activity that:

1. Identifies the learning goal(s) vis-à-vis a set of design principles and commitments
2. Develops cycles of learning that seek complex understandings of topics, genres, and texts
3. Identifies what knowledge and experience learners already might have about the topic/content to be learned; that is, their repertoires of practice
4. Identifies what learners still may need to know to develop robust understandings of subject matter as part of matrix of interdisciplinary knowledge and histories
5. Historicizes the curriculum such that the history of ideas and the historical contexts are objects of study and are situated in local everyday contexts and individual lives
6. Identifies what rich set of multimodal tools (materials, content, technology, reading/writing, translingual practices) and forms of assistance would best support individual and collective consequential learning
7. Identifies the social organization of learning (e.g., participation structures) that best supports expansive and equitable forms of learning for all participants
8. Identifies equity indices that support inclusive and meaningful learning throughout.

A critical English education in the end is about unsettling commonplaces in teacher preparation and pedagogical and curricular conventions and imagining them anew. It should be a "lived argument for the possible" (Gutiérrez, 2016, p. 195).

Notes

1. Social design-based experiments elaborated further in these articles: Gutiérrez, 2008, 2016, 2020, 2025; Gutiérrez et al., 2020; Vossoughi & Gutiérrez, 2014.

2. Principal Isken (and later Superintendent of Instruction at Lennox School District and UCLA Center X Director and Principal Leadership Program Faculty) and I forged a fifteen-year collaboration in which we codesigned a robust technology-mediated after-school program, *Las Redes*. Center X housed UCLA Graduate School of Education's Teacher Education Program.

3. *Las Redes* was a previously designed collaboration with Principal Isken and Moffett Elementary School, Lennox School District. This was a fifteen-year collaboration in which *Las Redes* was the crucible for learning to generations of children at Moffett and UCLA undergraduate and graduate students and postdoctoral fellows. It was also a site of learning for the school, its participating teachers, and staff. We also added making and tinkering to the design of another 5th Dimension in Colorado, *El Pueblo Mágico*, which provided expanded opportunities to engage in the playful imagination, creativity, and joint activity that generated rich learning and belonging for participants (Schwartz, DiGiacomo, & Gutiérrez, 2015).

References

Anzaldúa, G. (1987). *Borderlands/la frontera: The new mestiza*. Aunt Lute Books.

Becker, B. L. C., & Gutiérrez, K. D. (2021). Moving beyond linguistic bordering: Utopian designs for new futures. *International Studies in the Sociology of Education*, *31*(1–2), 104–123. https://doi.org/10.1080/09620214.2021.1990784

Castillo, A. (1994). *Massacre of the dreamers: Essays on Xicanisma*. University of New Mexico Press.

Cole, M., & the Distributed Literacy Consortium. (2006). *The Fifth Dimension: An after-school program built on diversity*. Russell Sage Foundation.

Cole, M., & Engeström, Y. (2007). Cultural-historical approaches to designing for development. In J. Valsiner & A. Rosa (Eds.), *The Cambridge handbook of sociocultural psychology* (pp. 484–507). Cambridge University Press.

Collins, P. H. (2000). *Black feminist thought: Knowledge, consciousness, and the politics of empowerment.* Routledge.

Crenshaw, K. (1991). Mapping the margins: Intersectionality, identity politics, and violence against women of color. *Stanford Law Review, 43*(6), 1241–1299.

DiGiacomo, D., & Gutiérrez, K. D. (2015). Relational equity as a design tool within making and tinkering activities. *Mind, Culture, and Activity: An International Journal, 23*(2), 141–153.

DiGiacomo, D., & Gutiérrez, K. D. (2017). Seven *chilis*: Making visible the complexities in leveraging cultural repertoires of practice in a designed teaching and learning environment. *Pedagogies: An International Journal, 12*(1), 41–57.

Domínguez, M. (2019). Decolonial innovation in teacher development: Praxis beyond the colonial zero-point. *Journal of Education for Teaching, 45*(1), 47–62.

El'konin, D. B. (1971). The problem of stages of mental development in childhood. *Voprosy Psikhologii, 17*(4), 6–20.

Espinoza, M. (2008). Humanization and social dreaming: A case study of changing social relations in a summer migrant educational program [Doctoral dissertation, University of California, Los Angeles].

Freire, P. (1970). *Pedagogy of the oppressed*. Seabury Press.

Galeano, E. (1997). *Open veins of Latin America: Five centuries of the pillage of a continent.* Monthly Review Press.

Goodman, N. (1978). *Ways of worldmaking*. Hackett Publishing Company.

Griffin, P., & Cole, M. (1984). Current activity for the future: The zoped. In B. Rogoff & J. Wertsch (Eds.), Children's learning in the zone of proximal development (pp. 45–64). Jossey-Bass.

Gutiérrez, K. D. (2005, April 13). *Intersubjectivity and the grammar of the Third Space* [Conference lecture]. 2005 Annual Meeting of the American Educational Research Association, Montreal, Canada.

Gutiérrez, K. D. (2008). Developing a sociocritical literacy in the Third Space. *Reading Research Quarterly*, *43*(2), 148–164.

Gutiérrez, K. D. (2015). *Equity by design*. Digital Media and Learning Conference 2015, Los Angeles, CA.

Gutiérrez, K. D. (2016). Designing resilient ecologies: Social design experiments and a new social imagination. *Educational Researcher*, *45*(3), 187–196.

Gutiérrez, K. D. (2018). Social design-based experiments: A proleptic approach to literacy. *Literacy Research: Theory, Method, and Practice*, *67*(1), 86–108.

Gutiérrez, K. D. (2020). When learning as movement meets learning on the move. *Cognition and Instruction*, *38*(3), 427–433. https://doi.org/10.1080/07370008.2020.1774770

Gutiérrez, K. D. (2023). When learning is made consequential: A methodological note on repertoires. *Review of Research in Education*, *47*(1), 84–99.

Gutiérrez, K. D. (2025, April 25). *Mutual constitution, learning as movement, and developmental ecologies* [Distinguished Contributions to Research in Education Award Lecture]. Annual Meeting of the American Educational Research Association, Denver, Colorado.

Gutiérrez, K. D., Baquedano-Lopez, P., Alvarez, H., & Chiu, M. (1999). Building a culture of collaboration through hybrid language practices. *Theory Into Practice*, *38*(2), 87–93.

Gutiérrez, K. D., Becker, B., Espinoza, M., Cortes, K., Cortez, A., Lizárraga, J. R., Rivero, E., Villegas, K., & Yin, P. (2019). Youth as historical actors in the production of possible futures. *Mind, Culture, and Activity*, *26*(4), 291–308. https://doi.org/10.1080/10749039.2019.1652327

Gutiérrez, K. D., Cortes, K., Cortez, A., DiGiacomo, D., Higgs, J., Johnson, P., Lizárraga, J., Mendoza, E., Tien, J., & Vakil, S. (2017). Replacing representation with imagination: Finding ingenuity in everyday practices. *Review of Research in Education*, *41*(1), 30–60. https://doi.org/10.3102/0091732X16687523

Gutiérrez, K. D., Higgs, J., Lizárraga, J. R., & Rivero, E. (2019). Learning as movement in social design-based experiments: Play as a leading activity. *Human Development*, *62*(1–2), 66–82. https://doi.org/10.1159/000496239

Gutiérrez, K. D., & Jurow, S. A. (2016). Social design experiments: Toward equity by design. *Journal of the Learning Sciences*, *25*(4), 565–598.

Gutiérrez, K. D., Jurow, S. A., & Vakil, S. (2020). Social design-based experiments: A utopian methodology for understanding new possibilities for learning. In N. S. Nasir, C. Lee, R. Pea, & M. McKinney de Royston (Eds.), *Handbook of the cultural foundations of learning* (pp. 330–347). Routledge.

Gutiérrez, K. D., & Rogoff, B. (2003). Cultural ways of learning: Individual traits or repertoires of practice. *Educational Researcher*, *32*(5), 19–25.

Gutiérrez, K. D., & Vossoughi, S. (2010). Lifting off the ground to return anew: Mediated praxis, transformative learning, and social design experiments. *Journal of Teacher Education, 61*(1–2), 100–117.

Gutiérrez, K. D., Zitlali Morales, P., & Martinez, D. (2009). Re-mediating literacy: Culture, difference, and learning for students from nondominant communities. *Review of Research in Education, 33*(1), 212–245.

Kondo, D. (2018). *Worldmaking: Race, performance, and the work of creativity*. Duke University Press.

Lave, J. (2009). The practice of learning. In K. Illeris (Ed.), *Contemporary theories of learning: Learning theorists . . . in their own words* (pp. 200–208). Routledge.

Levitas, R. (2013). *Utopia as method: The imaginary reconstitution of society*. Palgrave Macmillan

Mills, C. W. (1959). *The sociological imagination*. Oxford University Press.

Morrell, E. (2005). Critical English education. *English Education*, *37*(4), 312–321.

Rogoff, B., Callanan, M., Gutiérrez, K. D., & Erickson, F. (2016). The organization of informal learning. *Review of Research in Education*, *40*(1), 356–401.

Schwartz, L., DiGiacomo, D., & Gutiérrez, K. D. (2015). Designing "contexts for tinkerability" with undergraduates and children within the El Pueblo Mágico social design experiment. *International Journal for Research on Extended Education, 3*(1), 94–113.

Scribner, S., & Cole, M. (1999). *The psychology of literacy.* Harvard University Press.

Street, B. V. (1984). *Literacy in theory and practice.* Cambridge University Press.

Street, B. V. (1995). *Social literacies: Critical approaches to literacy in development, ethnography and education.* Routledge.

Vossoughi, S., & Gutiérrez, K. D. (2014). Studying movement, hybridity, and change: Toward a multi-sited sensibility for research on learning across contexts and borders. In J. Vadeboncoeur (Ed.), *Learning in and across contexts: Reimagining education* (pp. 603–632). Teachers College Press.

Vygotsky, L. S. (1978). *Mind in society: The development of higher psychological processes* (M. Cole, V. John-Steiner, S. Scribner, & E. Souberman, Eds.). Harvard University Press.

Wynter, S. (2003). Unsettling the coloniality of being/power/truth/freedom: Towards the human, after man, its overrepresentation—an argument. *CR: The New Centennial Review, 3*(3), 257–337.

INDEX

The letter *f* following a page locator denotes a figure.

Editors

Ernest Morrell is the Coyle Professor of Literacy Education, a member of the faculty in the English and Africana studies departments, and the director of the Center for Literacy Education at the University of Notre Dame. He is also director of the NCTE James R. Squire Office for Policy Research in the English Language Arts. He is an elected member of the American Academy of Arts and Sciences, an elected member of the National Academy of Education, an elected fellow of the American Educational Research Association, and a former president of the National Council of Teachers of English (NCTE). Morrell is also the recipient of the NCTE Distinguished Service Award, the Kent Williamson Leadership Award from the Conference on English Leadership, and the Divergent Award for Excellence in 21st-Century Literacies. His scholarly interests include critical pedagogy, English education, literacy studies, and youth popular culture. He is the author of fifteen books and more than a hundred peer-reviewed articles and chapters.

Nicole Mirra is an associate professor of teacher education in UCLA's Department of Education and faculty director of the UCLA Teacher Education Program (TEP). Her research utilizes participatory design methods in classroom, community, and digital spaces to collaboratively create learning environments with teachers and youth that disrupt structures of social injustice and creatively compose liberatory futures. Her scholarship is animated by critical sociocultural theories of democracy, literacy, race, and pedagogy. She previously taught English language arts and debate in Brooklyn, New York, and Los Angeles, California. Her books include *Doing Youth Participatory Action Research: Transforming Inquiry with Researchers, Educators, and Students* (2015), *Educating for Empathy: Literacy Learning and Civic Engagement* (2018), and *Civics for the World to Come: Committing to Democracy in Every Classroom* (2023).

Antero Garcia is a professor in the Graduate School of Education at Stanford University. His research explores the possibilities of speculative imagination and healing in educational research. Prior to completing his PhD, Garcia was an English teacher at a public high school in

South Central Los Angeles. He has authored or edited more than two dozen books about the possibilities of literacies, play, and civics in transforming schooling in America. He currently coedits *La Cuenta*, an online publication centering the voices and perspectives of individuals labeled undocumented in the US. Garcia received his PhD in the Urban Schooling division of the Graduate School of Education and Information Studies at the University of California, Los Angeles.

Cati de los Ríos is an associate professor of language, literacy, and culture at UC Berkeley's School of Education. She is a former English language development (ELD), Spanish, and ethnic studies high school in California and Massachusetts's public schools. She holds a PhD in English education from Teachers College, Columbia University, and her research interests include bi/multilingual adolescents' civic, folkloric, and translingual literacies. Her research has been funded by the Ford Foundation, the National Academy of Education/Spencer Foundation, and the National Council of Teachers of English. She is the recipient of Early Career Awards from American Educational Research Association's Division G, Grassroots Community and Youth Organizing Special Interest Group, and Language and Social Processes Special Interest Group. She has also received the Early Career Achievement Award and the Arthur Applebee Award for Excellence in Research on Literacy from the Literacy Research Association.

Jamila Lyiscott is an associate professor of social justice education and the founding co-director of the Center of Racial Justice and Youth Engaged Research at UMass Amherst. She is the author of *Black Appetite. White Food: Issues of Race, Voice, and Justice Within and Beyond the Classroom*. Her research examines the liberatory capacity of Black language, racial healing, and youth-led activism. Lyiscott holds a faculty fellowship at the University of Notre Dame and is the recipient of the AERA Outstanding Public Communication of Education Research Award, the AERA Scholar-Activist & Community Advocacy Award, a Fulbright-Hays Award, and the CIES Emerging Scholar Award. Coupled with publications in leading academic journals, her publicly engaged scholarship has led to several invited media features including Hulu, NPR, BBC Radio, NowThis, *Cosmopolitan*, Spike Lee's "2 Fists Up," and her TED Talk, "3 Ways to Speak English," which has been viewed over 5 million times.

Contributors

Mollie V. Blackburn is a professor in the Department of Teaching and Learning at the Ohio State University. Her research focuses on literacy, language, and social change, with particular attention to queer youth and the teachers who teach them. She is the author of *Moving Across Differences: How Students Engage LGBTQ+ Themes in a High School Literature Class* and *Interrupting Hate: Homophobia in Schools and What Literacy Can Do about It*, the editor of *Adventurous Thinking: Fostering Students' Rights to Read and Write in Secondary ELA Classrooms*, among coauthored and coedited books. She has received NCTE's LGBTQ+ Advocacy and Leadership Award; WILLA's Inglis Award for work in gender, sexuality, sexual orientation, and young people; AERA's Queer Studies Special Interest Group's Body of Work Award; and the Alan C. Purves Award for an article in *Research in the Teaching of English* deemed rich with implications for classroom practice.

Limarys Caraballo is an associate professor of English education in the Departments of Arts and Humanities and Curriculum and Teaching at Teachers College, Columbia University, and Doctoral Consortium faculty in urban education at the CUNY Graduate Center. Her research, which has been recognized by organizations such as the American Educational Research Association, the National Council of Teachers of English, and the American Association of Teaching and Curriculum, seeks to reframe deficit discourses about minoritized youth by amplifying their multiple voices, literacies, and identities in classrooms and beyond. She is also the cofounder and director of *Cyphers for Justice*, a youth-engaged research organization that supports intergenerational participatory inquiry. Entering her thirtieth year as an educator, she is deeply committed to scholarship-in-praxis and is currently co-developing the Latinidad Curriculum Initiative for New York City Public Schools.

Ofelia García is professor emerita in the PhD programs in urban education and Latin American, Iberian, and Latino cultures at the Graduate Center, City University of New York. García has published extensively on language education, sociolinguistics, and translanguaging. She has received numerous awards, including Distinguished Scholar Lifetime Awards from the Literacy Research Association (2024), the Modern Language Association (2022), and the American Education Research Association (Social Contexts in Education, 2019, and Bilingual Education, 2017). She has been elected to the Academy of Arts and Sciences (2023) and to the National Academy of Education (2018). Her website is www.ofeliagarcia.org.

Rubén González, proudly from Greenfield, California, is an assistant professor in the Department of Learning and Instruction at the University at Buffalo. He earned his PhD in race, inequality, and language in education and curriculum studies and teacher education from Stanford University. He examines how K–12 students and teachers of Color develop, sustain, and enact a critical sociopolitical disposition in classroom, school, and broader community settings. His research has been supported by the National Council of Teachers of English (NCTE), the Ford Foundation, and the National Academy of Education (NAEd)/Spencer Foundation. González began his career as a high school English and English language development (ELD) teacher in Sacramento, California. As a first-generation college student, he earned a bachelor of arts degree in English at California State University, Sacramento, after transferring from Hartnell College with an associate of arts degree in general studies.

Kris D. Gutiérrez is the Carol Liu Chair and Distinguished Professor at the University of California, Berkeley. Gutiérrez's expertise is in the learning sciences, literacy, and qualitative and design-based approaches to inquiry. Gutiérrez is a member of the National Academy of Education, the American Academy of Arts and Sciences, and a fellow of the British Academy; an ISLS and AERA fellow, an Osher Fellow-Exploratorium, and a fellow of the Center for Advanced Study in the Behavioral Sciences. Gutiérrez's research examines learning in designed environments with attention to culture, historicity, and ecological resilience, and the affordances of syncretic approaches to literacy and STEM learning. Her work in social design-based experiments foregrounds issues of equity in learning and design. Gutiérrez's numerous awards include the 2025 AERA Distinguished Contributions to Research award, the AERA Division C Sylvia Scribner Award for influencing the field of learning and instruction, and the 2016 Oscar Causey award for influencing the field of literacy.

Gloria Ladson-Billings is professor emerita and former Kellner Family Distinguished Chair of Urban Education at the University of Wisconsin-Madison. She is a fellow of the British Academy, a fellow of the American Academy of Arts and Sciences, and a fellow of the

Hagler Institute of Texas A&M University. She is an elected member of the National Academy of Education and its former president.

Sabine Little's research focuses on multilingualism in society, exploring the intersectionality between language, identity, and belonging. Her work spans both formal and informal educational settings, as well as public spaces such as libraries. Her development of a heritage language identity framework has led advancements in research, policy, and practice, working toward normalization of multilingualism in society and helping organizations and practitioners to support multilingual children. She is co-lead of the Sheffield City of Languages initiative in the UK, and her work on Sheffield's multilingual children's library has won the international Brenda Eastwood Award for Diversity and Inclusion. Working at the University of Sheffield (UK), she is regularly called upon to share her work internationally.

Kahdeidra Monét Martin is a Black American priestess of Haitian Vodou and scholar of language, education, and Africana religions. She is an assistant professor of education at Vassar College, where she is a member of the Africana Studies Steering Committee and an advisor to the Office of Religious and Spiritual Life and Contemplative Practices. Dr. Martin teaches courses on issues in contemporary education, adolescent literacy, and multilingualism and linguistic variation in schools and society. She uses the lens of translanguaging and community participatory methods to illuminate notions of linguistic and spiritual citizenship, religious racism in schools, and liberatory religious literacy curricula. Dr. Martin is the creator and host of the *Embodied Memories: Oral Histories of African Diasporic Religious Communities* podcast and the Embodied Memories: Africana Religion and Oral History curriculum.

Jennifer Rowsell is a professor of digital literacy and director of research and innovation at the University of Sheffield. Her research interests include multimodal, makerspace, and arts-based research with young people; digital inequalities research; and applying posthumanist and affect approaches to literacy research. She has worked and conducted research in Australia, Canada, the United Kingdom, and the United States. Her most recent book is *The Comfort of Screens: Literacy in Postdigital Times*. She is lead editor of *Reading Research Quarterly* and is coeditor of the *Routledge Expanding Literacies in Education* book series with Gerald Campano and Carmen Medina.

Laurence Tan is currently a doctoral student at Stanford University and was most recently a fifth-grade teacher at the Oakland Academy of Knowledge. A twenty-five-year educator in Watts and Oakland, he is most proud of openly employing a community and culturally responsive pedagogy centered around youth culture and a decolonized, social/racial justice, ethnic studies lens while conducting youth participatory action projects, STEM, and computer science curricula that allows students to problem-solve and transform their community. His biggest accomplishments have been his youth work within the community and the formation of many youth groups (including the Watts Youth Collective), and creating critical youth educator pipelines. Tan is an adjunct at the University of San Francisco and Santa Clara University. He is passionate about creating positive change in the conditions for the BIPOC communities, families, and youth he serves through education and action.

Stephanie Toliver is an assistant professor of curriculum and instruction at the University of Illinois Urbana-Champaign. In her research, Toliver employs creativity and imagination as tools to confront systemic inequities and to promote more equitable education environments. Specifically, her scholarship focuses on three main areas: (1) investigating Black storytelling as a mechanism of social critique and transformation; (2) examining the applicability of speculative fiction (i.e., science fiction, horror, fantasy, etc.) as a tool to assist Black youth in articulating and challenging social injustice; and (3) exploring the use of creative and arts-based literacy pedagogies to help preservice English teachers develop strategies to address racial injustice in their future classrooms. She is the author of the award-winning book *Recovering Black Storytelling in Qualitative Research: Endarkened Storywork*, and her academic work has been published in several journals, including *Equity, Excellence, & Education; Journal of Literacy Research;* and *Teachers College Record.*

Maisha T. Winn is the Excellence in Learning Professor in the Stanford Graduate School of Education, where she also serves as the faculty director of the Stanford Accelerator for Learning's Equity in Learning Initiative. She is the Principal Investigator for the Futuring for Equity Lab. Her scholarship examines how nondominant youth and communities have developed literate trajectories across a range of historical and contemporary settings within and outside formal schooling. She seeks to understand how communities that have been depicted as underresourced create practices, processes, and institutions of their own—and what we can learn from those examples to build more just, more collaborative, and more equitable futures. An ethnographer by training, Winn also engages in historical research focused on social movements in education. She is the author of *Futuring Black Lives: Independent Black Institutions and the Literary Imagination.*

This book was typeset in Sabon LT Pro by Barbara Frazier.
Typefaces used on the cover include Cera Bold and Black
and Garamond Italic.